PARENTING BY HEART

An International Board Certified Lactation Consultant (IBCLC), certified infant massage instructor and sought-after keynote speaker at conferences for parents and health professionals internationally, Pinky McKay is the author of *Toddler Tactics*, *Sleeping Like a Baby* and *100 Ways to Calm the Crying*. She runs a busy private practice in Melbourne and, thanks to modern technology, also supports clients around the world with gentle baby care, breastfeeding, settling and sleep solutions through her e-newsletter, web site, blog, teleseminars, workshops and private consultations.

The mother of four adult 'children' and a now-teenage 'bonus baby', Pinky's greatest pleasure is enjoying the precious giggles and cuddles of her delightful grandchildren. Visit her web site at www.pinkymckay.com.

By the same author

Sleeping Like a Baby
100 Ways to Calm the Crying
Toddler Tactics

PARENTING BY HEART

Sleeping, feeding and gentle care for your baby's first year

PINKY McKAY

VIKING
an imprint of
PENGUIN BOOKS

VIKING

Published by the Penguin Group
Penguin Group (Australia)
250 Camberwell Road, Camberwell, Victoria 3124, Australia
(a division of Pearson Australia Group Pty Ltd)
Penguin Group (USA) Inc.
375 Hudson Street, New York, New York 10014, USA
Penguin Group (Canada)
90 Eglinton Avenue East, Suite 700, Toronto, Canada ON M4P 2Y3
(a division of Pearson Penguin Canada Inc.)
Penguin Books Ltd
80 Strand, London WC2R 0RL, England
Penguin Ireland
25 St Stephen's Green, Dublin 2, Ireland
(a division of Penguin Books Ltd)
Penguin Books India Pvt Ltd
11 Community Centre, Panchsheel Park, New Delhi – 110 017, India
Penguin Group (NZ)
67 Apollo Drive, Rosedale, North Shore 0632, New Zealand
(a division of Pearson New Zealand Ltd)
Penguin Books (South Africa) (Pty) Ltd
24 Sturdee Avenue, Rosebank, Johannesburg 2196, South Africa

Penguin Books Ltd, Registered Offices: 80 Strand, London WC2R 0RL, England

First published by Penguin Group (Australia), 2011

3 5 7 9 10 8 6 4 2 1

Text design by Karen Scott © Penguin Group (Australia)
Cover design by Laura Thomas © Penguin Group (Australia)
Illustrations by Maxim Savva at illustrationroom.com.au
Cover photograph © FOTO
Typeset in Berkeley Oldstyle 11/16pt by Post Pre-press Group, Brisbane, Queensland
Printed and bound in Australia by McPherson's Printing Group, Maryborough, Victoria

National Library of Australia
Cataloguing-in-Publication data:

McKay, Pinky, 1952–
Parenting by heart: sleeping, feeding and gentle care
for your baby's first year / Pinky McKay.
9780670075089 (pbk.)
Includes bibliographical references and index.
Parenting.
Parent and child.
Child rearing.

649.1

penguin.com.au

FSC
www.fsc.org
MIX
Paper from
responsible sources
FSC® C001695

53869384

Contents

Trust yourself. Trust your child. Trust your feelings.

To my own five babies, who taught me so much about surrender, trust and unconditional love. And to my grand-babies, who really are nature's reward for nurturing our young, and a reminder that:

Time which passes swiftly by
won't stop to hear us, though we cry
for days long gone and smiles missed,
For damp curls that we should have kissed.

Introduction

♥

Every parent, every child and every parent–child relationship is unique. *Parenting by Heart* is not about advocating a single parenting 'method' because there is no one-size-fits-all. Rather, the spirit of this book is about encouraging you to trust not only your innate wisdom but also your child's response to your nurturing, just as women have throughout time, in cultures all over the world. Sadly, our confidence in our ability to nurture our young has gradually been undermined to the point that few women in our own time and culture seem to trust their intuition or their child's responses.

Each day, in my work as a lactation consultant and baby massage instructor, I hear from parents (mostly mothers) who feel confused, frustrated and overwhelmed by immense pressure to live up to unrealistic expectations. Many are burdened by feelings of inadequacy and guilt because they don't have a 'good' baby (who is, they believe, a reflection of their own competence). Mothers express fears that if they do hold and cuddle their babies as their instincts are urging, they may encourage 'bad habits'.

In our culture, values such as independence and control are prized. The pressure to be seen as 'coping' (or 'in control') perpetuates the myth of the 'good' baby. Many parents are afraid to speak openly about how their babies behave: those whose infants don't simply feed, play and sleep (preferably in that order) often feel as though they are somehow abnormal if

1

they 'give in' to their baby's cries; mothers whose babies 'fail' sleep training fear that they too have failed, as they secretly soothe little night howls; and many mothers exist in isolation because they are afraid of the stares and advice they will attract if they venture out in public with a baby who happens to cry – as all babies tend to do, at times!

'I was terrified of going out, and didn't really get over this for four months. I couldn't handle the feeling that my skills (or, more to the point – lack of) as a mother were on display for the world to see.'

Rachelle, mother of a nine-month-old

There is also pressure on the other side of the pendulum. The mother who 'confesses' that she is having a difficult time and perhaps has responded to her child harshly, or not as she may have if she'd had more help, is likely to be criticised too. Then there is the mother who is making conscious choices about her parenting but not fitting into the rigid ideas of a fundamentalist parenting group. Sometimes, mothers themselves create the worst kind of pressure.

'I popped my baby into her pram and walked to a nearby attachment parenting group – I needed to meet some other mums with small babies. I was breastfeeding and had had a natural birth at a birth centre, so I expected to meet some "kindreds" at such a group. Instead, I was criticised for having my baby "separated" from me in a pram, and also because she had a dummy. I went home feeling shattered and like a failure.'

Lexie, mother of a three-month-old

For many parents in our culture, having a baby is an enormous shock, rather than a rich experience in the continuum of life, celebrated and supported by the community. Many women today have never held a baby before their own is thrust into their arms. Invariably, as new mothers struggle with the notion of the 'good' baby, they are also struggling with an identity crisis – who am I now? Even when she looks in the mirror, the face (and body) reflected back at the new mother is virtually unrecognisable in comparison to the smart, savvy woman who used to have a clearly defined job description and a life that would fit neatly into her electronic organiser.

'I think it was the fact that I had always been so independent and success-ful that made it so much harder for me to surrender to these feelings of vulnerability. I was a health professional – I felt I should have known what to do. I felt that everyone was watching me – testing me, waiting for me to slip up. Even amongst my girlfriends with babies, it felt like we were all competing as to who was the perfect mum with the perfect baby.'

Melissa, mother of a toddler

Fathers can of course also experience shock at the new responsibilities and changed lifestyle involved with parenthood.

'People would say, "You must be so happy." Part of me was thinking: *I should be happy, I am a father.* But our lives had changed so dramatically that we were tired and stressed for weeks and months. There was a lot to get used to, especially the changes in our relationship. I would wonder: *Does this mean there is anything wrong with me, or with me as a father?'*

Richard, father of a one-year-old

When our sense of self is eroded, it is extremely difficult to trust our feel-ings or to believe we possess any wisdom at all. It is easy, then, to see how uncertainty and doubt creep in, and how new parents, desperate to regain a sense of control over their lives, not to mention their partner relation-ships, are all too willing to grasp at whatever promises are being made by whoever is offering advice. And, no matter how unrealistic these promises, or whatever the trade-offs involved, the promise of a 'good' – that is, 'con-venient' – baby is almost irresistible, even when it is being made by men in suits, in offices or clinics, or by childless 'celebu-nannies' who have never experienced the profound effects of the hormonal chemistry between a mother and her own infant. Without this amazing biological connection, it is almost impossible to fathom the awesome responsibility that you feel as you gaze into the eyes of your trusting baby, knowing that you are everything to her and that everything she needs comes from you.

Babies magically draw people together, even before they are born. It seems that everybody loves to share in the delight that a baby brings. Suddenly, too, it seems as though everyone is an expert – about your child. You can put yourself in the hands of these 'experts' or you can put yourself in charge. This doesn't mean you have to ignore or dismiss advice – after all, most of it is given with good intent. Nor do you have to go it alone without seeking support or professional help. Taking charge is about trusting yourself and your connection with your child, but it is also about becoming informed by asking questions, reading and listening so that you can make the most appropriate choices for your situation.

From now on, you are choosing on behalf of your child. You will live with your choices and so will your child. But as well as being your child's advocate, you are also his or her most important role model; your strength and support will make your child feel safe, even when you don't have all the answers.

You are unique. Your child is unique. To slavishly follow any method of parenting as though it were a religion, or to expect your child to fit a preconceived stereotype of success, is to deny your child's individuality as well as your own. But it is also a fact that the connection between you can be weakened when you are under stress, lack support or feel you are in unknown territory. At such times, you may question your own wisdom and become vulnerable to pressure and inappropriate advice. When your connection with your child is strong, you will find it easy to parent by heart, to ask yourself, 'How do I feel?' as well as, 'What do I think?' And to trust your feelings and thoughts.

'My husband and I have two little girls: Matilda, who is two years, and Genevieve, who is three months. I am so lucky to have a wonderful child-health nurse whose favourite saying is, "Trust your intuition." In those early days of sleep deprivation and sore nipples, I didn't think I had any intuition! But the more I listened to that little voice, the louder it became. And now I'm the proud mum of a smart, sweet, loving toddler and a happy, healthy baby. And all I can attribute it to is just being there when they want me, for whatever they want.'

Jo

When you follow your heart, rather than a single parenting 'method', you seldom fit neatly into a stereotype. Sampling various options from the stack of child-rearing techniques to form your own rich collage can often mean going against popular opinion. At times, following your heart can also result in challenges as you confront the wider (child-free) world. My two-year-old at my breast, I remember rocking up to weekend workshops with creative directors from some of the city's top ad agencies; these people were more familiar with the association between breasts and fast cars!

Like all parents, I have experienced criticism and self-doubt. To parent while ignoring mainstream opinions (which seem to change according to which 'expert' is currently popular) takes courage – and a deaf ear. To care for children and to nourish their identities requires a strong sense of self: you need to know where you are coming from in order to know where to go to find support.

There are as many ways of caring and loving as there are families. So, as well as evidence-based information, in this book I have included the voices of other parents, who share their experiences and their feelings – of joy, sadness, fear, frustration, hope and humour. Realising that other people make the same mistakes and feel the same fears validates your own experience and can give you new courage. You can, of course, also learn from others' experiences and apply this knowledge to your own situation, when it is relevant.

Having a child changes your life. Forever. It changes your body, your soul, your mind and your bank balance. It affects your relationships – with your partner, your parents, your friends and your community. This book shows you how to stand strong against those who undermine or oppose your choices. In other words, it acknowledges the real experts – you and your child. My aim is to help you unlock your intuition so that you nurture with confidence.

Seize your power! Whether you are making birth plans, choosing health care, education or child-rearing practices, or confronting the pain (and blame) of things gone wrong, explore all your options and take charge. Trust yourself. Trust your child. Trust your feelings. Take good care of yourself. Laugh, love, enjoy, and remember to be as gentle on yourself and your beloved as you are with your child.

P.S. Because children come in both genders, I have alternated the terms 'she' and 'he' throughout the book – no sexism intended. Boys and girls have equal ability to tickle your funny bone and pluck at your heartstrings, and, as babies, they are equally delightful.

Families come in more than one form, too – not just the traditional nuclear family. I would like to acknowledge this but apologise in advance if I haven't used the perfect terms to describe your unique family structure, whatever this may be for you and your child – single parent, blended, two mummies, two daddies and so on.

In some of the personal stories, the names of parents and children have been changed to protect their privacy.

1

Bonding with your unborn child

♥

Whether your baby was consciously conceived and you know the exact moment you welcomed her in, or whether your pregnancy came as a surprise and took you some time to get used to, bonding with your baby begins long before you actually meet each other face-to-face or, rather, skin-to-skin. By developing a strong bond with your baby before birth, you will know your child when she is born, and she will feel as though she knows you, too.

As you feel your baby growing inside you, you can begin to connect with her, emotionally, spiritually and physically. At first, simply allow yourself time to dream and feel present with your baby, visualising yourself being with this new little person: imagine the first time you hold her against your chest when she is born; breastfeeding her; taking her for walks; the delight of her first smile. Soon, you will feel tiny movements within your belly and, as your baby develops, she will begin to respond as you communicate with her by talking and stroking.

Here are some things you can do to help you bond with your unborn child:

- **Create a 'baby shrine'.** You might include a candle, baby photos of yourself and your partner, some baby 'objects' such as a pair of bootees, or whatever else you like. One mum-to-be, Roberta, sent me a photo of a whiteboard she'd set up in her kitchen. The board contains lovely written affirmations about pregnancy and birth, a pregnancy photo, and updates such as, 'Our baby is now 37 weeks', along with a description of the baby at that stage ('I'm 39 cm tall and weigh 2.9 kg'). By updating her whiteboard, Roberta and her partner were keeping track of the pregnancy and also sharing the excitement of growing and bonding with their baby.

- **Visit and hold a friend's baby.** This is a great way to make your baby and your imminent parenthood 'real' for you and to give you a bit of confidence. I often find women at antenatal classes, as well as new mothers, who have never held a baby before. I have also known women having difficulty conceiving who have held a newborn and, soon afterwards, become pregnant. If you have other children, visiting friends with babies can also help you introduce them to the reality of a new baby in your home.

- **Feel and watch.** As your 'bump' grows and begins to move, make some time each day to connect with your unborn baby and to feel how he responds to your voice and your touch. If this isn't your first baby, you may find that you are rushing through your day trying to get things done, but this really is a special time that you deserve to share with your baby.

- **Enjoy a candlelit bath.** Gently massage your baby while you bathe; watch her tiny limbs move and picture holding her in your arms.

- **Read to your baby.** You could read a children's book or a book of your own – whatever feels right.

- **Play music to your baby.** Humming or singing a favourite tune to your baby before she is born will not only help you feel connected but the vibrations will gently massage her and help her feel secure and connected to you. And, after she is born, these same songs and music will soothe her as they help her to recall her safe womb world.

- **Join a pregnancy yoga class.** A good teacher will incorporate meditations and visualisations that will help you bond with your baby. Making this a regular practice will also give you space and time to relax and enjoy this special connection, as well as allowing you to share your journey with other women who are pregnant.

- **Give your baby a name.** This will make her feel like a 'real' person. The name doesn't have to be the name you will finally give your baby (especially as you may not know whether you are naming a he or a she) – it can simply be a nickname.

Your partner and any older children will each connect with the unborn baby in their own ways and it is important to encourage this so that they can begin to enjoy their own unique relationships.

2

Your body, your baby, your birth

♥

Giving birth is a rite of passage: it is our first step into the unknown for the love of our child. Again, because each of us is unique and there are many variables involved, there is no one-size-fits-all set of instructions that can promise us a perfect outcome or a smooth passage. However, you do need to remember that it is your journey – your body and your baby. You are the one in charge. Taking responsibility will empower you by developing your confidence and helping you to trust your intuition. By becoming an active, informed participant in your birth experience – by asking questions, understanding your body and how to make birth easier, choosing carers and support people who are respectful and include you in decision-making, and finding a birthplace where you feel safe – you will learn valuable skills that are transferable to all parts of your life. You will discover strength and a depth of feeling you may never have believed possible. And you will develop reserves of courage that will sustain you later as you face other challenges on your parenting journey.

'My whole perspective on motherhood is one of surrender. Birth is a huge lesson in surrender. Our body becomes a vehicle for our baby. In labour, our body takes over, and at the same time we are stretched to the outer edges of our soul. Normally, I am quite a modest person. It was so different [in labour]. I had two friends with me and I was wandering around naked. It was a different me. Then, there is all the stuff of bearing down and being in touch with the spirits of all the women who have been there before, then pushing your own baby out. I felt I was at my "most" during that process. It is about losing control and being okay with that.'

Anne, mother of one

Be prepared

I am amazed at how many women seem totally preoccupied with preparing a nursery and buying baby products yet barely seem to give a thought to preparing their bodies and minds to give birth. You wouldn't approach any other major event without preparation – think of the lead-up to a wedding, a sporting competition, a new job or even a holiday to an exotic destination. You would, of course, want to give yourself the optimum chance of being in peak condition to manage any event like this.

You can prepare your mind and body for birth relatively easily, in a number of ways.

- **Good nutrition.** Eat a wide variety of fresh, colourful vegetables and whole foods (i.e. foods that have been processed and refined as little as possible) and perhaps include a multivitamin designed for pregnant women, as well as zinc and vitamin C supplements to aid muscle elasticity during labour. It's also important to include omega-3 fatty acids (found in oily fish such as salmon, sardines, tuna and trout or vegetarian sources such as walnuts, pumpkin seeds or flaxseed oil) in your pregnancy diet. Omega-3 fatty acids will assist your baby's brain and nerve-tissue development, and will help foster better sleep patterns after birth. They are also good for your own brain and will elevate your mood both during and after pregnancy. (Low levels of omega-3 have been associated with depression.) For more information about nutrition during pregnancy, consult a dietician or naturopath, or read a book such as the *The Natural Way to Better Babies* by Francesca Naish and Janette Roberts (see **Further Reading**).

- **Exercise.** A class for pregnant women, such as antenatal yoga or a pregnancy exercise class run by physiotherapists (such as Preggi Bellies or Fit to Deliver), will include squats and stretches to strengthen muscles for an active labour. In the later stages of pregnancy, regular walking and swimming are particularly beneficial because they encourage your body to produce more of the hormone relaxin, which helps ligaments stretch during labour.

'Having just gone through my second labour, with no pain relief (I had an epidural for my first), and going home four hours later, my two pieces of advice are:
1. Make sure you're physically ready for what's ahead – try to get in shape as much as possible. I did Pilates and it was great.
2. Read up on active birth positions because finding the right position can help you carry on for that bit longer. And make your partner/birth support aware of these positions, too, as there are times during labour when you can't remember anything you've read!'

Bryony

- **Physical rest.** It is important to listen to your body and respect signals that mean you need to rest. Growing a baby is a huge physical challenge and making time to rest will help you become more attuned to your body and reduce stress hormones (which can slow labour). Resting each day during the later weeks of pregnancy will ensure that you go into labour with good reserves of energy. This means you will be better prepared to manage the physical challenge of labour and your hormonal response to labour will be more effective because you aren't already feeling exhausted. (See **Helpful hormones**, page 27.)

- **Mental preparation.** Just as you get your body ready to cope with the physical rigours of birth, it is important to prepare yourself mentally, especially by practising relaxation during pregnancy. Giving birth is about letting go, and that can take some practice (see checklist below)! And, of course, if relaxation during pregnancy enhances your wellbeing, it will also enhance your child's – before birth and after.

'I did Calmbirth classes – anything to stop being the control freak I was. Calmbirth really helped me to relax and stop – just to be and to go with the flow a bit more, and to surrender to the birth and, later, to being a mum.'

Hannah

✳ CHECKLIST : **RELAXATION DURING PREGNANCY**

- You may find it helpful to listen to soothing music and to condition yourself to relax to a particular piece. You can then use this during labour and later, when you are breastfeeding. Some mothers report that this approach also has calming effects on their baby after she is born.
- Athletes use mental imagery to help them achieve peak performance. Conjure up some relaxing images and peaceful scenes (rolling waves, waterfalls, walking along a beach – whatever soothes you) and meditate on these during the later months of pregnancy so that you can also recall them and relax during labour.
- Deep, slow abdominal breathing can help you relax your body and your mind, as well as easing stress and discomfort during pregnancy and labour. For most of us, this requires a conscious effort and some practice. Start by sitting in a comfortable, supported position. Relax. Place one hand on your abdomen and inhale through your nose, breathing deeply into your abdomen. (If you are experiencing nasal congestion, which is common during pregnancy, breathe in through your mouth.) Your abdomen should move outward as you inhale. If only your chest is moving, then you need to inhale more deeply.

When you have inhaled as much and as deeply as you can, pause for a few seconds. Then, slowly exhale through your mouth as your abdomen returns to its normal position. Repeat these deep breathing exercises several times, working up to about 10 breaths twice each day, or more often if you like. If you feel yourself becoming lightheaded or dizzy, you probably need to slow down your breathing — try breathing in to the mantra 'I am breathing in,' and out to 'I am breathing out.' When you breathe, allow every part of your body to relax completely.

You can use deep breathing whenever you feel tired, stressed or nauseous. As you exhale, visualise yourself 'letting go' of negative feelings such as nausea or tension and releasing them from your body.

Pregnancy and birth-care choices

Your experience of pregnancy and birth will have lasting effects on your baby, your body, your mind and your soul. It will colour your relationships with your child and your partner, and it will affect your sense of self. By being an active participant, you may discover reserves of strength and a depth of feeling you would never have believed possible.

Whatever birthing approach you choose, how positive the experience is depends to a large extent on your commitment to educating yourself about the process, and seeking support people and a birth environment that suits you. You can only have each baby once. If you understand all the options, and weigh the pros and cons of various birthing styles, you can make informed choices. And if you choose carers who respect your priorities, you can work together as partners in the birth process. Remember, health professionals are no different from any other professionals in that their levels of competence vary. You would choose a mechanic or a builder with care, wouldn't you? Your body and your baby deserve the best care you can access.

Who?

For antenatal care, you have a range of options.

- **A public hospital clinic.** This is the least expensive option. You will be in good hands but not necessarily the same hands at each visit.
- **Shared care.** This is an in-between option, in terms of cost. Most pregnancy care will be provided by your local GP or midwife, interspersed with a few visits to hospital. During labour, you will be tended by hospital staff before returning to your GP for postnatal care.
- **Your GP, if they are a GP-obstetrician.** GP-obstetricians are not the same as specialist obstetricians, but they have completed extra training in obstetrics and have the advantage of being familiar with your medical history. GP-obstetricians are well-equipped to manage a normal birth and will refer you on if complications make it is necessary.
- **Your own obstetrician.** This is the most expensive option and only feasible, for many people, if they have private health insurance. If you choose this path, during labour you will be tended by hospital staff who will be guided by your obstetrician. Your obstetrician will attend your delivery (unless it happens very quickly) and will see you for your post-natal check-up.
- **A midwife.** Midwives may work independently or as part of a team based in a major public hospital. In the latter case, you will get to know a small group of midwives during your pregnancy and so will be familiar with the person who attends you when you give birth. Increasingly, women are employing independent midwives for hospital as well as homebirths. This can be especially helpful for first-timers, as hospital birthing suites are notoriously busy places: not only will you have to share a hospital midwife, but the one you're most familiar with might have to change shifts at the crucial moment. It can be reassuring to have a professional who has come to know you and your wishes during pregnancy.

Where?

The best place to give birth is where you feel safe and supported. This may be in a hospital; in a birth centre, which offers not only a more homey environment but a philosophy that encourages trust in the natural process and caution about the use of technology; or at home. The options available to you may be affected by where you live.

If you want to find carers who will respect your choices and a birthplace where you feel relaxed, it is worth taking some time to shop around. Before you decide, ask friends, local parent support groups and childbirth educators about their impressions of various options. If you are contemplating a hospital birth and want to choose an obstetrician, ask friends and family or your GP for recommendations.

Below is a list of good questions to ask the hospital or birth centre where you are considering having your baby.

✳ CHECKLIST : **WHAT TO ASK THE HOSPITAL/BIRTH CENTRE**

- What antenatal education do you offer?
- How do you encourage partners to participate during pregnancy, labour and the newborn period?
- Will my partner be able to stay with me throughout labour and the birth, whatever the outcome?
- Will my partner be able to stay with me during the postnatal period? (Birth centres and some hospitals provide double beds so the whole family can stay together.)
- How do you feel about me having my own support people at the birth?
- Can I bring my own midwife? Do any independent midwives have delivery rights at this hospital? (They generally don't, unless there is a special relationship between a particular midwife and hospital, or your midwife is connected to a government-funded homebirth or community midwifery program.)
- Will I be encouraged to move around during labour? (Being mobile during labour will help your baby move down the birthing passage more easily.)

- Is a bath/birthing pool available? (This can help ease discomfort during labour.)
- Can I give birth in water or will somebody 'pull the plug'? (Some places have 'birthing' pools but only allow water births if there is an accredited staff member on duty.)
- Can I give birth in any position? (Some obstetricians insist on birthing on the bed, but an active upright labour can decrease the length of your labour by 40 per cent.)
- What are my options for pain relief?
- What are your episiotomy rates? What are your caesarean rates? (Every obstetrician knows their figures – the value in this question is whether or not individual practitioners will divulge this information. A doctor who has reasonable rates and is not overly interventionist will be willing to share their statistics and their views on interventions during labour.) Printed information about these procedures and what they entail – so that you can understand and alleviate any fears or concerns – is usually available from your carer, clinic or hospital.
- Are mothers and babies separated after birth? If so, why?
- If I have a caesarean:
  - Will I be able to have skin-to-skin contact with my baby immediately, in recovery?
  - Can my partner discover the gender of the baby?
  - Will I be able to have my own support person as well as my partner stay with me in theatre and recovery? (This would be especially important if your baby needs special care, in which case it is desirable for your partner to be able to stay with your baby.)
- Can the APGARS (the baby's wellbeing check score) be done while I am holding my baby, instead of him being taken away to be examined?
- What breastfeeding assistance and support is available? For instance, are there lactation consultants on staff? Do you offer day-stay breastfeeding clinics, if I need further help? Does this hospital have 'Baby-friendly' accreditation? (This is an initiative of the World Heath

Organization and the United Nations International Children's Fund, acknowledging maternity facilities that implement specific practices that support breastfeeding.)

- If it proves necessary, what level of on-site special care is available for newborns? (Some hospitals need to transfer seriously ill babies and you may not be transferred with your baby.)
- What is your discharge policy? (This is especially important to ask if you are considering having your baby at a birth centre because the general policy at most centres is that you are discharged after twenty-four hours. If you need or want to stay longer – and many first-time mothers do – you will usually have to be transferred to a maternity ward, depending on whether this is an option at the birth centre you choose.)
- Do you offer any follow-up services after discharge? (Most birth centres will organise a midwife to visit you at home for a few days to check on you and your baby.)
- What are the costs involved? (It's important to establish what your health insurance will cover and what extras you will have to pay for.)
- You may also want to find out about more general issues such as visiting policies and meals.

How?

To gain support for your choices during pregnancy and labour, you may at times need to assert yourself with family, friends and health professionals. Contrary to popular opinion, being assertive does not mean being aggressive, nor does it mean telling people where to shove it. Assertiveness is about asking for what you want and explaining how you feel without hostility. Try saying, 'I would like . . .', 'It would help if . . .' or, 'I would prefer . . .'

Practise your assertiveness skills while you are pregnant; apart from anything else, they will come in handy for fobbing off all the uninvited advice you are sure to receive once your baby arrives. If, for instance, you are feeling pressured about your birthing choices by family or friends, steer clear by simply telling them, 'I don't feel comfortable talking about this.

Can we change the subject?' and then bringing up another topic. Or, smile sweetly and say, '[Your partner's name] and I have decided . . .' or, 'Our doctor/midwife says . . .' Remain confident by being well-informed and surrounding yourself with positive voices (don't hang out with negative family members or friends). As preparation for labour, when you may feel distracted and vulnerable, try role-playing with your partner or a friend: 'What is the procedure and what are the alternatives?'; 'This is important to me. Could you please explain this again?'

If friends or family members persistently ask you the gender of your baby or what name you have chosen, and you don't know or prefer not to tell them, respond with, '[Your partner's name] and I want it to be a surprise.' Or throw them completely off the track by suggesting the most ridiculous name you can think of. It's unlikely you'll please everybody with the name you've chosen anyway, but people are less likely to express their disapproval once your little bundle has actually been born.

When dealing with professionals, don't feel you have to accept everything they say as gospel and never be afraid to ask questions. Your birth plan (see **The best-laid plans**, page 21) can be a handy tool for discussion. It can also help to write down any questions that occur to you between check-ups, so that you remember to raise them at your next appointment. Enter all discussions at eye level with your health carer. For instance, if you need to ask questions, wait until you are sitting up; it is very difficult to be assertive when you are lying nearly naked on a trolley bed. If you are feeling intimidated by a health professional, imagine them naked or in their underwear (or wearing a spangly white Elvis suit, if the thought of them in the buff brings on an attack of nausea!). And remember that sometimes it is worth giving in on things that aren't really important in order to gain something that really matters to you.

Testing times

When your pregnancy is confirmed, one of the earliest decisions you will be confronted with is whether to have antenatal tests such as routine ultrasounds or an early ultrasound for nuchal translucency (this is used as an indicator of the risk, but not the presence, of Down's syndrome). If early screening or family history indicates some risk, or if you are an older mother or have had problems with previous pregnancies, more intrusive testing such as chorionic villus sampling or amniocentesis may also be proposed.

While carers are medically obliged to offer these tests and there are, of course, legitimate reasons for having them, it is essential to ask:

- Is this the only option?
- What are the risks?
- What are the benefits?
- What will happen if I don't have the test?

Also, consider what you will gain from the results of such tests: will they alleviate anxiety, or will they make you more anxious if you are faced with tough choices such as further intrusive tests or even termination of the pregnancy? And even if the course of your pregnancy will not be altered by test results, might waiting for the results or knowing in advance about a birth defect prevent you from enjoying your pregnancy? Or might it enable you to prepare for a special-needs baby? For each couple, the answers to these questions will be different.

'When early tests indicated that our baby could have Down's syndrome, we were offered an amniocentesis. I didn't think there would be anything wrong and I had no intention of having a termination, but my husband really wanted me to have the test. His theory was that if our baby had Down's syndrome, we could educate ourselves and get into a support group and be ready before the baby came. He looked after me totally and wouldn't let me out of bed for two days after the procedure. Everything was fine.'

Erika

Another consideration when deciding whether to have testing is its role in helping you to bond with your baby. Might it subtly affect your trust in your own body or undermine the magical experience of your baby growing inside you, which is so much a part of connecting with your unborn child? This is also a consideration when it comes to finding out whether you are having a boy or a girl.

'When I was pregnant with my first baby, I decided against having a scan. This was a rather unusual decision, as my partner and I are both doctors and had even done pregnancy scans ourselves while training in GP obstetrics a few years earlier. What influenced me the most was my feeling that I would lose something important as a mother if I allowed someone to test my baby. I knew that if a minor or uncertain problem showed up – and this is not uncommon – I would be obliged to return again and again, and that after a while, it would feel as if my baby belonged to the system, and not to me.'

Dr Sarah Buckley, author and mother of four

The choices we make are personal. We are the people who live with them, however we choose. It may be appropriate to accept some tests and to decline others, but you don't have to have any tests unless that is what you want.

The best-laid plans

Writing a birth plan is a good communication tool for you and your carers. It is also a useful exercise to educate yourself and your partner, and to define your priorities.

The ideal way to record your birth plan is to do it together with your health carer. This way, you can learn about each other and build up a sense of trust. It also helps to clarify your wishes and intentions as early as possible, since you may well find you feel less decisive when you're in labour or in those first hours after the birth. (Don't underestimate how vulnerable you can feel, naked and in a strange environment, with a little group of people peering into your vagina.)

Most importantly, be flexible and consider what you would like if the birth doesn't go exactly as you anticipate. And, regardless of the type of birth you might experience – natural delivery, caesarean section or some variation – don't forget to think beyond the actual birth and consider all the possible outcomes. What if you have planned a homebirth and later require a transfer to hospital, or a natural drug-free birth at a birth centre but end up being transferred to a regular maternity ward because you need some form of intervention, or perhaps a labour that results in an unplanned caesarean section? Thinking about other outcomes can mean the difference between a gentle beginning for your baby and your family life, or feelings of disappointment and loss.

For example, if you have your heart set on a particular birth experience and things don't pan out the way you'd hoped, you might find yourself totally preoccupied with feelings of regret. This can use up a great deal of precious energy at a time when you need all your reserves, and can also affect the way you are able to relate to your baby. On the other hand, if you think through all the possible outcomes and have a back-up plan, you can begin your mothering journey feeling strong and confident because you were involved in decisions, either directly or through your support people, who were fully aware of your wishes.

By going through the list below with your midwife or support person during your pregnancy, you will be able to work out what feels right for you. It is also a great way to educate yourself about the process of birth – what may make it easier, what support you might need, and whether you have chosen a birthplace and carers that fit with what is important to you. Many of these points can be put into your birth plan.

✳ CHECKLIST : BIRTH AND THE BIRTH ENVIRONMENT

- Would you like to birth or labour in water?
- What birthing positions (such as squatting, using a birthing stool or giving birth on all fours) might be useful and comfortable?

- What natural pain-relief options are available? Consider movement – rocking, walking, bellydancing; hot compresses or wheat bags; water – bath, shower or birthing pool (pools can be hired); TENS machine (mild electrical stimulation to divert the pain of contractions; you may need to ask about this option, as it is not always promoted); or acupuncture. TENS and acupuncture require advance preparation.
- If you have an elective caesarean, you can request an epidural (which numbs the lower half of the body but leaves you awake) rather than a general anaesthetic. This way, you can see and touch your baby immediately. If a caesarean is unplanned but becomes necessary, your partner can request early contact with the baby if you aren't up to it.
- Who will be with you or nearby to welcome your baby?
- Do you want your baby to be allowed to breathe before the cord is cut? By having a 'natural third stage' of labour (instead of having an injection of Syntocinon in your thigh and immediate cord cutting), you will gain maximum benefit from the release of hormones that help you bond with your baby and reduce bleeding, and your baby will receive up to 50 per cent extra blood volume from the placenta. This will reduce stress for your baby and also reduces the likelihood of low iron levels in your child. Also, when we consider the amazing properties of cord blood, especially the stem cells, it makes sense to see that your baby gets his full quota of cord blood as well as the stem cells, which will migrate to his bone marrow soon after birth, transforming themselves into various types of blood-making cells.
- Who will cut the cord? Will you keep the cord? Will you cut the cord at all or will you have a 'lotus birth' (keeping cord and placenta intact until the cord separates naturally)?
- What kinds of sights, sounds and smells would you like to be surrounded with as you welcome your baby?
  - Some mothers like music during labour. Perhaps there is a special piece your baby has come to know while in the womb. But keep the

volume low, for although your baby could hear in utero, the sounds were muted.

* Aromatherapy can be helpful during labour but do bear in mind that once your baby is born, it is vital for her to be able to familiarise herself with your smell, unadulterated by anything else – and vice versa. Please be aware, also, that although aromatherapy is a natural treatment, it is powerful and some oils are contraindicated during pregnancy. Please check with a qualified practitioner about which oils might be helpful and which to avoid.

• Make it clear beforehand if you want uninterrupted private time after the birth to breastfeed, cuddle and be together as a family.

'During labour, I used an affirmation that I was made to do this [give birth]. I also think that a support person who knew both me and my partner was what made my first labour an empowering experience. She knew what to say, how to say it and when.'

Suzanne

3
Birth

♥

Fear can have negative effects on how women labour and give birth. Learning to trust in your body and understand its natural hormonal processes can help you create an environment that makes birth easier for you and your baby.

It is difficult to avoid having our ideas about labour and birth contaminated by frightening stories and dramatic movie portrayals that often suggest birth is a dangerous business. Images like this can make you anxious and fearful; it may be a general fear of the unknown, or a more personal fear – perhaps because somebody close to you had a difficult birth experience. Whatever the case, fear not only affects our attitude towards birth but can affect the actual process itself: fear can inhibit the hormonal processes of labour and this, in turn, can make labour more painful and also increase its length.

This is not, though, a reason to call for an epidural at the first contraction or to opt for a caesarean simply to avoid labour altogether. These procedures pose risks to mother and baby that are best avoided unless there are medical reasons for intervention. For example, an epidural increases the likelihood of intervention (such as an episiotomy and/or forceps) during your baby's birth because you are not able to move around into optimum positions during labour. And a caesarean, which constitutes major abdominal surgery, means a longer recovery period for you. Instead, overcome any fear you might have about giving birth by educating yourself about the process and learning how your body works, so that you can participate in the experience with courage and confidence.

It's a birthday, not a party

Whoever you choose to support you at the birth needs to be aware that they are there to do exactly that – support you. Give some thought to how many people you want in attendance; some women find that the more people who are there, the more stressful they find the occasion. The hormonal effects of labour are much more productive when women feel safe, protected and private (see **Helpful hormones**, page 27). The optimum environment for birthing a baby, from a hormonal perspective, is the same as for making a baby. So consider: could you comfortably make love with an entourage of spectators? Just because you may want your mother with you, don't feel obliged to invite your mother-in-law or other family members as well. On the other hand, especially if this is your first baby, a support person other than your partner is likely to be invaluable, particularly someone with experience in the field such as a doula (trained attendant) or your own midwife, who can keep you going when you are fizzling out and your partner doesn't know what to do next. This extra person can guard your space and advocate for you if she knows your wishes; she can also do practical things such as dimming lights or opening windows, preparing drinks for you and your partner or heating wheat bags so that your partner can stay with you and totally support you. Also, if your partner needs to take a break, having a support person means you will not be left alone at any crucial moments. Your own midwife will be able to help you understand hospital protocol and support your partner to advocate for you if she feels this is necessary.

It's a good idea for your prospective support people to attend childbirth classes with you, so they understand the process and what your wishes are. Warn them that you could ask them to leave at any time during labour, but that this won't mean they're being 'fired' – it's just that you're not sure how you will react when the time comes. If you have a midwife or doula, it could be her job to sort out who goes and who stays, according to your needs at the time.

Helpful hormones

Dr Sarah Buckley, a GP-obstetrician/family physician and the author of *Gentle Birth, Gentle Mothering* (see **Resources** and **Further reading**), reassures women that our bodies are superbly designed for birthing babies and describes how this design can maximise safety, ease and pleasure. If you have not had the good fortune to be surrounded by women who have had positive birth experiences, or if you have previously had a difficult birth yourself, you may be thinking that birth and pleasure cannot be put in the same sentence. But Dr Buckley explains the hormonal processes of labour and what she describes as the four 'ecstatic hormones': oxytocin, beta-endorphin, adrenaline and prolactin.

Oxytocin – the hormone of love

Making and having a baby, and breastfeeding, are important social behaviours that involve the hormone oxytocin. During pregnancy, high levels of oestrogen in our body stimulate a dramatic increase in the number of oxytocin receptors in our brain. This makes us highly responsive to the presence of oxytocin. As well as releasing oxytocin during labour, we also release it in huge quantities when making love as well as during breastfeeding, when it causes the release of milk (this is called the 'let-down reflex'). Oxytocin is released when we're interacting with other people in a pleasant way, such as sharing a meal or cuddling. Because oxytocin's release in the brain switches down the fear centre (called the amygdala), we feel less fearful and more sociable.

Oxytocin is naturally produced within the limbic system (the part of the brain that largely controls our emotions), and is released in pulses during labour. Each of these pulses travels to the mother's uterus and stimulates the uterine muscles to contract. The rhythmic contractions of labour are caused by the pulsating release of this hormone within the mother's brain.

When we release oxytocin during labour and birth, not only does it cause the rhythmic contractions of labour, but it also gives mothers a boost to push their baby out. When the baby's head is coming low into her cervix and lower vagina, it causes what is called a positive feedback loop: the mother gets a surge of oxytocin, which helps her to deliver her baby quickly and easily.

After the birth, the mother continues to have high levels of oxytocin, and when she is left alone with her baby immediately after birth, eye-to-eye and skin-to-skin contact will stimulate further oxytocin release. The early pre-breastfeeding behaviour that every baby is programmed to engage in – massaging the mother's nipple and sucking his fists before he actually attaches to the breast – also stimulates oxytocin release in the mother. This is very important because after she has given birth, the uterus shrinks and the placenta begins to peel off, leaving a raw wound that can bleed heavily. If the baby is on the mother's body, as nature intended, the mother releases oxytocin, which causes her uterus to contract, preventing bleeding.

Beta-endorphin – the hormone of pleasure and transcendence

Beta-endorphin is one of the body's natural opiates. It has properties in common with drugs like morphine, pethidine, fentanyl and some other synthetic opiates, which bestow feelings of pleasure or euphoria. Of course, we also use those drugs to relieve pain, and beta-endorphin is a powerful pain-relieving natural hormone as well.

We release beta-endorphin when we're under stress or in pain. For example, marathon-runners release it as they compete (it is the cause of 'runner's high'). We release large quantities of beta-endorphin when we're in labour, which is an intense and often stressful event. The further on the woman is in labour, the more dilated her cervix is and the more pain she reports, the more beta-endorphin she will release.

Of course, beta-endorphin doesn't completely abolish the pain of labour, like an epidural does, for instance. Instead, it puts a woman into an altered state of consciousness, just as drugs do, and this helps her to transcend the stress and pain of labour. It also puts her in tune with her baby so that she knows, for example, exactly what to do with her body to help her baby come down the birth canal. (Birth in humans is a much trickier event, anatomically, than birth in other species. Because we began to walk upright several million years ago, our birth canals developed twists and turns, so human babies have to do a bit of a corkscrew to come out.) This altered state of consciousness is a very important safety feature as well because as the mother feels attuned to her baby, she will move into optimum positions to help facilitate birth, and she will feel calmer, reducing the effects of stress hormones that may inhibit and slow the labour process.

Beta-endorphin is also released by the baby during labour, because birth is a stressful event for the baby, too. Like oxytocin, beta-endorphin activates the pleasure centres in the brain. As with oxytocin, mother and baby have peak levels of beta-endorphin in their brains immediately after birth, putting them in an optimal state to bond and fall in love.

Adrenaline and noradrenaline – the hormones of excitement

You probably know adrenaline and noradrenaline as the 'fight-or-flight' hormones but, in the context of birth, they are the hormones of excitement. The release of these hormones during labour ensures maximum safety of mother and baby during birth.

Early in labour, the mother needs to have low levels of adrenaline and noradrenaline for labour to progress and for the birth to continue optimally. If a labouring woman feels unsafe in any way, she will release high levels of these hormones. Females in labour are genetically programmed to be incredibly sensitive to their surroundings; this sensitivity ensures that labour is safe, particularly for mammals giving birth in the wild, where a rustle in the bushes could indicate a predator coming to attack.

If the mother has a rush of adrenaline and noradrenaline early in labour (what Dr Buckley calls the 'sabre-toothed tiger effect' – it was what would happen in the wild if a sabre-toothed tiger appeared), these hormones slow things down, turning off uterine contractions to give the mother a break in order to find somewhere safe so that labour can resume. They also divert the blood to her major muscle groups (the part of the body she needs for fight or flight), taking the blood away from the uterus and baby. We know from medical studies that women who have high levels of adrenaline and noradrenaline early in labour have more signs of foetal distress – because their babies aren't getting the blood and oxygen that they need – and slower labours.

In our present maternity-care system, women in labour are often brought into an extremely foreign environment (hospital) full of people they don't know, strange noises and all of those things can activate the fight-or-flight response in our primal body, slowing down labour. This is why, according to Dr Buckley, the basic requirement for women in labour is to feel private, safe and unobserved. It's not that they have to be absolutely private – we don't have to retreat to a cave to give birth – but a sense of being totally safe is important to facilitate the hormonal response that makes labour easier.

Prolactin – the hormone of tender nurturing

Prolactin is the major hormone of breast-milk production and is also known as the hormone of tender nurturing. During pregnancy, its milk-producing effects are inhibited by the hormone progesterone.

During labour, prolactin is released along with oxytocin. The mother has high levels of prolactin for the first eight to nine hours after birth, which is probably for optimal milk production. (Once the baby is born and the placenta comes out, prolactin triggers milk production.) This release of prolactin after birth also switches on the instinctive mothering behaviours that all mammals exhibit and that are critical for survival – breastfeeding and bonding.

When we understand these natural hormonal processes, we can see that the whole system of human birth is designed for safety (adrenaline/noradrenaline), efficiency (oxytocin and prolactin) and pleasure (beta-endorphin). This is nature's way of encouraging us to have lots of babies!

Special delivery

If your baby needs special care and you must be separated from him immediately after the birth, you may not be able to cuddle and feed him as you
had planned. You may find yourself overcome by emotion because your
baby is not the healthy newborn you expected, not to mention feeling anxious about his wellbeing and treatment. In order to help both yourself and
your little one, there are a number of things you can do.

- Maintain your connection with your baby in whatever way you can. For
  example, don't feel self-conscious about singing into an incubator – he
  will recognise your voice and feel safe even if you are out of tune.
- Be assertive about being taken to visit your baby if you are unwell
  yourself.
- Ask your partner or a friend or relative to speak for you if you are having trouble communicating effectively and would like more information
  about your baby's treatment or more involvement in his care.

Great expectations

Our experience of birth doesn't always live up to our expectations. Perhaps
you had expected a natural birth but complications during labour meant
that things turned out otherwise. Perhaps you ended up having a caesarean
birth or an epidural and didn't experience the euphoria you were anticipat-
ing. Although we can prepare for birth, we can't plan for every eventuality.

If your birth experience was traumatic or disappointing at any level,
you will need to be gentle on yourself as you take time to process this.
Try to accept that you did all you could at the time, while still acknowledging your emotional pain and disappointment. Your emotional journey,
including grieving the loss of shattered expectations, can be made easier
by finding an appropriate counsellor or support group that will help you
process your experience. Although it may take several months before you
are ready to revisit your birth experience through counselling, it is sensible to find an experienced professional to help you work through what

happened, especially if you are planning another pregnancy. Talking to someone will help you to explore different options of care or seek different support the next time around. This will be both healing and empowering and will help you enter your next labour and birth with confidence rather than fear, which may affect the progress of your labour (see **Helpful hormones**, page 27).

'My first birth was a vaginal delivery with forceps. They put me on my back with my legs in stirrups. It was a traumatic experience all round. Although I would have done it all over to have another baby, I had learnt the hard way that I didn't have good carers the first time. This time I chose another doctor. He was young with little kids of his own, and was very supportive and listened to me. I had an elective caesarean, but I was able to plan a positive experience. I have recovered so easily this time. The first time I think my body was in shock and I probably had postnatal depression. This time I feel so well and happy.'

Wendy, mother of a three-year-old and a three-month-old

'I've had two very different labour experiences, each one teaching me so much about myself and my ability to trust. In my first labour, interventions were high and, begrudgingly, I handed over responsibility to the medical team around me. It was looking back over this that led me to choose a homebirth for my second pregnancy. Being surrounded only by people we had chosen and trusted meant that our second birth was a much more satisfying and empowering experience for us. I felt safe, nurtured and entirely capable of birthing our baby without the need to guard my space or body. The one-on-one care we received in pregnancy, birth and the postnatal period was an essential ingredient for giving me confidence in my mothering. Trusting our instincts is so easy when we embrace what our hearts tell us.'

Donna, mother of two

Planning your babymoon

Many people spare no expense or effort to plan an elaborate wedding and a romantic honeymoon, and yet the greatest change of life – having a baby – is often expected to be a mere blip on the radar, or just another event to fit into an already busy schedule. In fact, many couples assume that this time will be a great opportunity to renovate – after all, you will have time off work! Be warned: I have seen many unfinished projects and stressed-out families who hadn't anticipated the unrelenting needs and unpredictable sleep patterns of a newborn.

Just as a honeymoon has traditionally been a time for couples to get to know their partners more intimately, a 'babymoon' is a very special time for you, your partner and your baby to put aside expectations, shut out the world until you feel ready, and simply enjoy bonding as a family. It is a time to take things slowly and delight in every moment – you'll need to do lots of watching and wondering to get to know your baby's little quirks and foibles, and how he expresses his needs in his own way. I am not advocating that you spend a fortune on a retreat to an exotic destination or that you check into a five-star hotel; your own bedroom and living room are ideal.

Becoming attuned to your baby and beginning to understand his needs in these early weeks will set up a foundation of confidence that you really do know your baby best, as well as a bond between you and your little one that helps him feel secure and encourages his development. Although your baby has only simple needs at this stage (affection, food and sleep), it can help to consider the enormous sensory changes he has experienced in going from 'womb to room', and to offer 'womb service' as you help him to adapt (see **Missing the womb**, page 224). To do this, and to heal your own body after such a momentous experience as growing and birthing a baby, plan your babymoon with as much care as you would plan a honeymoon.

'It is a great gift for a baby and family to have a quiet time with a newborn. The more babies I have had, the more I have enjoyed that time and the more careful I have been about protecting it. I feel very psychically open and easily overwhelmed in the newborn period. This time, for the first ten days, we had all our meals in the bedroom and the kids came in and coloured in and read books. The school community brought meals. I had asked for offers of help before I had this baby. With each baby, I have become more open to receiving help and people do want to be involved with a little baby. Everyone can share the magic of a baby.'

Sarah, mother of four

When you truly respect the changes that a baby will bring – even though you can't possibly imagine these before the baby arrives – and when you set aside time to welcome your baby by setting up supports and postponing unnecessary work obligations, you will avoid a mountain of stress and be able to enjoy this precious time together as you gently introduce your baby to the world beyond the womb.

4
The essential items

♥

Preparing to welcome your baby into the world is a rite of passage and, of course, it is your right to choose which equipment will best suit your needs. However, before you part with your money, it might be worth considering how disappointed you might feel if your little cherub doesn't share your enthusiasm for designer baby gear (the most expensive cot in the catalogue won't guarantee a better night's sleep). Rather than making your baby feel loved and precious because he has the best gear money can buy, a lot of baby 'equipment' is not only completely unnecessary but might actually make your baby feel less loved. (The pressure that goes with designer labels makes some people feel that they need to 'get their money's worth' by making the most of their swish nursery furniture; sadly, this can unintentionally result in separation between baby and mother – the person the baby most wants to be close to.)

Few modern parents could imagine living without a pram, whether flash or basic, but the majority of the world's babies never ride in one; they receive much more sensory stimulation as they are held and transported in a loving pair of arms. When you carry your baby, she hears your voice as you chatter to her; she feels your touch as you stroke her face and her delicious little body; she smells your familiar scent; and she feels the textures of your clothing and your bare skin and hair. Plus, her view of the world is the same as yours, rather than just bums and legs or the dark inside of a pram hood. Another concern is that few strollers or prams are designed so that babies can see their mothers, making it more likely that your baby will feel alone and that you will miss out on the chance to read her subtle cues. Research carried out by Dr Suzanne Zeedyk from Dundee University in 2008 found that children in prams facing the front are less likely to talk, laugh and interact with the person pushing them. However, babies facing whoever is pushing them are twice as likely to be talked to, boosting their language and emotional development. This study also revealed that the infants' heart rates also fell slightly when they were facing their mothers (a sign that they were more relaxed), and that they were twice as likely to fall asleep, which could indicate reduced stress levels.

Many baby products are very useful in small doses. Few isolated mums without other loving arms to share the load can manage to carry their babies constantly, and nobody would argue that car restraints are non-essential or that a desperate mother should feel guilty when a few minutes in a rocker or baby swing can buy her a quick shower. But overuse or inappropriate use of 'baby containers' can hinder infant development, as they restrict movement and sensory stimulation. And some items, such as baby walkers, can be potentially dangerous as well.

Rather than feel guilty that you haven't spent a small fortune on nursery gear, hold your little one close, look into those dark-blue eyes and remind yourself that the best baby playgym is a clean floor and the very best 'product' for her wellbeing and development is – you! As the Beatles sang, 'Can't buy me love'.

Baby gear

There are, nevertheless, some items you will need to buy. Your list will depend on your personal preferences, your lifestyle and your priorities as a family. But when buying any baby gear – from tiny adorable clothing to a larger item such as a cot – I think it's a good idea to ask yourself a few questions when deciding what is helpful and/or useful.

✳ CHECKLIST : **BUYING BABY GEAR**

- **Is it safe?** This is your number-one priority. For equipment such as cots and prams, look for the Standards Australia mark (this confirms that the product has been manufactured according to quality-assurance guidelines) and also check the web sites productsafety.gov.au and babysafety.com.au. But do remember that the standards mark does not guarantee safety; you need to remain aware of how you are using the product. Remember, too, that it is perfectly okay to look a gift horse in the mouth if you are being offered goods that don't fit your requirements or that may be potentially unsafe.
- **Will it help our baby feel loved?**
- **Will it help our baby's development?**
- **Is it congruent with our parenting style?**

With these questions in mind, let's look at some essential items and how you might make choices with regards to bonding with your baby and enhancing her development.

Car restraint

Whatever your budget or parenting style, you will need a safety standards-approved car restraint for your precious cargo. The restraint needs to be fitted professionally by an authorised fitter. And you must ensure that every time your baby rides in a car, he is securely strapped in according to the directions on the particular safety restraint being used. If a baby is on your lap and you are in an accident, or even if your car stops suddenly, you may not be hurt, but your child will become like a little missile and could be seriously injured, or worse.

The safest way for a baby to travel in a vehicle is in the rear-facing position. The guidelines (these vary slightly from state to state, so you will need to check) advise that all babies under 9 kilograms should be in a rear-facing seat and that they should stay in this position until they outgrow the restraint. You may be able to hire an infant capsule from a safety-restraint hire centre or a local council. Or, check out convertible car restraints that can be turned to face forward as your baby grows.

If a grandparent is going to be transporting your baby on a regular basis, it might be worth investing in a second restraint so that you don't have to keep re-installing from one car to the other. Car restraints might seem a bit expensive, but when you think about the possible consequences of not having the safest option available, they are worth every cent.

Pram/stroller

Getting out for a walk with your baby is a sure-fire baby and mummy calmer – a bounce over bumpy footpaths will banish cabin fever as it lulls your little one to sleep and helps you to release endorphins (feel-good hormones).

When you choose a pram or stroller, it is worth remembering that you will probably use it more when your baby is a toddler. Initially, you might use a sling or baby carrier more often, especially if you have a baby who isn't happy in a pram (this can happen if you have a baby who suffers from reflux and is uncomfortable lying down) or if you just want to duck into the shops without lugging a pram in and out of the car. However, it can be a false economy to use a stroller that is designed for a toddler to transport a newborn, as it isn't healthy for their tiny backs to be propped up in an almost-sitting position; your newborn's pram needs to lie flat.

Perhaps the most important consideration when choosing a pram is where and how you will use it. If you do a lot of walking, it's best to choose one that has large wheels that will be able to handle uneven surfaces easily (three-wheeled 'jogger' prams are often best for this). However, if you do buy a three-wheeled pram and want to use it for shopping or visiting friends, check that the wheel base isn't too wide to get through doorways or checkout lanes, as this can be very frustrating!

If you will need to lift the pram in and out of your car regularly, check whether it folds easily, how heavy it is to lift (by both parents – mothers will have reduced muscle strength for a few months after having a baby), and whether it will fit easily into the boot of your car (along with the shopping!).

✳ **CHECKLIST : CONSIDERATIONS WHEN BUYING A PRAM/ STROLLER**

- **Harness**. Does the pram have a five-point harness? All prams should have one – and it needs to be used. Even young babies have been known to wriggle upwards into unsafe positions or have falls when not properly strapped in.
- **Hood**. Will the hood provide good shade or can you easily add a shade if necessary?
- **Height**. Does the pram have height-adjustable handles so that it's comfortable for both parents to push?
- **Size**. Will the pram you choose for your young baby also be suitable for a toddler, and how will it steer with a large, active child on board? Will it convert to a stroller later? Some people invest in both a heavier pram for walking and a lighter ('umbrella') stroller to leave in the car, or a pram for the early days and a stroller for the toddler years.
- **Second-hand**. Consider getting a second-hand pram – some of the older-style prams (such as an Emmaljunga) have well-sprung wheels, are very stable and are great for young babies because they face you. Many of these also convert to a sitting position for toddlers, too.
- **Siblings**. Do you want to use your pram for more than one child? If so, consider spending a little extra to buy a good-quality pram that will last well. And make sure that you can attach a child seat if your children might be close together in age.

Baby carrier

Carrying your baby in a sling enables you to use your hands while still keeping your baby close. Also, this constant contact helps you to become familiar with and respond to his pre-cry signals. Lower levels of stress hormones in your baby's bloodstream in turn result in a more relaxed, happy baby – and parent! And while your baby is in a sling, he is exposed to a smorgasbord of sensory experiences: the different textures of your skin, hair and clothing; a range of sights and smells; and the sound of your voice.

When you carry your baby chest-to-chest against your body, your heartbeat, rhythmic movement and respiration have a balancing effect on your baby's irregular rhythms of waking, sleeping and digestion; it is also thought to help him regulate his developing nervous and hormonal systems, and promote day waking and night sleeping. Carrying your baby upright against your warm body will also help relieve symptoms of colic and reflux. And yes, your baby is safe sleeping in a sling, although, as in any situation, it's up to you to be active in caring for your baby (see the checklist below).

Start carrying your baby in a sling as early as possible to get your own body used to his weight before he becomes too heavy. If you find baby-wearing a strain at first, use the sling for shorter periods and gradually increase the length of time as your muscles adapt. Before you buy a sling, try on various different brands (preferably with a baby in them).

✳ CHECKLIST : CHOOSING AND USING A BABY SLING

- Does the sling have good head and back support for a newborn? (Some slings, such as the ERGObaby carrier, have an insert to support newborns; it can be removed as your baby grows.) Ensure that your baby's head isn't slumped forward against his chest inside the sling, as this can restrict his ability to breathe. Also ensure that the sling allows good airflow around your baby's face so that he isn't constantly re-breathing the same air.
- Are the leg openings wide enough?
- Does the fabric chafe?
- Could a newborn baby slip out or an older baby climb out?
- Will your baby be supported if he falls asleep?
- Can your baby get his fingers caught anywhere?
- Is the sling easily washable?
- Are the fasteners easy to do up properly?
- Can you get the sling on easily without help? (This may take some practice and perhaps a few lessons from another mum who is an experienced sling wearer, but it is essential to be able to do it yourself.)

- Can the sling be used horizontally as well as upright? (If your baby is very small, it may be wise to carry him horizontally until he can hold his own head up.)
- Although it's easy to get on with things around the house when your baby is calm and quiet in a sling, do remember to check on him frequently.

'With the arrival of my second baby, Chela, ten years after the first, I was much more relaxed as a mother and trusted my intuition when it came to my baby's needs. She very clearly communicated that she did not like to be left alone (even if I was close by), and having her close against my body in a baby carrier just felt so right. She was happier, cried so much less, slept longer and deeper, and I had both my hands free to get on with my day. I feel baby-wearing not only strengthened my confidence as a mother, it deepened the bond between us – and that is forever.'

Suzanne, mother of two

Clothing

There are some beautiful baby clothes available and no doubt you will be tempted by many of them before your baby is born. Remember, however, that you are likely to be given plenty of gorgeous but impractical clothing as gifts when your baby arrives. So, when you are purchasing clothes in preparation, take the checklist below into account.

✳ CHECKLIST : **PRACTICAL BABY CLOTHING**

- Will the clothing allow easy access for skin contact? All-in-one jumpsuits do not. You can stroke tiny backs or rub tummies more easily with two-piece suits or nighties. Your gentle touch is comforting to your baby as well as important for the release of the hormones (in you and your baby) that encourage bonding (see **Helpful hormones**, page 27).
- Are the clothes likely to fit so snugly that they cause overheating or restrict your baby's movements? Comfort must come before style:

larger, loose clothing is better. Natural fabrics (pure cotton, wool or silk) are preferable to synthetics, which don't absorb perspiration and may irritate sensitive skins. Babies may, though, find direct skin contact with wool irritating, so if you need wool for warmth, purchase a pure cotton t-shirt for underneath.

- Do the clothes have envelope necks or front openings? Some babies cry as you pull clothing over their heads and it is less stressful if you can minimise the need for this.
- Is there easy nappy-changing access? Again, all-in-one jumpsuits might not be the most practical; press-studs can be frustrating, particularly in the middle of the night!
- Is the quality good? In particular, check seams under arms and at the crotch: are they well-stitched and overlocked, or will they fray easily? (Loose threads can irritate and catch around little body parts like fingers and toes.) Do zippers go up and down easily (if not, they might pinch delicate skin)? Are buttons sewn on firmly (so they won't fall off and become choking hazards)?

Skincare

Becoming a parent changes your perspective on many things, including what you eat and drink while you are pregnant and how this will affect your unborn baby. Your baby is not only affected by what you eat and drink, but by what your skin eats. Our skin is our largest organ and around 60 per cent of what we apply to our bodies is absorbed into our skin. In traditional Chinese medicine, the skin is called the 'third lung' because is it such a direct pathway to our bloodstream. It makes sense, then, to choose skincare that is as safe and as chemical-free as possible while you are pregnant. After your baby is born, you will want to continue protecting your little one from potentially harmful chemicals being absorbed through delicate newborn skin.

Read labels and avoid products that contain mineral oils (these are petroleum-based) and chemicals such as parabens. The general rule of thumb is: If you wouldn't eat it, don't put it on your baby's skin. And remember that even though they may cost a bit more, organic products are not only healthy for our children and ourselves, they are healthy for the planet, too. (When buying 'organic' products, do check that all the ingredients are organic rather than just a small percentage of them.)

Before you apply anything to your baby's skin (for example, massage oil), no matter how natural, do a test first: apply a small amount to the skin inside your baby's leg or forearm and leave overnight. If there is no rash or redness by the next morning, the product is usually safe to use on a wider area.

Bedding

Attachment, the process of 'learning to love', is a behavioural system that operates twenty-four hours a day. It does not deactivate during sleep, where your baby spends an awful lot of time in the early days. In fact, when it is dark and your baby cannot see, skin-to-skin contact, your touch and your familiar smell are even more important for him.

In many cultures, parents would never be faced with the question, 'Where will our baby sleep?' because it goes without saying that he would sleep snuggled against the warm body of his mother. However, while sharing a bed is a lovely option when practised safely, it may not be one that you have considered or that you and your partner feel comfortable with – at least not on a full-time basis. So, you will most likely need to shop for some sort of baby bedding.

There is a range of bedding choices, but the most important consideration is how you can ensure proximity with your baby. This is important for the following reasons:

- Kids and SIDS (the organisation dedicated to reducing the number of sudden infant death syndrome cases in Australia) believes that having your child sleeping in the same room as you for 6–12 months is a significant protective factor against SIDS.
- Touch and proximity are essential elements of bonding.
- Since prolactin levels (prolactin is the milk-production hormone – see page 30) are highest during night-time breastfeeding, it makes sense that

proximity to your baby at night enhances your milk supply. Continued breastfeeding maintains the release of hormones that aid mother–infant bonding, and breastfeeding is more likely to be successful for a longer duration when mothers and infants share sleep. So, co-sleeping (that is, sleeping within arm's reach of your baby, not necessarily sharing the same bed) would seem to be a biologically valid and valuable practice to enhance bonding.

The following products support close night-time parenting:

- The Arms Reach Co-sleeper can be placed against your own bed with one side removed so that your baby has his own space while he sleeps close to you. Because this bed is height-adjustable and attaches to your bed, there are no gaps or crevices for your baby to get caught in.
- My Little Bed is a soft-sided bed for small babies that can be placed in your bed between parents, giving your baby his own safe space while allowing you to attend to him quickly.
- Baby hammocks and cradles that are suspended are likely to make the 'womb-to-room' transition easier for your baby. As he moves around, he starts the hammock or cradle swaying or rocking, much like the way he was lulled to sleep while in the womb. The modern versions of these beds have a flat mattress so that the baby can be placed safely on his back to sleep (according to SIDS guidelines). Some can be suspended from a hook in the ceiling and/or have a stand so that you can easily move your baby around the house; this means that you can keep your baby near you when it isn't convenient or easy to be carrying him in a sling or holding him as he sleeps.

For more information about safe infant sleep, see chapter 8.

'Our daughter, Mika, enjoys an extraordinarily strong, trusting and loving relationship with her father. We attribute it, at least in part, to having a "family bed". Mika is now 4½ months old, and she has been sleeping in our bed since birth. Between the rush to leave for work, and the chaos of dinner and bathtime rituals, her contemporaries appear to spend precious few waking hours with their working fathers. While this is no different for our Mika, she lies in our bed at night, listening to her father's breathing (or snoring!), enveloped in his smell, sensing his heartbeat. When she stirs in the wee hours of the morning, she shows no prejudice in snuggling up to either of us. Even as the weather cools outside, she's never shown any signs of a cold, and her father's arms are always there to welcome her and keep her warm. It's a real moment of joy for me to see Mika wake in the morning and, with a beaming smile, proceed to place her little hand on her father's cheek to let him know it's time for all of us to wake.'

May

Baths

You can spend a lot on a fancy baby bath or you can simply bath your baby with either parent or an older sibling in the big bath. A baby bath will be useful in the early weeks and may allow you to save water for a few months, but it isn't going to be used for long so a simple 'no frills' bath is probably your best bet economically. One new concept is a 'tummy tub' – a baby bath that looks rather like a bucket: your baby can sit in it in a similar position to when he was inside your tummy. As well as saving water, this can be very comforting, especially if he has tummy pains, as these will be relieved by his position, and the warmth and depth of the water will help him to relax. Bathing with a parent is a lovely way to bond and the deep water of a large bath will allow your baby to experience the buoyancy of his body as well as helping him relax. I advise against using a baby bath seat – it's just one more gadget that really doesn't have a purpose. You won't be leaving your baby unattended anyway (this is an absolute safety rule!), and by holding him naturally, with your arm supporting his neck and your hand holding the armpit furthest from you, he will experience floating, which will help him feel comfortable in water and later with swimming. (Yes, even babies can float and swim, but do book in for baby swim lessons if you want to learn more.)

5

The first six weeks – a survival guide

♥

Here you are, gazing at your amazing newborn, completely overawed that you could feel so in love and protective of somebody you have just met. And yet, despite your wonder at the beautiful little being you have produced, you are probably a little overwhelmed, too, wishing there was a red button on the wall to summon help – at all hours!

There is a conspiracy of silence about how overwhelming it can feel to be in sole charge of your own precious little baby. And it seems that people rarely tell the truth about the realities of newborn behaviour or how unrelenting it is to be the primary carer. It is stressful just getting through your day. Who would have thought one tiny being could create so much washing? Or that they could breastfeed for an hour every two hours? Or that their squeaks and snuffles are loud enough to keep you awake all night? Or that getting out of the house before 2 p.m. could be an impossibility? Or, most surprisingly, that all this is *completely normal*? On top of these stresses sits the incredible barrage of advice about how you 'should' be caring for your baby. Is it any wonder you feel overwhelmed?

'People told me that all newborns did was eat and sleep. Boy, were they wrong!'

Natalie

'I cried the first night I had my new baby at home because she wasn't in my tummy any more and I couldn't protect her from the world as easily as before.'

Lynne

Even if it seems difficult to believe right now, you *do* have it in you to be the mother you want to be. Firstly, it can help to understand what is normal and how to work with your individual baby so that you can enjoy this precious time instead of obsessing over doing things 'right' (according to whichever person you are currently listening to). Feeling confident about the things you can predict and control will help you to accept the other unpredictable things that are part and parcel of caring for a newborn. This way, you can give your baby a gentle welcome to the world as well as being gentle on yourself as you learn new skills and adapt old ones so that they serve you better in this new and awesome role.

Ditch the rules

You may have read a dozen books and been to a number of classes, and you may have decided exactly what sort of parenting style will work for you. But what seemed completely sensible before you had a baby may not actually fit *your* baby, or be practical, now that he is here. For instance, I have seen women with neatly printed and ruled routine charts and checklists, all ready to slot their baby in. When their unique baby doesn't eat, sleep and play according to the chart, the poor mother is thrown into chaos. Instead of considering that the routine (prescribed by somebody who doesn't know *your* baby) might simply be unhelpful right now, mothers tend to think that they are doing something wrong, and this self-doubt begins to erode their confidence.

I have also seen women who write down every feed (how many minutes, which side), how many wees and poos, and how many minutes of sleep their babies have each day. They strive to find a pattern in an effort to feel more in control. However, they become so obsessed about what their baby is doing (or not) that they not only create an enormous amount of extra work, but they end up so focussed on outcomes that they don't spend any time enjoying their baby – gazing and smelling and smooching and 'drinking in' their beautiful new being. This time is what really matters – not how long your baby sleeps, how often she feeds or whether you have her in a routine.

Remember, there are no rules. So, you may be asking: How do I know what is right and who do I believe? My criteria for discerning what is right is to step back and ask three questions before you try anything:

- **Is it safe?**
- **Is it respectful?**
- **Does it feel right?**

If you want to try out some new advice or a new way of being with your baby and it fits these criteria, then go ahead. If what you are doing works for you and your family, feels right and is safe and respectful, then do it. Of course, babies change so quickly that just when you feel you have things sorted and working well, you're back to the drawing board! This is the time to reassess and perhaps try another strategy. (Looking after a baby requires some experimentation.) Again, if you have any doubts about what you are doing, check in: Is it safe? Is it respectful? Does it *feel* right? You can also use these criteria if you are given advice that undermines your parenting. This is *your* baby and *you* are your own best expert.

Although there is no other baby exactly like your baby, there is some typical baby behaviour and development that it is useful to understand. It will help you to have realistic expectations, and you will feel more calm and accepting of your baby's very intense needs during the early weeks. If you can appreciate that your baby's behaviour patterns (or lack of them) are often related to developmental changes, you will be able to step back, breathe and accept the wonderful baby you have. And you will be able to nurture him gently and respectfully.

Day 1

Congratulations! You have birthed your amazing baby and now you are getting to know her. It's awesome, exciting and overwhelming! Depending on your birth experience, you may be high on hormones or totally exhausted; a mix of both; or, especially if you had complications and are separated from your newborn, you may be anxious. In this section, I am going to talk about what is normal care for your baby; if there are complications or a situation that requires extra care for you or your baby, you will be guided by your health carers. If you are affected by medication that could make you drowsy or reduce awareness of your baby, it is best to have your partner or a support person to supervise and help you handle your baby.

Wait to weigh

There is no need to weigh your baby before he has his first feed; it is much more important for him to be placed straight on your body. When it does come time for weighing, later on, please ask for your baby to be placed in the scales on his tummy, on top of a warm towel; it can be very frightening for a newborn to be placed flat on their back after they have been snuggled in your womb. Also, lying on his back will trigger your baby's startle reflex, which will increase his feelings of fear. Speak to your midwife about this so that she is aware of your wishes.

Your baby's first feed

After birth, allow your newborn to lie between your breasts against your bare skin (with a blanket over you both – your baby must be kept warm). Newborns who are kept warm and allowed uninterrupted skin-to-skin contact with their mother will often seek and latch onto the breast without very much help at all (you can see a video of this at breastcrawl. org). Research shows that when babies are held skin-to-skin against their mother's body, they instinctively search for the breast by lifting their heads and thrusting their chin and mouth forward, which in turn has the effect of tilting their head backwards. This posture facilitates good attachment and feeding.

If you are patient and allow your baby to take his time – it may take up to an hour for your baby to complete the natural pre-breastfeeding behaviours such as kneading your breasts with her fists, grasping and licking your nipples, then attaching and sucking – this first feed can last anywhere from about half an hour to a couple of hours.

This first feed is important because it provides your baby with colostrum (the yellowish fluid that precedes breast milk; colostrum is high in antibodies and other important elements that prime your baby's immune system), and also helps your baby to imprint a sucking technique.

If you have a shower after this first feed, it is best not to wash your breasts because when your baby next feeds, he will be guided by the smell of the amniotic fluid he left on your breasts at his first attempt. After this, it's fine to wash your breasts, but don't use any soaps yet, as the perfume could confuse your baby.

Hey, Dad, your first cuddle

Dads and partners, it's best to have a threesome cuddle at first, as your baby lies on Mum's body, so that your baby gets to know the smell of his food (Mum's breasts) without confusion. However, if for any reason your baby is separated from Mum immediately after birth, it is important that you provide skin-to-skin care for your baby, if he is healthy: remove your shirt and cuddle your baby close or tuck him inside your shirt like a tiny kangaroo and snuggle.

If baby needs help to feed

Some babies may need a little help to start feeding but please don't force your baby; instead, hold him close, skin-to-skin, and place him near your nipple (see **Position matters**, page 108). Squeeze out a drop of colostrum so he can lick and taste. This will encourage him to stick out his tongue in a way that will make it easier for him to latch onto your breast. Most importantly, don't let anybody grab your baby and your breast and shove them together! If a midwife looks as though she is about to do this, put your hand up in a 'stop' sign and say, 'I would like to have a go myself. Can you just watch and give me some tips, please?'

If your baby isn't interested in feeding yet

If your baby isn't interested in feeding straight after birth, please don't stress – allow skin-to-skin contact and let him come around in his own time. Your baby won't be hungry – he has stores of brown fat that help to keep him warm, and his stomach will be full of amniotic fluid that will sustain him for the first day or two. If you have had medication or complications during the birth, or if you and your baby are separated initially, be reassured that nature allows ongoing opportunities to bond with your baby and establish feeding – but you may need extra help. If your baby is having difficulty attaching to the breast in the early days, hand-express and give colostrum to him in a syringe or with a small spoon (ask a midwife for assistance).

Keep your baby close

After his first feed, your baby will probably have a long sleep. This is also your recovery time so please keep visitors, other than immediate family, away for the first day or two, and spend this time resting and snuggling with your newborn and your partner. Keeping your baby near you in the first days, snuggled kangaroo-style against your bare chest, helps you get to know each other and will encourage your body to produce the hormones oxytocin and prolactin (see pages 27 and 30), which will help your milk 'come in' i.e. change composition from the initial sticky colostrum and start to flow. If hospital staff discourage this or suggest that you regulate feeding times because this is 'hospital policy', insist (politely) on doing what works for you. By keeping your baby close to you, you will be able to see immediately when your baby begins to stir and make signals (rooting or sucking movements with her mouth or moving her hand towards her mouth) that indicate she is ready to try feeding.

Day 2

Just as you realise you have survived your first day as parents and are wondering whether you have hit the jackpot with the proverbial 'easy' baby, all hell breaks loose! Your baby wakes and yells. You offer the breast. He sucks a bit and calms, then falls asleep. You gently wrap him and place him back in his cot. Moments later, he is awake and yelling – again! You begin to wonder whether he is hungry. Should you give him a 'top-up' bottle? As he continues to yell, you become more and more anxious, not to mention exhausted.

Unsettled behaviour is common in newborns around two days after birth. And it isn't due to hunger. In fact, your baby has woken to the world, and the sensory changes between his cosy womb world and the 'outside' are overwhelming him. The closest place to 'home' for him now is snuggled in your arms against your comforting heartbeat, sucking at your breast.

To help your baby settle, snuggle him close and let him breastfeed (he needs the practice before he has a large volume of milk to contend with, and this close contact will help your milk come in more quickly). When he falls asleep at the breast, gently move him so he can lie against your chest in a comfortable position. Let him rest there until he is in a deep sleep (his arms will become limp), then move him to his bed or to your partner's arms if you need a rest.

You may also have some fussy days like this later on, especially after a busy day with lots of environmental changes such as outings or lots of cuddles with other people. Nursing at your breast and cuddling in your arms will comfort your baby quickly and help him through these unsettled periods. Remember that for your baby, breast is home.

Jaundiced babies

Jaundice, characterised by a yellowish tinge to the skin, is one of the most commonly occurring conditions in babies a few days old. The most common cause is that the baby's immature liver is not yet able to process and excrete bilirubin (a normal by-product of broken-down red blood cells) quickly enough.

One side-effect of jaundice is that babies become very sleepy. However this isn't the time to let your baby sleep for as long as he likes. Sleepy, jaundiced babies can be difficult to arouse for feeds, but letting them sleep can lead to more severe jaundice and, in turn, more intensive treatment. This is a good reason to take preventative measures. Early and frequent breastfeeding without supplements of water, sugar water or formula, which may be suggested by hospital staff, will encourage the baby to pass meconium (those first black, tarry bowel motions) so that he will more quickly establish good gut flora that will break down bilirubin. So, if your baby isn't waking and demanding to be fed at least by the second day, even if he's not jaundiced, it is important to wake him and offer feeds every two to three hours.

Days 3–5

If you had a hospital birth, you may be heading home with your newborn now. Please don't under-estimate how exhausting that single car ride can be, even if it's short. It isn't just the trip that's tiring, but the anticipation and excitement of being a family – and the trepidation about being left totally in charge of your newborn!

Don't plan on *any* stops at shops on the way home – your partner or a good friend can grab anything you need, preferably before you leave hospital. And partners, please note: clean sheets, clean towels, a clean toilet and some prepared food at home are *essential* to keep this childbearing woman as emotionally stable (as possible) right now.

You, your body and your baby

Your milk will come in sometime between days three and five (it can be slower if you had a difficult birth, a caesarean or excessive bleeding after birth, and it usually comes in a bit sooner if this isn't your first baby). As your milk comes in, the hormonal changes that occur can leave you feeling vulnerable and emotional (see **Crying more than your baby?**, page 277) and your baby may also be quite cranky. This may be partly due to discomfort as his tiny tummy gets used to a larger volume of milk, and perhaps partly because he is missing the womb. There are incredible sensory changes between the safe warm womb world where he has been tucked up for all of his tiny life so far and the big new world that he has been born into. See chapter 10 for tips on helping your baby through this stage.

Whether you are at home or in hospital, try to plan quiet days of nurturing (see **Planning your babymoon**, page 33) and limit visitors so you get as much rest as possible. This way, you will find it easier to manage the challenges that these days inevitably present, and your recovery will be quicker and with fewer tears for you and your baby.

How often should I feed?

After birth, your baby's stomach is only the size of a marble and, about ten days later, it is still only about the size of his tiny fist, so his stomach can't hold enough food to go long between feeds, day or night. Also, breast milk is very quickly and easily digested. So, at least in the early weeks, your baby will need frequent feeds. It is perfectly normal for a breastfed baby to need 8–12 feeds in twenty-four hours during the first few weeks. This could mean that she will feed as often as every two hours – and that means two hours from the beginning of one feed to the beginning of the next, not two hours between feeds!

To make feed times nurturing for you, rather than having them feel like an added stress because you 'can't get anything done', set up a comfortable 'headquarters' for feeding and cuddling. You'll be sitting around an awful lot in the first few weeks, so borrow some good books and DVDs. Keep a basket handy containing some healthy snacks to keep you going as well as your book, phone, water bottle, pen and a writing pad. Then, if you feed your baby in different places (inside or outside), you can simply take your basket with you. The pen and pad are for keeping track of things you need to do later, though don't put too many things on your list – the idea is to feel less stressed.

And don't worry: feeding your baby won't take this long forever. In a few weeks, he will be much more efficient and may take only 10–20 minutes to feed. This change from long to short feeds, which often occurs quite suddenly, often has mothers worried that their babies aren't 'getting enough'. But if your baby is having plenty of wet nappies and putting on weight, he is fine. Having said that, if your baby's typical patterns – feeding or otherwise – suddenly change and you're worried in any way, don't hesitate to have a check-up with your child-health nurse or doctor.

Continue to keep your baby close

Being separated from you will be stressful for your baby in her early days, when the only familiar things in her new world are the sound of your heartbeat and voice, and the comfort of your body close to her. Based on observations of the animal world, many researchers claim that babies have an innate need for close physical contact with their parents. There are two types of infant-rearing amongst animals: caching and carrying. 'Caching' species, such as deer, are adapted to their mothers being absent for long periods; babies of these species do not cry (this would attract predators), and their mothers' milk is extremely high in protein and fat so that it can sustain them for long periods.

Humans are much closer to continuous-feeding, 'carrying' mammals such as anthropoid apes; our milk is identical to theirs in fat content, and our babies – like theirs – suckle slowly and cry (often loudly!) when they are distressed or out of contact with a parent's warm body. Research shows that human babies thrive on skin-to-skin contact, which provides warmth as well as the comforting scent of a loving parent. Holding your baby close will enhance bonding as well as neurological development. So, relax and enjoy snuggles with your little one – you're not only helping him feel secure, but making him smarter as well! Hold him against your bare skin, nuzzle against his soft downy head, and inhale his delicious baby smell.

'What surprised me most about having a baby was how it brought me completely down to earth. It made me realise that we really are just another mammal. That no matter how educated, rich or powerful we

may be, in the end, we are all the same. My baby was just a little sweet
bundle of instincts and reflexes! It amazed me that a cry would cause my
breasts to 'let down', and that I felt so *fiercely* protective (just like a lioness
and her cub). I imagined so many things, but I never expected to feel so
connected to the earth and its animal kingdom.'

Amanda

Week 2

Ideally, at first, your partner will be at home to support you, and you
will be able to muddle through together as you get to know your baby,
sleeping when your baby does and generally taking it easy. However, we
don't live in an ideal world, and we don't always have other supportive
people around when partners have to return to work. By two weeks,
most partners are heading back to work, if they haven't already. If you're
at home alone, caring for your newborn, the barrage of advice that may
be coming at you from various angles can play on your mind and you
might begin to worry about your baby: Is he getting enough food? Why
won't he sleep? How long should he sleep? What is he trying to tell me?
Why is he crying? . . .

At about two weeks, your baby is quite likely to go through another
cranky spell. We don't really know why this happens, but if you are
forewarned, at least you can put it down to 'a stage' and remain relatively
calm as you respond to your baby instead of worrying that you might be
doing something 'wrong'. Of course, any time you are concerned about
your baby's health or wellbeing, trust your instinct and have him checked
by an appropriate professional – you are *never* an overanxious mother!
The good news is that unsettled stages that are due to developmental
changes only last a day or two before everything settles down again. Your
best friends right now will be a rocking chair or any other form of rocking (see page 188) and a baby carrier (see page 39): the movement will
soothe your baby and, with a sling, you will have your hands free to do
a few chores.

Weeks 4–5

As your baby starts to get into some kind of a pattern of periods of wakefulness and alertness during the day and (if you are lucky) sleep during the night, you might begin to feel more confident. He will still need frequent feeds (every two or three hours) and help to get to sleep. During the first 3–4 months, your baby will enter sleep through an 'active' sleep phase and his startle reflex can wake him easily as his tiny body jerks uncontrollably. So, if he can't stay asleep when you put him down awake (as you may have been advised), rather than stressing, hold him until he has actually fallen asleep. To make sure he is in a deep sleep phase, wait until his arms are floppy – this can take around twenty minutes – then gently place him into his bed. This way, he will sleep longer without tears. (See chapter 8 for more information on sleeping).

If you are feeling more confident, you might be eager to get out and about. Be careful not to pack too much into your days, though. If you overdo things, you're likely to become exhausted and your baby will be unsettled as a reaction to too much stimulation. This doesn't mean you have to stay home, but it is worth pacing yourself carefully and being very aware of your own energy levels (see chapter 11 on how and why to nurture yourself). A good way to get out of the house is to go for an afternoon walk; this will help your baby to settle into a better day/night sleeping pattern and it will also stimulate your body to release endorphins, and help you feel fitter and more energetic, too.

Cluster feeds

I often have calls from parents of babies around 4–6 weeks because their babies are unsettled in the evenings. Many of these parents are trying desperately to settle their babies for several hours at night. They are worried about colic or reflux and, although discomfort can play a part in unsettled evenings, often the crying is because parents have been trying to get their babies to *sleep* when they actually need to *feed*.

This need for a cluster of feeds close together typically happens in the evening, but it can occur at any time of day. So, if this happens for you, instead of spending hours in a darkened room trying to rock or pat your baby to sleep and becoming increasingly anxious or even slightly resentful that you can't enjoy your evening, try relaxing and seeing this as 'family time'. You and your partner can sit together, cuddling or chatting, as you offer your baby frequent, almost continuous feeds (one side then the other then the other, without trying to space out these feeds). If it gets too much for you, your partner can hold, burp or rock your baby to give you a rest. Partners and grandmothers won't smell of breast-milk so, if your baby has had quite a good feed, he may settle easily in other loving arms instead of rooting around looking for more milk (a natural instinct when food is close by). Babies who cluster-feed in the evening get a tummy full of nutritious hind milk (the rich, creamy, higher-fat milk that will keep them satisfied for longer) and often take a long sleep when they do eventually settle – which can be very convenient if this is around the time you head to bed yourself.

Get practical

From new mothers, I often hear comments like: 'I can't even have a shower because I don't know how long she will sleep for.' Or: 'It takes so long to get her to sleep that we start cooking dinner at 9 p.m.' If your baby hasn't yet been born, these sorts of comments may sound ridiculous. But managing your day around a newborn can be a challenge, especially if you're used to order and punctuality.

Conserving your energy and learning to multi-task are keys to survival in these early days. There are lots of helpful strategies in chapter 11 but, for now, here are some quick tips for getting through your day. I'm not advocating a rigid routine, but it can be helpful for both you and your baby if you create a gentle rhythm based on her needs.

✱ **CHECKLIST : MANAGING YOUR DAY WITH A NEWBORN**

- Include your baby in your daily tasks. For instance, don't wait until she is asleep to have your shower. Instead, pop her in a rocker in the bathroom so that you can see each other. She will probably enjoy listening to the water running and the sound of your voice if you sing or chat while you shower.

- Get dressed early in the day – then you will feel at least slightly in control, even if things go pear-shaped later. And you'll be ready to head out for a walk with your baby if you suddenly feel overwhelmed by cabin fever or an unsettled baby.
- Plan your day around your baby's calm times. For example, if she tends to be more content in the mornings, pop her in a pram or sling and do your shopping then. Or prepare dinner early so that later, if (or when) she has her 'arsenic hour', you won't feel so stressed.
- Set up a comfortable feeding 'headquarters' (see page 54).

Week 6 and onwards

Everybody has warned you about the first six weeks and there's no doubt they are tough. You have a medical check at six weeks and you may have physically recovered from the birth experience by then. You may be feeling more confident about your mothering skills, and you may even have received the biggest reward of all – your baby's first smile. So, things will be a breeze from now on, right? Not necessarily.

In fact, weeks 6–8 can be another typically unsettled period for babies. If your baby wants to feed more often during this period, relax and allow him to do so; he will regulate the exact amount and composition of milk that he needs to grow and thrive. Regardless of your baby's reasons for fussiness and wanting to feed more often some days, it's easy to deflect any undermining comments from visitors ('Are you sure you have enough milk?' or 'Make sure you don't spoil him') by smiling and saying confidently, 'He's having a growth spurt at the moment' (see page 121).

When you have a good milk supply, you will make approximately the same amount of milk in twenty four hours, according to how much your baby drinks. Remember, too, that breastfeeding is not just about hunger;

it also provides comfort and encourages bonding, reduces stress hormones and boosts immunity. (If your baby has been exposed to somebody who is unwell, he will often feed a bit more often, as though his little body knows that he needs an antibody boost.) As long as your baby is having five or six heavy, wet nappies a day, and regular soft or runny yellow poos, you can be assured he is getting enough milk.

Another reason for your baby's restlessness at this stage may be that he is becoming much more alert and aware of his surroundings, but doesn't yet have the capacity to calm his tiny brain or shut out stimulation (see **Developmental changes**, page 219). Be sure to introduce your baby to the world gradually and respect his cues: if you are out and he starts to cry, looks unusually wide-eyed (startled), falls asleep when he would normally be awake, or otherwise seems distraught, take some time out together in a quiet place. Drape a wrap over your shoulder and your baby to block out excess visual stimuli, and offer him a breast/bottle/dummy or a clean finger to suck on, as sucking is a calming, familiar activity.

The most helpful thing to understand is that there will be challenging days and although the reason may sometimes be obvious (handling by lots of visitors, a reaction to the extra coffee you drank earlier, or whatever) there will be other times when you won't be able to work out why. Make sure you offer a feed even if it isn't his usual feed time; he may be needing extra nourishment in line with a developmental stage or he may simply be looking for some extra soothing. Once you have ruled out hunger and obvious causes of discomfort such as a full nappy or wind, try some of the techniques in the checklist below.

✳ CHECKLIST : CALMING YOUR UNSETTLED BABY

- Sit on a fit ball, holding your baby in your arms, and gently bounce as you hum. The movement will soothe your baby, and humming forces you to control your breathing, helping to calm you and changing your energy levels, which in turn makes it easier to calm your baby.
- Take your baby for a walk outside, in a sling or in your arms; around the yard is often enough to distract him. If you have a leafy tree,

try standing under it – the movement of the leaves will give him something to watch.

- As you hold your baby, close your eyes and feel yourself tuning into his energy as you remain still and breathe deeply. Let go of the advice that is clouding your mind and try to be present in the moment with your baby. This might sound a little 'out there', but you really do have a very special energetic connection to your baby and often, by calming yourself and connecting with your little one, the reason for his distress will become clear. And, even if you don't necessarily feel any clearer about the reason for your baby's crying, at least you will feel calmer – and this is good for you both.

Sucking for comfort

Sucking is a comfort to babies and helps them relax. In fact, your baby quite possibly sucked his fingers even before he was born. Especially in the early days, your baby will often indicate that he wants the breast – nature's most convenient pacifier – by 'rooting' (turning his head towards the breast and making grasping movements with his mouth) even when he isn't hungry. Some mothers may find a baby who wants to be almost constantly 'attached' quite disconcerting, but be reassured: as he gets used to the world and as his movements become more controlled so that he can more easily find his fingers, your baby will not rely on nursing so much as a form of comfort. Offering a dummy may buy you some short-term relief at times when your baby seems inconsolable, or it may be helpful if he is a 'high-needs baby' (see **Why do babies cry?**, page 218) – but do read the box below before deciding to offer a dummy.

Dummy alert!

Before you decide to offer your baby a dummy, consider the following potential disadvantages.

- Dummies/teats require a different sucking action from breast nipples and may cause 'nipple confusion', which may create or exacerbate breastfeeding difficulties such as effective latching. Instead, you might like to try offering your baby a clean finger to suck on; a finger holds the baby's tongue flat, in a similar position to breastfeeding, while a dummy encourages a 'thrusting' tongue action.

- There are no calories in a dummy. Inadvertently popping a dummy in when your baby is actually trying to signal that he is hungry or in order to 'stretch out' feeds can have a negative effect on his weight gains and your own milk supply.

- Dummies can turn out to be more trouble than they are worth, as some babies who sleep with dummies are woken – and start crying – every time the dummy slips out. For this reason, if you do use a dummy to help your baby relax, it's wise to use it sparingly and to remove it once he has fallen asleep.

If you do decide to offer your baby a dummy and find that it helps to comfort him:

- Keep a supply of clean dummies so that you always have a replacement to hand if the one he's using gets lost or falls on the ground mid-wail.

- Never attach a dummy to your baby with a ribbon, as dangling ribbons are a strangling danger.

- Never sweeten a dummy (or dip it in any substance).

- Watch your baby's cues and if he spits out the dummy, don't keep plugging him up again, as you run the risk of blocking his only means of communication; he may want his needs met in other ways, such as being fed, played with or talked to.

Do I need a feeding routine?

There is increasing pressure on parents to enforce strict feeding and sleeping regimes as early as possible to foster a 'good' (read 'convenient') baby. While a gentle rhythm to your day may help you feel a sense of control as you adapt to your new lifestyle, and a feeding and sleeping routine may appear to suit some babies, being pedantic about enforcing a routine to 'train' your baby to fit in with your lifestyle or to sleep longer is likely to result in lengthy bouts of crying and can have adverse effects. Leaving a baby to 'cry it out' in order to enforce a strict routine when the baby may, in fact, be hungry, is similar to expecting an adult to adopt a strenuous exercise program accompanied by a reduced food intake. The result of expending energy through crying while being deprived of food is likely to be weight loss and a failure to thrive.

Also, apart from not being conducive to infant development, parent-directed feeding regimes (as opposed to responding to your baby's hunger cues) can result in low milk supply and premature weaning. In the early weeks, as your milk supply changes from being hormonally driven to baby-driven, your production capacity will be set by the amount of milk your baby removes as you establish breastfeeding. This is because, in the first three months postpartum, there is ongoing development of hormone (prolactin) receptors that facilitate an abundant and ongoing milk supply. Limiting your baby's access to the breast by stretching out his feeds in the early weeks can interrupt this process, and many women who may have been able to make a strict feeding routine 'work' initially can experience an abrupt drop in milk supply after around three months. Many of these women say, 'I have lost my milk,' or, 'My milk dried up.' At this time, a diminished milk supply may not respond to normal methods of increasing supply, such as more frequent breast-emptying or even medications. This is because the mother's hormone receptors didn't have an opportunity to develop in the early weeks, and there will now be an insufficient number. This sudden weaning can be very disappointing and stressful for both mother and baby, especially if the mother had planned to nurse for longer. On the other hand, by being sensitive to your baby's cues as you establish breastfeeding, and maintaining adequate breast stimulation and milk removal, you will ensure hormone receptor development and build a good milk supply, and your baby will probably be happier and sleep more soundly because he has plenty of milk to meet his needs.

If your baby is unsettled and not due for a sleep, it is likely that he is hungry and looking for a feed. If you learn to identify your baby's early hunger signals (see **'I'm hungry'**, page 90) and allow him access to the breast as soon as you see these, you will be able to avert hunger cries (crying is a late hunger signal for most babies), and know that he will take exactly the amount of milk that he needs.

Feed, play, sleep

One popular routine for babies consists of variations of 'feed, play, sleep'. Rather than watching the clock, this kind of routine is usually based on understanding your baby's cues or non-verbal signals (see page 89) and translates to feeding your baby and then giving her time to play before popping her into bed.

Babies are individual in the amount of time they may be awake between feeds. For instance, sometimes they may feed and doze quickly back to sleep without being awake longer than it takes for a nappy change. At other times, they may be awake for longer. But as a general rule, a newborn up to three months or so will stay awake for around 1–2 hours, at six months your baby may stay awake 2–3 hours, and your twelve-month-old will probably need a nap after around 3–4 hours awake. Watch your baby's cues: these are much more useful signals than the clock.

While this sounds reasonable and can help you feel more in control because you have a plan, it is often interpreted too rigidly. I have, for instance, heard of babies who have fallen asleep after a feed, then been woken (yes, really!) for their playtime, to avoid putting their routine out of whack. I have also seen mothers who have been advised that they must give clear messages to their baby about what part of the routine they are following, so that while the mother is 'allowed' to hold her baby while she feeds him (this is a safety issue – if you're bottle-feeding, never prop your baby to feed), she must put the baby down on the floor to play and then put him into the cot to sleep.

Being so rigid or trying to follow any style of routine very strictly can lead to you feeling out of control and confused when you can't 'make' your baby sleep or feed simply because he isn't ready! In fact, in the early weeks, as you get used to your baby's signals indicating that he is hungry or tired or wants to spend time engaging and having a little 'chat' to you, it may work better to follow a pattern of 'feed, play, feed, sleep'. To make this work, you would feed your baby, then have a short chat/playtime and change his nappy, then offer him a little top-up (you can't overfeed a breastfed baby – he will only feed if it suits him). Please don't feel stressed if he falls asleep on the breast; although you may be warned against this (on the premise that it will create 'bad habits'), it can be the easiest way to settle a newborn because of the amazing hormones in your milk and the relaxing effects of sucking. In a few months, he will naturally develop the capacity to fall asleep without so much help. Also, considering a newborn needs to be fed around every two hours at first, he is likely to need a top-up after almost an hour awake, and when you put him to sleep after this, he is likely to nap for longer. If he doesn't have the top-up, he may be awake again very soon because he is hungry.

Even if your baby seems to be 'all over the place' right now, he will soon fall into his own natural pattern and, often, the less you try to force this, the quicker it will happen. If you watch your baby and get to know his cues rather than relying on the clock, you will develop the confidence that you do really do know him best (see **Baby cues**, page 89). Above all, it's sensible to use any routine as a general guide rather than a set of rules, and before you try out any practice, go back to my criteria for discerning what is right for you and your baby (see page 48):

- **Is it safe?**
- **Is it respectful?**
- **Does it feel right?**

Then, do what works best and feels right for you and your baby – and remember, there is a difference between a gentle rhythm and a rigid schedule.

6

Bonding after birth

♥

How often do you hear the phrase, 'Babies don't come with a manual'? It's this kind of thinking that sees you looking outwards for answers to the myriad questions you have about caring for your baby, and worrying that you are not 'doing things right' or are 'creating bad habits'. It is this pressure that produces feelings of doubt and uncertainty as you are torn between current advice and what you feel in your heart as you are treading new ground, whatever the age of your child. Of course, it is useful to seek information and support, and to 'skill up'. However, it is also important to trust the connection between yourself and your child. As US psychologist Jan Hunt says, 'The baby is the book.' By taking time to bond deeply with your baby, you set up a strong foundation, giving you confidence in your intuition that will last long beyond your child's infancy. You will know that you are the expert about your child and, at any time, whatever struggles or advice you may be faced with, you will be able to listen to your child and your own heart, and to trust this amazing connection. You will be able to step up during difficult times and protect your little one, and you will know when you should step back and question advice that doesn't feel right.

Bonding and attachment

Bonding with your baby is rather like falling in love. It might be love at first sight: as soon as you meet this new little being, you might feel as though you already know him. Or, you may wonder at first, 'Am I meant to love you?', and those deeply tender feelings of connection will develop more gradually, over a few weeks or months.

Attachment and bonding are two separate processes. Attachment can be described as the process of 'learning to love'. A baby's first attachment to a loving caregiver is the prototype for all future relationships. When you are bonded to your baby and respond appropriately to his cues, with love, you will teach him that he is loved unconditionally – just the way he is. He will feel safe, learn to trust and be able to form a secure attachment to you. From this secure base, your baby learns to reach out and form relationships with others.

Sadly, a baby who doesn't learn to love is at risk of being unable to form close, loving relationships in the future. If he sees himself as 'unlovable', he will be susceptible to low self-esteem. And if his own responses are out of tune with those of his carers, he may also be in danger of abuse or, at least, neglect: a baby who cries a lot and doesn't respond to the care the parent offers, either because the parent isn't quite attuned or because the baby is extra-sensitive or 'high-interest' (see page 219), is more at risk of bearing the brunt of frustration as parents become exhausted. This frustration can quite easily result in anger that is expressed either verbally or physically, or the parent may be more easily tempted by advice to 'let him cry', which isn't fair on a baby who may be having difficulty at some level. (Imagine feeling upset or anxious and having somebody you love walk out and shut the door on you.) If you do have difficulties feeling connected or attuned to your baby, please seek help, starting with your child health nurse, or ask your GP for a referral to a psychologist (which is funded by Medicare) – and persist until you are heard.

Bonding may be delayed or adversely affected by trauma or unpredictable events such as physical separation at birth or emotional separation as a result of the death of a loved one, a relationship breakdown during pregnancy, a previous pregnancy loss or maternal depression. Bonding can also take a little longer if the baby you have seems different from your pre-conceived image of him or her.

If you don't fall in love with your baby instantly or the baby doesn't feel as though she is yours, please be reassured: there are plenty of opportunities for the bonding process to occur. It's never too late to connect with your child or to strengthen the bonds between you.

As with any relationship, conscious effort will strengthen your connection with your little one: making time to connect with your unborn baby and, after birth, cuddling skin-to-skin with your baby placed between your breasts (whether you are breastfeeding or not), as well as breastfeeding itself, will release hormones that enhance bonding and attachment.

'Imagine my surprise when I went for my first antenatal scan and found two babies! Wriggling little twinlings swimming around and talking to each other, oblivious to the mayhem they had caused. I was really unwell until around nineteen weeks, and was struggling emotionally with the idea of twins. The second half of my pregnancy was less sick, more hungry and stretched! To help with bonding, we found out the genders – two little girls. This made it easier for me to prepare my older daughter (two), and to build a connection with the twins and talk to them. Many people were disappointed that I didn't have a surprise. My response? "Trust me, I've *had* my surprise!"

'My GP-obstetrician was wonderful, and his team of midwives looked after me well. A last-minute scan at 37 weeks revealed (as suspected) a double-breech. A great obstetrician was brought in for an 'elective' caesarean, and I have to say, despite my preference for natural birth, it was all okay. The operating team were great: they chatted me through my nerves, listened to my concerns and wishes, and were really positive and happy for me. My twins were born with me wide awake and my husband there; he held them immediately and they finished the caesar with him there. Then the babies were able to come on the trolley with me to recovery, and back to my room. They got their first twin breastfeed in recovery, with the help of a midwife and hubby. They got weighed etc. later in the day when I was able to go with them. After a caesar at 9 a.m., I was up and around by 4 p.m. and having a shower, so I was pleased with the outcome of the operation (I had heard all the horror stories and expected much worse). Breastfeeding went well, although feeding them together caused such a strong let-down that we joked that if they didn't drink, they would drown!

'It was on the second day that I realised I felt a stronger bond with the second twin. I was surprised and perplexed – I hadn't even considered that might happen. None of the other twin mums had mentioned it, and my initial reaction was that I must be a bad mum. I realised, by the third day, that the second twin was more demanding and vocal – much like my older daughter. This seemed to me to be the source of the bonding issue: I felt I understood this baby and spoke her language, whereas the first twin was so quiet and contented that I felt I didn't know what she wanted. Once I realised this, I relaxed a little and followed her cues, and accepted that although they are identical twins, they are different, right from the moment they are born. They are still different, at one year, and although I haven't slept for what feels like years, they are happy babies that keep us very busy. Everyone says to me, "Gee, you've got your hands full!" to which I reply, "Ah, yes – but better full than empty!" and I hope it makes them think about the joys of twins rather than the difficulties.'

Amee

'I didn't realise that I hadn't completely bonded with my first baby. As much as I loved and adored her, I found being a mother challenging. I remember walking out of the birthing suite to my room and leaving her behind and a nurse reminding me to take her with me. I had a birth experience that wasn't ideal, she was a difficult baby with colic and we had awful breastfeeding problems. For the first three months she just looked like a scared little alien who seemed to be thinking, What the hell am I doing here? and I felt I that I could do little to help her. And to add to it all I found out later that I may also have had mild postnatal depression.

'My husband had spent a great deal of time caring for her when I couldn't cope with the colicky crying and needed to rest, so at least she had one very connected parent. I did baby massage and worked hard on trying to do all the 'right' things like carrying her around in a baby carrier, singing and reading to her. When she was nine months old I noticed a big shift and I felt a lot more connected with her. I really started to relax and enjoy her and being a mother.

'When our second baby girl was born nearly three years later, the experience was totally different. I bonded with her so deeply from the minute I laid eyes on her, I remember for weeks afterwards constantly kissing the top of her head and being so in love with her. Her birth was a much better experience and I slept with her and carried her around and I had a lot more support in place to help us through the first few months. She was a much more contented baby, and I found the whole experience much easier and more enjoyable. But at the same time, I felt guilty about not having that with my first and I am always constantly aware of the difference between the two. I try very hard to stay connected with my first, spending one-on-one time alone with her and telling her how special she is.'

Caroline, mother of two

The chemistry of attachment

A massive hormonal upheaval begins in your body during pregnancy and this chemical response is designed to help you and your baby feel an amazingly strong connection when you meet each other face-to-face or, rather, skin-to-skin, at birth. Ideally, this is nature's insurance that your baby will signal for exactly the care she needs to grow and thrive, and that your strong connection with her will help you understand and meet these needs as she adapts to the world outside the womb. Although various interruptions such as pregnancy complications or birth interventions can impact the effects of this natural hormonal chemistry, the powerful feelings of protection you feel for your baby are completely normal and not a sign that you are simply an overemotional, besotted creature who is at risk of 'spoiling' your child.

During the last trimester of pregnancy, your body brews a cocktail of hormones. By the time your baby is born, your pituitary gland (a pea-sized gland at the base of the brain that produces this 'mummy margarita'), has doubled in size and remains enlarged for up to six months postpartum. So, for as long as six months after your baby is born, your emotional mindset will be affected by shifting levels of hormones. This powerful hormonal hangover has such universally intense effects on mothers' inner lives that it is documented by researchers under a variety of labels, including 'maternal preoccupation' and 'motherhood mindset'. This more intuitive mindset can be quite at odds with our modern lifestyles and often comes as a shock to women who have been in a more goal-oriented and solution-focussed space prior to having a baby. Suddenly, it seems that logic has left the building, as the skills that used to keep things neat and tidy (literally) are no longer predominant.

Two of the major players in the mummy margarita are prolactin (see page 30) – a hormone that promotes milk production and is said to make you more responsive to your baby – and oxytocin (see page 27) – a hormone that encourages feelings of caring and sensitivity to others, and helps us to recognise non-verbal cues more readily. Oxytocin is part of a complex hormonal balance. A sudden release creates an urge towards loving that can be directed in different ways, depending on the presence of other hormones. In conjunction with a high level of prolactin, the urge to love is directed towards your baby.

Breastfeeding is also a powerful enhancer of the effects of these love hormones, which are released by both mothers and babies. (Babies produce their own oxytocin in response to nursing.) However, physical contact with your baby will also stimulate the release of oxytocin, so if you are bottle-feeding, you can chemically boost the bond with your baby if you nurse with cuddles and skin contact, rather than prop him up to feed (something you should never do anyway, for safety reasons) or hand him to others.

And fathers, you too can succumb to the influence of these love drugs of family-bonding (and you thought you were the voice of reason, didn't you!). Men's bodies are instinctively programmed to respond to their partner's pheromones (steroid hormones made in our skin that emit barely detectable odours). Through closeness with your baby's mother and signals from her pheromones, your own oxytocin and prolactin levels rise toward the end of the pregnancy, and then, when your baby is born, an even greater surge of these hormones occurs when you spend lots of time holding your baby. And so a self-perpetuating cycle begins: close contact with your baby releases your own oxytocin and prolactin, and encourages you to become more involved with your child.

Whichever parent you are – and whether you are the biological parent, an adoptive parent or a same-sex partner – the more you connect with your baby through touch, eye contact, smell and talking, the stronger your connection will be and the more difficult you will find it to misread or ignore your baby's signals. And this is exactly as nature intended.

Building the bonds

Despite there being an optimal period for bonding with your baby – ideally, you will have an opportunity to cuddle your baby skin-to-skin without any interruptions for at least the first hour after birth – there are many factors that may affect or delay this: you could be totally exhausted, unwell, or overwhelmed at the enormity of what you have achieved! If your birthing journey has been difficult or required intervention, you may have a range of feelings to deal with or you may be separated from your baby immediately after birth or for longer. Be reassured, though, that even if things don't go according to plan, nature provides ongoing opportunities for bonding to occur. Studies show that even premature babies who are given 'kangaroo care' (snuggling skin-to-skin between mothers' breasts) when it is medically possible, regardless of early separation, have good outcomes with bonding, attachment and development. So, as soon as you have the opportunity, snuggle, smell and breathe in your beautiful newborn; gaze into his eyes at least several times a day and tell him, 'I love you.' Even if he doesn't feel like he is 'yours' just yet, he will, very soon.

'As a father of two children, I have found the period immediately after birth to be a powerful time of connection and bonding with my children. Throughout their time in utero, I made every effort to actively connect through my voice and my touch. Once they emerged into the world, I had the opportunity to behold and marvel at their perfection completely. The hours, days and weeks that followed became moments of wonder and awe, where, without distraction, love and adoration formed the silent link.'

Damien

'When I was pregnant with my first baby, I was so worried that after it was born I wouldn't love it. I was so sick during the pregnancy, I just didn't bond at all with the unborn baby. A friend of mine said not to worry, I'd love my baby once I got to know it. He was right. It took a few months for us to get to know each other, but she became the most important thing in the world to me. When I was pregnant with my second baby, I was worried that I could never love another baby as much as I loved my first. My mother-in-law said she's a fickle mother with her own children, and always loves whichever one she's looking at right now the most. Now that I've had three babies, I understand what she means. I love all of them, but the greatest love I feel is for the person I am in the moment with. I understand much better now how it is possible for my capacity to love to increase endlessly as there are more children to be loved.'

Emma

Love through the senses

For most parents, research to show that mothers and babies feel best when they are close to each other is about as necessary as research to show that grass will grow if it rains. However, there is indeed scientific evidence that mothers and babies are hardwired to seek togetherness. Your baby is primed to bond with you through all of his senses as he:

- feels your touch
- hears your voice
- senses your smell
- meets your gaze

Loving sensory interactions between you and your baby are exquisitely designed to help you form a powerful bond with each other that not only ensures that he survives and thrives, but that the emotional and neurological development of his immature brain is kick-started. As you touch and talk to your child and share eye contact, you stimulate the development of connections between nerve cells in your baby's brain that form the foundations for thinking, feeling and learning.

And as you respond to your baby, you also develop connections in your brain that will help you to understand and meet your baby's needs. Studies show that intimate contact between you and your baby is mutually regulated by the reciprocal activation of your opiate systems. This means that with every interaction between you and your baby, both of you experience elevated levels of beta-endorphin – the hormone of pleasure and reward – in your brains.

Interestingly, nature has also ensured that you instinctively hold your baby in precisely the right way to aid his development: most mothers cradle their babies on the left (heart) side of their own body. This tendency is well developed in women (not in men), is independent of whether the woman is left- or right-handed, and is widespread in all cultures.

It has been suggested that this left-cradling tendency not only helps your baby feel secure, as he is connected to your heartbeat, but facilitates the 'right brain to right brain' connection between your own and your baby's emotional centres. This helps you read and interpret your baby's cues, as information flows most directly and effectively from your baby via his left ear and eye to the centre for emotional decoding that lies in the right hemisphere of your own brain.

Your touch

Kissing, tickling, blowing raspberries . . . How can you resist that delicious baby-fine skin or the precious giggles and chuckles as your little one responds to your touch?

Your loving touch (perhaps we should call it vitamin T!) is just as important a nutrient for your baby as the nutrition in the milk he drinks. Touch is the first sense to develop, just days after conception, and it is important in maintaining health and wellbeing for a whole lifetime.

Although it is difficult to measure the effects of spontaneous touch between parents and babies, studies of early skin-to-skin contact and baby massage show amazing benefits for babies. The best news is that you don't need to buy expensive equipment or make radical changes to your daily workload.

Skin-to-skin contact between you and your baby at birth has been shown to reduce crying, to encourage mother–baby interaction and to keep your baby warmer as his body temperature becomes stabilised by yours. It also makes breastfeeding easier because close contact stimulates the release of oxytocin, the hormone that makes your breast milk flow. Babies who are kept skin-to-skin with their mother immediately after birth for at least an hour are more likely to latch onto the breast without any help and are more likely to latch on well, especially if the mother did not receive medication during the labour or birth. (See also **Your baby's first feed**, page 49.)

If you miss skin-to-skin cuddles or are separated from your baby immediately after birth, studies of premature babies show that cuddling your little one skin-to-skin as soon as possible will still have profound effects on bonding, attachment, breastfeeding and your baby's development. This is reflected in the 1991 joint World Health Organization–UNICEF Baby-Friendly Hospital Initiative, which includes 'Ten steps to successful breastfeeding'. Step 4 advises: 'Place babies in skin-to-skin contact with their mothers immediately following birth for at least an hour and encourage mothers to recognise when their babies are ready to breastfeed.' (See unicef.org/programme/breastfeeding/baby.htm for more information.)

When we consider the biochemistry of breastfeeding and how it is designed to facilitate mother–infant bonding and the wellbeing of both mother and baby, it's easy to appreciate that early skin-to-skin contact is of critical importance in getting breastfeeding off to a good start. When breastfeeding is going well, the hormones released help you feel calmer, less anxious and more loving, and this peaceful, loving breastfeeding state of mind makes it easier to calm your baby and to manage his stress. Of course, if you aren't breastfeeding, you can still facilitate good bonding with your baby, although it may require a more conscious effort on your part: remember to offer skin-to-skin contact and hold your baby close as you bottle-feed, making feeds a time of loving interaction between you to activate the chemistry of attachment for you both (see **Bottle-feeding**, page 160, for more information).

A lot of the research into early skin-to-skin contact has been done on premature babies and shows that 'kangaroo care' has lasting effects on the baby's cognitive and motor development as well as the mother's wellbeing and her attachment with her baby. Skin-to-skin contact has been shown to positively affect a premature infant's alertness and gazing behaviour, which makes it easier for the babies to engage with carers and in turn helps parents to get to know their baby's cues and respond in a more attuned way.

For premature babies, the experience of touch is mostly painful, as they endure various medical procedures, so your gentle touch is very precious for both your baby's wellbeing and your own experience of bonding with your tiny infant. A study by Dr Tiffany Field of Miami University found that premature babies who were massaged gained 47 per cent more weight than babies in the control group (who were not massaged), and were able to be discharged from hospital six days earlier. Follow-up studies showed that these benefits had lasting effects. (See **Massage**, page 82, for some practical information.) Studies of kangaroo care that include fathers also show positive effects of skin-to-skin contact between father and baby.

Your gaze

The gazing that goes on between you and your baby is like a secret, intimate language between lovers: you look at each other as though you have both met the most wonderful person in the whole world. And this is exactly how it feels when you and your baby are perfectly attuned to each other.

Eye contact is an important element of parent–child bonding and the development of trust between parent and child. According to neuropsychologist Dr Allan Schore from the University of California and the UCLA Center for Culture, Brain, and Development, your face is the most potent visual stimulus for the growth of your baby's social and emotional brain. As you and your baby gaze into each other's eyes, endorphin levels rise in your baby's brain, producing feelings of joy. In turn, your own endorphin levels rise, and you and your baby become emotionally synchronised.

Sadly, many parents are being given advice that interrupts this exquisite bond. Some strict sleep-training regimes advocate avoiding eye contact with your baby at bedtime. Of course, it is wise to keep bedtimes calm and gentle. But imagine how you would feel if your partner repeatedly avoided your gaze.

If you have been trying to follow a rigid baby-care plan but feel it is interrupting the bond between you and your child, be reassured that you have not irreparably damaged your relationship, and that it is never too late to make changes. Spend a little time learning to read and respond to your baby's cues (see page 89) and, with interaction such as baby massage (see page 82) and games that involve eye contact (see below), you will soon be engaging with each other again. Look into your baby's eyes, say 'I love you', and wait for her to meet your gaze.

Some baby games to encourage eye contact

I'm a tiny baby . . .

As you say this rhyme to your baby, to the tune of 'Incy Wincy Spider', look into her eyes and move her little limbs to the rhythm. Please be respectful and conscious of her reactions – and have fun!

I'm a tiny baby,
I'm soft and round and small.
But when I'm busy stretching,

I feel so big and tall.
My arms are getting long,
And my legs are getting strong.
And the next thing you know,
I'll be learning how to crawl.

Crossing arms

Hold your baby's arms out wide, then cross them across her chest three times, first with one arm on top, then the other. Then gently stretch her arms out to the sides. The rhythm is *cross, cross, cross, open*. Repeat this sequence three times as long as your baby is comfortable. This exercise is not only great for engaging your baby, but helps provide important messages to your baby's brain that will stimulate movement and coordination, and lay pathways for later learning.

Diagonal cross-crawling pattern

With your baby lying on her back, take one of her arms at the wrist and the opposite leg at the ankle. Gently bring the arm down to the rib-cage and the foot up towards the shoulder (allowing the knee to bend), then cross the arm and leg so that the arm goes to the outside of the leg; cross again so the arm is under the leg, then cross one more with arm over leg again. Stretch them out in opposite directions (gently). The rhythm is *cross, cross, cross, open*. Repeat this pattern with the opposite arm and leg. Practising this pattern will help get your baby's brain ready to crawl, and then walk, later on.
Note: With an older baby, bring the knee, rather than the foot, up to cross with the arms.

Crossing legs

Cross your baby's legs over her tummy, alternating which leg is over and which is under, then gently stretch her legs out towards you. This is a good exercise for toning the digestive tract.

Gentle knee bends

Push your baby's knees together and up towards her tummy, then stretch them out straight. If she resists straightening her legs, bounce them gently and encourage her to relax. Repeat this three or four times.

Bicycle legs

Gently push your baby's knees into her tummy, one after the other, then bounce them out straight to relax. The rhythm is *push right, push left, push right, straighten* – alternating the leg you start with each time.

Your voice

Talking and singing to your baby are intuitive – no matter what your singing talent! The familiar sound of a mother's voice has been shown to regulate an infant's early, uncoordinated body movements as the baby synchronises his movements with the rhythm of his mother's voice. Talking to your baby face-to-face also enhances the effects of gazing (see page 76). As you talk and interact with your baby, please be respectful and take turns with him, allowing him to 'talk' back. Be theatrical with your gestures, laugh and giggle together, and reward your baby's efforts at communicating with smiles, cuddles and lots of attention. Also, remember to leave some quiet times for reflection.

Even the littlest baby will love a chat, and he will feel your respect for him as a person – rather than an object – if you speak intelligently to him right from the start. Tell him what is happening around him, and what you are doing as you change, dress and bath him. When he is a few months old, play little games like 'This little piggy' or 'Round and round the garden'. The more you talk to your baby and the more he is encouraged to respond, the sooner he will learn to talk. Provide a good model for your child by talking clearly and naturally, and when he begins to say recognisable syllables (like 'ooh', 'aaah' or 'goo') or words, reinforce these by repeating them back to him and telling him how clever he is. Your pleasure and excitement will boost his efforts, whatever new skill he is practising.

Rhymes to enjoy with your baby

Baby on the bus

To give your baby a mini workout to the tune of 'The Wheels on the Bus',
lay him on a blanket or towel and move his body parts as you sing.

(Bicycle your baby's legs as you sing the first four lines.)

> *The wheels on the bus go round and round,*
> *Round and round, round and round,*
> *The wheels on the bus go round and round,*
> *All through the town.*

(Lift your baby's arms up and down.)

> *The people on the bus go up and down . . .*

(Roll your baby from side to side.)

> *The wipers on the bus go swish, swish, swish . . .*

(Touch your baby's nose as you 'beep'.)

> *The horn on the bus goes beep, beep, beep . . .*

Tap, tap, tap . . .

Sit with your baby at the table, or across from him in his high chair. Start
tapping on the surface while you sing:

> *Tap, tap, tapping on the table,*
> *Tap, tap, tapping on the table,*
> *Tap, tap, tapping on the table,*
> *Till it's time to stop!*

On 'stop!', raise your arms. It won't be long before your baby does the
same. For variety, sometimes tap hard, other times softly; sometimes
fast, other times slowly. If you like, create new verses: 'Tap, tap, tapping
very softly,' 'very quickly,' – or whatever tickles your fancy. Your baby will
love imitating you, whatever you do, and will soon take the lead himself.

Reading stories is another delightful way to interact with your little one
through language, and you can read to your baby from birth – or even
before! In fact, popular children's author and reading specialist Mem Fox

claims that if all parents read three books a day to their babies from birth, illiteracy would be eliminated. At first, it doesn't matter what you read your baby (the *Financial Review*, if you choose!) – he will just love the sound of your voice. Soon, though, you will both discover that books provide a rich sharing experience: reading stories and looking at pictures exposes your baby to language, encourages conversation between you, and can be a lovely way to slow down during a busy day and connect with your child at his pace.

Because so much of your baby's development will depend on his under-standing of language, it is important to seek help from an appropriate health professional if you have any concerns about his hearing or if he seems unresponsive to your 'conversations' with him. If he has repeated ear infections, it is worth asking to see an allergy specialist, since allergies may cause a build-up of fluid in tiny ears.

Your smell

'I was so surprised when my beautiful boy smelled like warm sweet pastry! I wanted to smell him all day.'

Tanya

After your baby is born, snuggle into the top of his tiny head and inhale deeply – before anybody has an opportunity to wash him. In fact, there is absolutely no rush to wash your newborn: smelling your baby and allow-ing him to smell your scent is an important element of bonding for both of you, as it is for all mammals – just watch mother sheep with their lambs (yes, I did grow up in the country!). Below is a checklist for helping your baby to bond through smell.

✳ CHECKLIST : BONDING THROUGH SMELL

- When you have your first shower after the birth, after your baby's first breastfeed, don't wash your chest because your newborn needs to be able to find his way back to your breast by following the smell of amniotic fluid.

- Avoid using perfumed products of any kind (even those that are made from natural ingredients) on your skin or your baby's in the early months.
- Avoid essential oils (even many 'natural' products designed especially for babies contain essential oils) for 3–6 months after birth. Apart from their less than optimal effects on bonding, essential oils need to be processed by the liver and may create unnecessary stress or sensitivity reactions while your baby's liver is immature.
- If you are applying anything to your baby's skin (for example, massage oil), no matter how natural, do a test first: apply a small amount to the skin inside your baby's leg and leave overnight. If there is no rash or redness by the next morning, the product is probably safe to use on a wider area.

Massage

Massage is a skill well worth learning because it encompasses all the elements of bonding. I was taught infant massage by a Sikh woman and practised this ancient art with my own five babies. Later, I trained as an infant-massage instructor. I find this a beautiful, non-intrusive way for parents and babies to engage and get to know each other really well, and for parents to develop confidence in their ability to care for their little ones. I would encourage all parents to learn how to massage their babies because it not only encompasses all the elements of bonding, but the benefits to health and development are well-documented. Researchers from Warwick Medical School in the UK looked at nine studies of massage, covering a total of 598 infants aged less than six months (Underdown, 2006). These studies showed that babies who were massaged cried less, slept better and had lower levels of stress hormones compared to infants who did not receive massage. One of the studies also claimed that massage could affect the release of the hormone melatonin, which is important in aiding infants' sleeping patterns. An Australian study of infant massage and father–baby bonding (Scholz and Samuels, 1992), found that at twelve weeks old, babies who were massaged (by their fathers) greeted their fathers with more eye contact, smiling, vocalising and touch than those who were not massaged.

Introducing massage

At first, gently stroking your baby's legs and back is a lovely way to connect. (Remember that this is easier if you have clothing such as nighties or two-piece suits that allow easy access, rather than one-piece suits.) As you introduce more formal massage, it is important to choose a time of day when you and your baby are relaxed and your baby is receptive. Your aim is to help your baby develop an association between massage and relaxation; this can be a valuable tool in your parenting kit because you'll be able to use it to calm your baby at other times when he is unsettled.

The best time to introduce massage will often be about twenty minutes or so after a feed, when your baby is calm but alert. During the first three months, your baby will probably find a massage as well as a bath too stimulating, so it's best to massage and bath at separate times, or massage one day and bath your baby the next. If you move the two activities together as your baby gets a little older, try massaging before your baby's bath so he doesn't get cold.

Start by introducing a little bit of massage at a time: you might start with just a leg massage, adding extra strokes gradually over a period of several days or weeks, depending on your baby's age. Always watch your baby closely to check how he is responding. Which strokes does he enjoy? Massage of which body parts seem to make him most comfortable/relaxed? Are there any spots that seem uncomfortable? Some babies who have had painful procedures (such as heel pricks, for instance), may grimace as you touch their feet. If this happens, just hold that tiny foot in your hand and talk to your baby: 'You are safe now. Mummy will hold your foot if it's scary and soon you will be able to let me rub your foot again.' If your baby becomes restless or unsettled, it is better to stop massaging than to push him along and create extra stress.

Remember, too, that massage can make your baby feel thirsty, so always offer a top-up afterwards, no matter when he was last fed. For babies old enough to handle a massage and a bath one after the other, this routine and then a feed make a lovely bedtime ritual.

Setting the scene

If you create a special time and space for massage, your baby will soon associate the smells, sights and sounds in that space with the soothing experience of being massaged. Warm the room, play soft music and avoid harsh lighting. If you are massaging during the day, open the curtains and bathe the room in natural light. Take the phone off the hook, hang a 'Do not disturb' sign on the front door and have everything at hand, including nappies and a soft blanket, towel or lambskin for your baby to lie on.

The good oil

Studies show that babies prefer to be massaged with oil: they show fewer stress behaviours (like grimacing and clenched fists) and lower cortisol (stress hormone) levels when oil is used. Some babies may be sensitive to particular oils or additives, so read labels carefully to check for ingredients. A cold-pressed vegetable oil is nourishing to the skin, feels pleasant and won't hurt your baby if he sucks his hand and ingests a little. Don't massage your baby with mineral oils (contained in some brands of 'baby oil'): as well being petroleum-based, these can be absorbed through your baby's skin and, when excreted, may take some vitamins with them. If you have any concerns about your baby's sensitivity, test a sample of oil on a small patch of skin inside his leg or forearm. Leave the oil on overnight. If there is any reddening or a rash, don't use this oil on your baby's skin. And, for safety's sake, do remember that oily babies are slippery!

Always warm your hands before you massage your baby by rubbing them together or holding them under warm water, then dry them thoroughly. Remember to clip your nails and use hand lotion regularly to soften any rough patches on your palms (yes, dads too!). Warm the oil by rubbing it in your hands (never put it directly onto your baby), then allow it to warm or cool to your body temperature before massaging.

Connect with your baby

Before you begin to massage your baby, ask his permission or tell him gently, 'We are going to have a massage now. I am going to pick up your tiny foot and stroke it.' Watch and wait for him to respond. By respecting your baby's attempts to communicate, you are teaching him in the gentlest possible way that he is safe: his body belongs to him, his feelings are important and he has a right to refuse unwanted touching.

Make eye contact with your baby and watch his facial expressions as you massage. Talk to him and wait for him to 'reply'. Tune in to his responses and try to understand what he is communicating to you. Feel the tension in your baby's body. Is he relaxing, or does he tense up when you touch various areas of his body? If he expresses sensitivity in certain areas, you may need to stop and give your baby a cuddle or gently get him used to experiencing touch. Sometimes, your baby's response may mean abandoning the massage until another time.

If your baby resists massage, or if it isn't appropriate to massage him (if he is unwell or has been immunised within the past forty-eight hours), offer him skin-to-skin contact in other ways: snuggle him against your bare chest, bathe with him, or hold your hand against his bare back under his clothing.

How to massage

It is important that you are relaxed when you massage your baby, as your stress will be transferred if you are tense. Find a position that is comfortable for you both – lie him between your legs or on your lap facing you, or kneel on the floor beside him – and remember to connect with your baby before you begin to massage. You can start massaging your baby's head or feet first, but it is important to keep him warm, so if you undress him completely, cover body parts you aren't massaging with a bunny rug.

It will be beneficial for you, your partner and your baby to attend a series of infant-massage classes (check out a local infant-massage association such as Infant Massage Australia). If this isn't practical, you can learn how to give a complete massage, as well as specific strokes to relieve tummy pains and wind, in my *Baby Massage* DVD (see **Resources**). Meanwhile, you can follow these steps to give your baby a mini massage:

- Sit comfortably, take some deep slow breathes to relax yourself, then connect with your baby and ask his permission (as above).

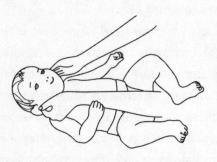

- Stroke the crown of your baby's head in a gentle, circular motion. Then, with both hands, stroke with flat fingers from his brow to his temples. With your fingertips, massage in small circles around his jaw. If you are massaging a young baby, avoid his cheeks near his mouth or you'll trigger the rooting reflex (and he will become frustrated when he can't find food).

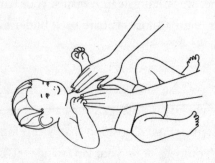

- Place both hands on your baby's chest. With flat fingers, stroke up your baby's sternum, around the top of his chest, out to his shoulders and down to the base of his ribs, then back to the base of his sternum, making a heart shape. Then stroke gently outwards over his shoulders. Cup your hands around your baby's shoulders and massage in gentle circular motions with your thumbs. 'Milk' his arms, one at a time, from shoulder to fingertips, and delicately massage his hands and each of his fingers.

- Imagine a clock-face on your baby's tummy, just below his ribcage. With the palm of your hands, start at seven o'clock and stroke firmly around his tummy in continuous clockwise circles, with one hand following the other. (Only do this after the umbilical cord has dropped off.) This massage follows the ascending, transverse and descending colon and, when alternated with bending your baby's knees up towards his chest, can be used to help relieve tummy ache.

- Starting at the top of your baby's thigh, 'milk' his legs, massage his ankles and then, supporting each ankle, use your thumb to massage along the sole of each foot. Give each toe a gentle rub.

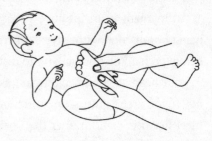

- Place your baby on his tummy (with his arms forward) across your thighs. Supporting his buttocks with one hand, stroke with your other hand from his shoulders to his buttocks. Finish off by lightly 'combing' his back with your fingertips, gradually making your movements slower and slower.

- As you finish the massage, it is important to gradually lighten and slow your movements, then place your hands on your baby's back or stomach for a few moments. (By massaging, you create a relaxed state for both you and your baby, and it may startle your baby if you stop massaging suddenly.) As you hold your hands on your baby, continue the mood you have created by breathing slowly with your baby and feeling the connection you have made. Keep your baby's clothes ready and make dressing an extension of the massage, or roll him in a towel ready for a bath if this is your routine. And, of course, always enjoy a cuddle with your calm, relaxed baby after a massage.

Attunement

Attunement means exactly that: tuning in to your baby's subtle cues and responding appropriately to her needs. So often we look outwards to try to work out what is going on for our baby. Mothers are often told to check the clock to find out whether it's time for a feed or sleep. But tuning in to your baby and responding to her signals will help her feel understood. You know how it feels when somebody 'gets' you? You feel they are there for you in a meaningful way. Rather than just going through the motions, they really understand.

Attunement is an intuitive process but can feel very difficult if you are being bombarded with advice, or feeling stressed or very tired. So, without being too hard on yourself, try to dismiss the advice that is playing like a tape in your head as you check in and ask yourself: *What is my baby trying to tell me?* If you aren't quite sure, watch how your baby responds when you try to meet her needs and, rather than being persuaded by advice that might not really be appropriate, ask yourself questions like: *Does my baby like being held this way? Does she settle when I follow this routine? How do I know what she likes?* By watching, waiting and wondering as you interact with your baby, and being respectful of her responses, you will discover her likes and preferences and how she expresses these. This is attunement in action.

For most parents, tuning in to your baby becomes increasingly natural as you get to know her and the subtleties of her body language, facial expressions and noises as she communicates with you. Cues, or non-verbal language, are your baby's way of telling you what she needs. Although it may take a few weeks to get to know your baby's cues, if you watch closely, you will be amazed at how even very young babies can give clear signals (see page 89).

Responding to your baby's cues, day and night, will help your baby develop a sense of trust in her ability to influence her environment, and will help her form a secure attachment to you. These are important prerequisites for later emotional development and relationships. Your responsiveness will also help your baby learn what psychologists call 'emotion regula-tion', which is the capacity to understand that we have control over our emotions. As you soothe your baby, you are teaching her that when she is upset, she can calm down. When a baby's signals are ignored, and they escalate to cries that are not responded to, the baby fails to develop the understanding that she can regulate her own emotions (see **Wiring tiny brains to manage stress**, page 212).

While tuning in to your baby may seem a tall order – especially at first – and a huge responsibility, please don't feel stressed if you are a bit confused about what your baby is trying to tell you or if you get it wrong sometimes. It's perfectly normal for parents to feel out of sync, then to get back in tune with their littlies – in fact, this process is so common that it even has a label: 'rupture and repair'. When your baby has an occasional yelling bout at a difficult time – perhaps you are driving the car and can't pull over to attend to her, or you need to get that last potato peeled in order to feed your other hungry children – it might feel awful, but don't worry that you will damage your baby for life! Most of the time, these small ruptures are just that – a few minutes of distress followed by comfort that shows your baby that she can calm down again.

Baby cues

Every baby will develop her own mix of cues or signals. For instance, one tired baby may lie still and watch her tiny fist as she becomes increasingly drowsy, while another's movements may become jerky and uncoordinated, and yet another baby may rub her eyes and fuss. As you play with your baby, take your time getting to know her way of communicating when she is enjoying playing, when she is feeling a bit overwhelmed and needs a break, and when she is becoming hungry or tired.

Your baby's signals may seem unclear at first, but by spending lots of time just watching your little one, along with some trial and error as you work out what she is telling you, you will soon become attuned to each other. By staying close and getting to know your baby, you will be support-ing her development as you strengthen the connection between you both. After a while, your awareness of her needs will become almost subcon-scious: you won't have to wonder, 'What kind of cry is this?' or, 'What does that squirming or grimace mean?' You will simply respond, moving her to a more comfortable position, feeding her or changing her environment so that she feels more secure. Your baby will develop her own unique way of communicating with each person in her world, and you and your partner will learn to respond in just the way that suits your baby.

Having said this, there are some typical cues that most babies use to elicit the care they need – although individual babies will not use all of these cues all of the time.

'I'm hungry' Long before they begin to cry, babies give a lot of subtle cues that they are ready to feed – from rooting with their mouths, making sucking noises and trying to suck on their fists or fingers, to little noises that say, 'I'm working up to a cry.' If these signals are ignored, they will probably cry. Crying is a late hunger cue and when we repeatedly wait until a young baby cries – for example, because we are trying to implement a strict feeding schedule – we can set ourselves up for unnecessary feeding problems. Of course, sometimes it is impossible to respond to your child straight away; when this occurs, you will need to help your baby calm down before trying to feed her. When a baby is yelling, her tongue is up against the roof of her mouth and she won't be able to latch on to feed. Even if she calms enough to latch on and feed, her suck is likely to be disorganised, or she may be exhausted from crying and only take a small feed before falling asleep. This, of course, means that she will probably sleep for only a short time then wake for another feed.

At night-time, it may take you longer to arouse from your own sleep to respond to your baby's signals, but she will usually give a few small 'warning' calls before she works up to distressed wailing. If your baby sleeps near you in the early months, you will be surprised how intuitively you respond to her movements and noises, even if they aren't very loud.

'Play with me' Tiny babies have very short periods during which they can actually engage and interact with you, but as she grows, your little one will be able to play for longer periods and her signals will become much clearer. When your baby wants you to play, her eyes will become wide and bright, and she may purse her tiny lips as though she is saying 'ooh' as she turns towards your voice or looks at your face. Movements of her arms and legs will be smooth (as opposed to jerky) as she reaches out to you – she might grasp your finger or hold on to you. If you respond, your baby will make eye contact and smile, coo, babble or 'talk'. These engagement cues are your baby's way of saying, 'Please play with me.'

'Give me a break' When your baby needs a break from what she is doing, she will give very clear 'disengaging' signals such as looking away (little babies can only maintain eye contact for short periods, so may look away then continue gazing at you after a break), turning her head away, squirming or kicking, coughing, spitting up or arching her back. Some babies will even put up their hand in a sort of 'stop' sign. More subtle cues that your baby is tiring of engagement or needs a change of pace or activity may be yawning, wrinkling her forehead or frowning, or hiccupping. If you keep playing when your baby tries to tell you she wants to stop, she will become agitated and make thrashing movements, or she will start fussing and crying.

'I'm sleepy' None of us likes being kept awake when we are craving sleep so, rather than waiting until your baby is 'past it', put her to bed as soon as she shows sleepy signs, such as becoming quiet, losing interest in people and toys, making jerky movements (young babies) or becoming very still (these babies relax and fall asleep easily), yawning, frowning or knotting her eyebrows, clenching her fists into tight balls, rubbing her eyes and ears, and generally fussing. If you miss this window of opportunity, your baby is likely to become grumpy or overtired and find it difficult to settle.

A little respect, please

It is easy to simply do things *to* small children and babies without considering how intrusive or disrespectful it might feel to them. Just for a moment, put yourself in your baby's bootees: what if you were working on a task (play is a child's work) and somebody scooped you up and began removing your clothes without so much as a 'please' or 'thank you'? And what if they then popped you into bed and walked out of the room, expecting you to go to sleep without a fuss?

Empathy is about putting yourself in your baby's place and seeing things from her perspective. We can all be more mindful about how we look after babies and small children. We can tell our baby what we are about to do, rather than just sneaking up on her. If we want to do something with our littlie that isn't absolutely necessary (of course, tasks such as changing a nappy aren't optional – but it is respectful to at least talk to your little one about what you are doing), such as giving her a massage, ask her consent first. It might sound strange to ask consent from a baby, but as I have discussed, even a tiny baby will be able to give you clear signals that she wants to play, or be picked up, or that she would prefer to be left alone. By responding sensitively to your baby's cues, you are teaching her to say 'yes' and 'no' – an important part of the development of communication.

The independent child

Although right now you may enjoy some dreamy image of having a loving family of cooperative, placid children as a result of your gentle, connected parenting, I would like to offer a word of caution. Whatever parenting style you choose is hard work, but it can seem particularly intense to implement a very conscious, attached parenting style like the one I'm suggesting. It can also be a shock to discover that these empathically parented children can become strong-willed, independent and often quite feisty individuals. There will be days when you question whether it might have been better all round to have kept your baby in a darkened room with little stimulation (so she wouldn't be so smart); or perhaps to have been more rigid in your style of discipline (so she would be more compliant). On days like these, it can help to remember why it is so important to nurture an independent child who can think for herself:

- Independent children are more likely to have good self-esteem, which will impact their entire lives and how they allow others to treat them.
- Independent children are less likely to be compliant to peers (this becomes especially pertinent in their teenage years).

Although independent children are likely to experiment, explore and push the boundaries as much as any children, if the connection between you and your child is strong, you will intuitively sense when they need some extra support or firmer boundaries.

As a connected parent, you will have the confidence in yourself to do what is best for each child (this might mean seeking referrals for extra help or support for yourself, at times). You will be secure enough in your role as a guardian of and model for your child that you won't need to be 'best friends' to ensure your child's love.

'As a teenager, my youngest tried it on with me when I told him that something he planned to do wasn't acceptable. He tried to cajole me into changing my mind, saying, "But I'll be your best friend." I told him, "I don't need any new best friends. I am your mother and it's my job to keep you alive until you're twenty-five!" Although this was a spontaneous response, I later learnt that it does take around twenty-five years for young male brains to develop a total sense of safety, wellbeing and understanding of the consequences of their actions.'

Pinky

Daddy rejection?

When they are upset of hurt, it is normal for babies to favour or be comforted more easily by one parent – usually their mother. This isn't a rejection of the other parent, although it can seem this way. It is a good idea, though, to encourage time with the parent who isn't the primary carer. With small babies, this can be done gradually – dad could carry baby in a sling when she is happy, or massage her while mum holds her. As she becomes more comfortable with dad, introduce an activity such as bathing that is solely dad's domain. This way, dads become more confident and have an opportunity to bond deeply, too.

7
Feeding

♥

How you feed your baby is one of many choices you will make on behalf of your child. As with all the choices you'll be faced with, it's important to make an informed decision. If there is a physical reason why you cannot breastfeed, or if you encounter insurmountable difficulties and wean earlier than you'd planned, you may feel you have failed another one of those mythical motherhood tests. Well, you haven't! Although breastfeeding, when it is going well, elicits a hormonal response that makes mothering easier by reducing your own stress levels and facilitating the bond between you and your baby, it is no guarantee of good mothering. Feeding your baby is about so much more than milk: *how* you feed your baby with cuddles, eye contact and loving interactions is just as important in developing a close connection with your child as *what* you feed him.

'Our first child had a difficult birth and wouldn't feed well at first. He lost a significant amount of weight, so they told me, "You can't go home unless that baby is on a bottle." I was in such a state of shock, I did what I was told. Then, at home, I had a series of maternal and child-health nurses who all seemed to offer different advice, and I felt really confused. I think I felt a mixture of grief and depression because I thought that my body should have been able to do this [breastfeed].

94

'I was determined to learn from my experience, so I searched around before I had Claire (my next child) and found a maternal and child-health nurse who was a certified lactation consultant. When I was in hospital, I requested a particular nurse, who was really good. She supported my need to have a plan so I wouldn't run into the same trouble as last time. I fed then expressed, so I had lots of milk this time. I also asked for no visitors while I was there, so I didn't get any unwanted advice. At home, I got great support from my maternal and child-health nurse. This time, I am much more relaxed and Claire is happy.'

Wendy

Why breast is best

The key to successful breastfeeding is to know *why* you are doing it. If you understand in your heart and mind why breast milk is best for your baby and breastfeeding is best for your body, then you are more likely to be proactive in resisting inappropriate advice that undermines your efforts to breastfeed. You will also be motivated to persevere through any challenges that arise.

Immunity

Breast milk is like a daily vaccination against every bug your baby comes into contact with: it is a living fluid containing healthy bacteria, antibodies, white blood cells, antimicrobials, cell-wall protectors and proteins that all offer protection against bacteria and viruses. Recent research shows that human breast milk can destroy cancer cells and also contains substances that can cure teenage acne (when applied as an ingredient in a topical cream).

If you catch a bug, specialised white blood cells will appear in your breast milk to protect your baby. Conversely, if your baby becomes sick, the transfer of germs from your baby to your breast will trigger the production of specific antibodies. These antibodies will be deposited into your milk to boost your baby's immunity and help her fight off illness.

Without this natural protection, your baby is defenceless against common bacteria in our environment and more susceptible to respiratory and gastrointestinal infections, diarrhoea and allergies. A 2007 analysis from the US Department of Health and Human Services (Ips, 2007) looked at over 9000 studies on breastfeeding, weeded out the ones with poor methodology, and came up with an overall percentage for each. They found that breastfeeding reduces babies' risk of:

- lower respiratory tract diseases by 72%
- gastrointestinal infections by 64%
- acute otitis media (middle-ear infection) by 50%.
- atopic dermatitis (often called 'eczema') by 42%
- type 2 diabetes by 39%
- sudden infant death syndrome (SIDS) by 36 per cent
- asthma by 27%.

A more recent study (Bartick, 2009) observed: 'The United States incurs $13 billion in excess costs annually and suffers 911 preventable deaths per year because our breastfeeding rates fall far below medical recommendations . . . The vast majority of extra costs incurred each year could be saved if 80 to 90 per cent of women exclusively breastfed for the medically recommended six months. Most of the excess costs are due to premature deaths. Nearly all (95 per cent) of these deaths are attributed to three causes: SIDS; necrotising enterocolitis, seen primarily in preterm babies and in which the lining of the intestinal wall dies; and lower respiratory infections such as pneumonia. Breastfeeding has been shown to reduce the risk of all of these and seven other illnesses studied.'

Baby's brain development

As well as building your baby's immune system, breastfeeding provides the optimum nutrition for your baby's developing brain. Breastfeeding has been shown to increase hand–eye coordination, visual development, and language and social skills. Breastfeeding is also protective against illnesses such as ear infections, which have been linked to later learning problems.

Mother's health

Mothers who breastfeed experience less postpartum bleeding because hormones released while breastfeeding cause the uterus to contract and return to pre-pregnancy size. Breastfeeding also delays the return of menstruation after childbirth and accelerates the loss of fat stored during pregnancy. It is also related to a reduced incidence of obesity later in life as well as protection against osteoporosis, ovarian cancer, premenopausal breast cancer and type 2 diabetes.

Bonding

One of the most important benefits of breastfeeding is the exquisite bond you develop with your baby. Although breastfeeding isn't a guarantee of good mothering, just as bottle-feeding doesn't mean you can't foster a lovely closeness with your baby, the hormones you release when you breastfeed help you become more attuned to your baby. If you listen and watch carefully, you will more easily get to know your little one's non-verbal signals. Soon, you will be able to care for her without as much guessing about when she is hungry and why she is crying. And, because you can often settle her quickly at the breast, there may even be less crying to contend with. (If you aren't breastfeeding, offer lots of skin-to-skin contact as you bottle-feed and remember to change sides to stimulate both sides of your baby's body – as each side faces outwards – and both your baby's eyes.)

Environmental considerations

Consider the fuel needed to produce infant formula – from producing milk and transporting it to processing a finished, packaged product and transporting it to stores, as well as the chemicals used for sterilisation of feeding equipment and the disposal of packaging (which will inevitably become landfill). Breastfeeding saves food, resources, fuel and energy – no chemicals or packaging required!

Family finances

As well as saving a substantial amount on your weekly grocery bills by not buying formula, you will also save on medical bills because your baby is unlikely to be very unwell with common bugs. Breastfeeding can also save on orthodontic bills later, as the sucking action enhances your baby's jaw and facial development.

Convenience

What could be simpler than having the perfect food ready to go at any time – day or night? No bottle-washing, sterilising or measuring formula etc. Travel is easy, too, whether it's accepting an impromptu invitation to stay at friends' for dinner or a trip to a holiday destination where clean drinking water may be an issue – your baby will be safe, fed and comforted at the breast, even in an unfamiliar environment.

How long should I breastfeed?

As your baby grows, the composition of your breast milk changes to meet her changing needs. Some immune compounds in breast milk have been shown to increase at around six months (just when babies become mobile and are exposed to a greater range of germs), and also as they get older and are breastfed less.

While it is generally agreed that 'breast is best', there can be disagreement, even among health professionals, about how long breastfeeding will benefit your baby. The World Health Organization recommends exclusive breastfeeding (i.e. no other fluids or foods) for the first six months, and that breastfeeding continue for two years and beyond. Despite this, if you choose to breastfeed beyond even six months, you may hear comments such as, 'But there's no goodness in your milk any more.' In fact, the nutritional and immunological benefits of breastfeeding last for as long as breastfeeding continues.

In many instances, the long-term protective effects of breastfeeding are related to its duration. Children breastfed for more than six months have one-third the number of middle-ear infections in the first three years of life than formula-fed babies, the incidence of allergies is reduced sevenfold, and they are also protected against bacterial meningitis in their first five years. The risk of a number of serious disorders increases when babies aren't breastfed: coeliac disease, insulin-dependent diabetes, leukaemia, childhood lymphoma, multiple sclerosis and chronic liver diseases.

When you breastfeed your baby girl, you reduce her risk of developing breast cancer later in life by 25 per cent (Freudenheim, 1994). Breastfeeding lowers the mother's own risk of breast cancer, too, so you could be saving two lives! A study of Chinese women found that their breast cancer incidence dropped by 63 per cent when they breastfed for six years. Though that tends to be longer than most women choose to do here, your reduced risk can be determined by the cumulative amount of time you've spent breastfeeding over the course of your life. For example, if you had three babies and nursed each for six months, your cumulative breastfeeding time of 18 months would serve to reduce your risk of developing breast cancer. And because maternal bone density increases with each child who is nursed, breastfeeding mothers experience less osteoporosis in later life.

Misinformation

Despite all the scientific evidence about the benefits of breastfeeding, lots of old wives' tales persist – for example, that the size of your breasts affects the amount of milk you produce (this, of course, is utter rubbish!). Overall, we still don't have a breastfeeding-friendly society and, as a lactation consultant, I encounter many women for whom breastfeeding has become an exercise fraught with pain and despair due to misinformation and a paucity of practical help, even from health professionals.

Information about breastfeeding is often withheld on the premise that if we promote breastfeeding, we will make mothers who bottle-feed feel guilty. This strategy hardly makes sense. Can you think of any other area of health prevention where this happens? We have no hesitation about informing people that smoking causes lung cancer, that failing to apply sunscreen may result in skin cancer, or that parents can reduce the risks of SIDS by putting their babies on their backs to sleep. And can you imagine the furore if new parents attempted to take their baby home from hospital without an approved safety restraint? Would concerns about making parents feel guilty even be considered? Hardly – in fact, they wouldn't even be allowed to take their baby home.

When we properly examine mothers' feelings about not being able to breastfeed, or not being able to do so for as long as they would have liked, they are rarely feelings of straightforward guilt. A well-informed mother who reaches for the bottle after a struggle with breastfeeding knows that she has done the best she could with the resources she had at the time. She may feel disappointed but generally doesn't feel guilty.

A mother who later discovers that she was 'short-changed' by receiving inadequate information is likely to feel angry or betrayed rather than guilty. And a mother who gives up on breastfeeding because she allowed herself to be talked into something that was less than perfect for her baby is likely to find that her self-image as a competent mother is compromised. It is perfectly normal for a mother to feel she would die to protect her baby – most mothers would! So, when a mother gives in to external pressures to wean her baby, she loses confidence in her ability to protect her young.

Above all, breastfeeding is more than simply about the milk. It is a relationship, an integral part of a woman's life and an intrinsic aspect of our biological femininity. When the breastfeeding relationship is ended prematurely, most mothers feel a deep sense of loss. This feeling is grief, not guilt, and women need permission to grieve the loss of this intimate relationship.

'When my first-born son, James, was five months old, I was diagnosed with Hodgkin's lymphoma, a malignant disease of the lymphatic system. Naturally, this was a huge shock, as I had assumed that cancer only happened to other people – especially older people. It certainly should not be happening to a 26-year-old who had just begun a family. I was admitted to hospital for tests over a one-week period, during which time baby James was not allowed to stay with me. I was told to wean him straight away, as I would have to undergo chemotherapy and the drugs would be secreted in my breast milk.

'Looking back on that time now, I remember the pain and grief of the initial diagnosis. But the major cause of my suffering was the enforced weaning and separation from my baby, rather than the threat of a potentially terminal illness. Weaning was such a trivial issue to the doctors (and friends and relatives) when my life was at stake. But not to me! My baby was the focus of my life at the time, and it was such a wrench to discard such an effective, healthy and almost 'mystical' bond between us. Platitudes such as, "You've done a good job," and "He's had a good start," seemed like an insult to the importance of this special aspect of our relationship.'

Catriona

Whose breasts?

Even in the twenty-first century, the act of breastfeeding is still something of a taboo, except amongst consenting mothers in private. We are accustomed to seeing breasts used to advertise anything from cars and horse-racing to flavoured cows' milk, but many people seem to feel uncomfortable when they are confronted, up close and personal, with breasts being used for their natural purpose.

Men, too, can be less than supportive about their partner breastfeeding in public or even in private. I met a woman at a playgroup whose husband wouldn't let her breastfeed because (he said) he was allergic to milk! Another was left at home while she was breastfeeding because her husband didn't want other guys 'perving' at her. She 'compromised' and weaned her baby at three months, even though she wanted to continue.

So, to all you male partners: although your own conditioning may affect your attitude to breastfeeding, please bear in mind that your support is a crucial factor in your partner's breastfeeding success.

'I have heard other guys say that breastfeeding can be convenient for them (because it is something that they can't do in the middle of the night!) and I know that the cost saving of not buying formula is attractive to some, too. Those things haven't rated highly with me. I know that breastfeeding has enabled my boys to enjoy the best possible start to life in terms of health and nutrients, while the boys have also developed an incredibly strong bond with their mum. I am enormously proud that my wife breastfed both our boys for the better part of two years. (The little bloke is still feeding, with no sign of giving up.) It's been an amazing journey through the boys' "booba" time.'

Jon, father of two

A confidence game

Breastfeeding is as old as forever and as new as tomorrow. Women have been breastfeeding babies since the beginning of time, in all sorts of societies, in poverty and in war, without any academic understanding of the physiology of lactation.

These days, despite a plethora of information about the amazing properties of human milk and the incredible benefits of breastfeeding to mother and baby, breastfeeding rates are low. In our efforts to research human milk and infant feeding, we seem to have lost sight of the simplicity of breastfeeding. Instead of an art handed down from mother to daughter, during which a very special relationship is fostered between mother and baby, breastfeeding has become a science taught by professionals.

It is wonderful that many professionals are motivated to support breastfeeding and that so many studies have been done on the benefits. After all, mothers' milk can't be duplicated, despite medical advances and claims by pharmaceutical companies. But despite all the information, sadly, confidence among mothers-to-be – the only people who can actually do the breastfeeding – is at an all-time low. I constantly hear pregnant women say, 'I will breastfeed *if I can*.'

The difference between us and women in traditional societies is that they grow up around babies, handle them from an early age and are accustomed to watching them being fed at the breast. In other words, without even realising it, these girls learn about infant behaviour and breastfeeding long before they become mothers. Many mothers in 'advanced' societies, on the other hand, have never even picked up a baby before their own is thrust into their arms. So, they learn to breastfeed at the same time as they are learning to understand basic baby behaviour, and at a time when they are probably feeling vulnerable and unsure of themselves.

When a mother doubts her body's ability to nourish her young, these doubts turn to stress and, as this stress inhibits her lactation hormones, often her milk supply dwindles, along with her confidence. Soon, she is reaching for the bottle (of milk, that is!). After all, no mother wants to risk starving her baby.

Also, there is a barrage of misinformation out there about how breasts work and how babies feed. Much of this is due to formula-feeding principles being inappropriately applied to a breastfeeding situation. For instance, recommendations to strictly schedule infant feeding so that babies will fit into a modern mother's lifestyle have no basis in the physiology of breastfeeding. Rather than resulting in convenience and control, efforts to impose these schedules can result in mothers spiralling downwards in despair as their breastfeeding becomes fraught with problems that range from insufficient milk and mastitis to anxiety about a baby who does not comply with a parent-directed routine. Some mothers and babies may be able to manage these suggested regimes without a problem, but they are in the minority. For most, breastfeeding can only work – and last – if the mother and baby find their own natural rhythm.

Preparing to breastfeed

Although breastfeeding is a natural process, it is also a learning process for you and baby and it may take several weeks to master. For mothers, breastfeeding is like learning to dance with a partner who is also new to the steps. And for babies, not only are they learning this new dance (how to coordinate sucking, breathing and swallowing) but they are also adapting to a whole new environment. You will have a head start if you learn as much as you can about breastfeeding before your baby arrives. After the birth, if you have any concerns – no matter how small they may seem – ask for help as soon as possible rather than leaving it until things become really difficult and you lose confidence.

To make the path as smooth as possible for yourself, take the following three steps before the birth.

1. Look forward to a natural birth

Attending childbirth classes that will prepare you for a natural birth, so that you can avoid unnecessary drugs during labour, will be an advantage when it comes to breastfeeding. All medications pass through the placenta and can affect your baby's ability to breastfeed. An epidural, for instance, can affect some babies' feeding ability for up to four weeks. However, even if you get off to a 'slow' start with breastfeeding because of a difficult birth, a long labour or a caesarean (your milk will often take five to seven days to come in after surgery), this doesn't mean you won't be able to breastfeed, so please don't be put off by people who try to advise you otherwise.

Whatever birth experience you have, the most important thing you can do is to allow your baby uninterrupted skin-to-skin contact with you as soon as possible after birth. With support and positive help, you and your baby will then be able to 'catch up' on the breastfeeding front. Remember, there is absolutely no need to interrupt early bonding by weighing and measuring your baby before you have had getting-to-know-you time, and if your baby is a little slow to latch on, ask hospital staff to allow you to try yourself; having your breasts grabbed and your baby shoved on is upsetting to you and your baby, and it can make feeding more difficult as your baby arches away from the breast in an instinctive effort to breathe.

2. Check your breasts

Your nipples need to pop out easily for your baby to be able to grasp hold and feed effectively. Some women have flat or inverted nipples, so it's a good idea to find this out before you actually have a hungry baby to feed.

To check for flat or inverted nipples: hold your breast just outside the areola (the dark part behind the nipple), with your fingers underneath (at six o'clock) and your thumb on top (at twelve o'clock), then squeeze gently. If your nipple pops inwards or stays flat, you may have inverted or flat nipples. In this case, gentle sucking by your partner during foreplay later in your pregnancy will help to draw your nipples out and make breastfeeding easier. If you aren't sure about your nipples and how effective they'll be for breastfeeding (after all, women don't actually go around comparing nipples!), ask your midwife or a lactation consultant to check. And remember that even if your nipples seem flat (or large or small), the good news is that your baby hasn't had experience of *any* nipples, so he doesn't know what nipples are supposed to look like! Also, he needs to attach onto the areola rather than the nipple itself, so with correct latching, his suction will soon draw the nipples out. I have supported women with all nipple shapes and sizes to breastfeed, despite some very undermining comments from health carers. The important things are:

- to allow your baby plenty of practice suckling before your milk comes in
- to avoid any other teats (bottles or dummies) because they are longer and firmer than your nipples and may confuse your baby when he attempts to latch onto your breast.

With practice and positive guidance, a hungry baby soon will figure it out.

3. Seek support

As well as becoming informed, it is important to find a 'cheering squad' of support people so that you aren't trying to find help as you juggle a crying, hungry baby. Attend some meetings at a breastfeeding support group such as the Australian Breastfeeding Association (breastfeeding.asn.au) or La Leche League (the foremost international authority on breastfeeding, which has groups in many countries: laleche.org/public), where you will get to know the people who can help you if you have difficulties; it is always easier to call somebody you know or have spoken to before than a complete stranger. At these meetings, you will also see babies being fed and pick up some tips to boost your confidence about mothering in general as well as breastfeeding.

Lactation consultants are allied health professionals who are experienced and trained to solve breastfeeding difficulties. Many offer antenatal breastfeeding education, either as private sessions or classes. It is important to check that anyone claiming to be a lactation consultant is a member of a professional body such as the Australian Lactation Consultants Association (ALCA) or the International Lactation Consultant Association (ILCA) and is Board-certified (the title 'International Board Certified Lactation Consultant', or IBCLC, identifies someone trained in lactation management). Many lactation consultants will do home visits if you need extra help but are finding it difficult to get out to a clinic (see alca.asn.au).

Breastfeeding 'equipment'

In theory, all you really need to breastfeed your baby is a breast (yes, plenty of women have nursed their babies with just one breast). However, being a modern consumer, you will probably also want a few other bits and pieces to help you breastfeed more comfortably.

- **Nursing bras**. A good nursing bra will keep you comfortable as your breasts become heavy with milk. When choosing a bra, the most important thing to consider is that your baby needs to have easy access to your breast – your bra cups need to open so that your breast is fully exposed and your baby can latch on well. The bra also needs to have the capacity to stretch a full size larger because when your milk comes in, your breasts will be up to a size larger than they are immediately after birth. Avoid bras with under-wires or other bands that exert pressure on your breast tissue, as these can cause blocked ducts, which may lead to mastitis. You will need at least two nursing bras – one to wear and one to wash.
- **Breast pads**. These absorbent pads fit inside your bras to protect your clothing when your milk comes in (there can be a lot of leakage,

especially in the early weeks). You can use washable pads made from cotton fabric, which are very soft and allow air to circulate around your nipples to promote healing if there is some soreness. Or you may prefer disposable pads that can be thrown out after use. Many women find a combination of both types useful.

Tip: If your breast pad gets stuck to your breast between feeds, express a few drops of milk to moisten the pad before you remove it so that you don't cause damage to your nipple.

- **Nursing clothes**. There are some great clothes designed to allow discreet breastfeeding – but you don't need to lash out on expensive items. During the early days, you will need clothing that you can relax in at home, such as tracksuits or separate tops and bottoms. These clothes need to have easy access for feeding and also be comfortable enough to allow you to rest when baby does without having to change your clothes. For a few weeks, at least, you probably won't fit into your pre-baby clothes, so make sure you have some casual clothes that fit comfortably for when visitors arrive.

  Tip: To nurse discreetly, pull tops upwards (if you are wearing a shirt, unbutton from the bottom rather than unbuttoning from the top and 'flopping out' a breast); your baby will cover your bare tummy and your breasts won't be exposed.

- **A suitable chair**. Many breastfeeding difficulties can be attributed to poor positioning (see **Position matters**, page 108). One big step towards avoiding this is to have a comfy chair to sit in for feeding. Of course, the beauty of breastfeeding is that you can breastfeed anywhere. But you will be sitting at home, holding your baby, for many hours each day and night and, in order to avoid back strain and shoulder pain, you need to be sitting in a comfortable, supported position. A rocking chair is especially relaxing as you comfort your baby, and a foot stool (you can improvise with phone books) raises your knees higher than your hips; this takes pressure off your back and helps you hold your baby high enough to bring your baby to the breast, rather than leaning over your baby, which can cause back strain. You shouldn't have to go out and buy a new chair for breastfeeding. Check your chairs at home for one that has a seat that is:

- wide enough for you to fit a pillow next to you, in case you need this support
- not so deep that you find yourself slouching
- high enough so that your feet reach the floor comfortably (or where you can use a foot stool to raise your knees higher than your hips).

Also, it's helpful if the chair has nice wide arms to rest your own arms on. Even an office chair with arms may be comfy enough if it is height-adjustable.

- **A good breastfeeding book**. Read a helpful book before your baby is born. Take it with you to hospital so that you can dispel conflicting information there and refer to it later, once you're back home, when you don't have a midwife at the call of a buzzer. A small paperback is best because you can hold it with one hand as you feed your baby. Try one of the following (details appear in **Further reading**):
  - *Breastfeeding Simply* (Pinky McKay) – you can print and bind this ebook or download and listen to the recorded version.
  - *Breastfeeding Naturally* (Australian Breastfeeding Association) – you get this great book free when you become a member of the ABA.
  - *Baby Magic* (Sue Cox) – published by the Australian Breastfeeding Association, this is a lovely book with a gentle approach to mothering.
  - *The Womanly Art of Breastfeeding* (Torqus and Gotch) – published by La Leche League.

Position matters

Latching your baby onto the breast in a good feeding position can prevent early breastfeeding problems such as sore nipples or insufficient milk. Some nipple tenderness is normal in the early days (a little like breaking in a new pair of shoes), but breastfeeding isn't supposed to be painful. If your nipples really hurt or look squashed when they come out of your baby's mouth, get an expert to watch you feed, as the problem may be due to incorrect latching and/or positioning.

I see a large number of women who have been taught breastfeeding positions that might facilitate a good baby-to-nipple latch and might be useful for babies in special circumstances, but which don't take into account the newborn reflexes of rooting and seeking a nipple. (The cross-cradle hold, where the breast is held with the hand on the same side and the other hand is used to support the baby's neck/head, is once such hold.) These positions also tend to feel rather awkward to most mothers. In these positions, the baby tends to arch away from the breast if her tiny head is pushed towards the breast, and/or the mother experiences severe pain as her nipple becomes distorted or squashed in the baby's mouth. Many mums also suffer from back and shoulder pain as a result of unnatural posture in these positions.

While positioning and latching onto the breast are two different aspects of breastfeeding, one facilitates the other: if you are holding your baby comfortably, it will be easier for her to latch on properly and feed effectively without hurting you.

Tip: If you do use the cross-cradle hold, please ensure that you support your baby between her shoulders; don't ever push her head.

Getting comfy

At first, holding your baby skin-to-skin (with your bra off or well out of the way and a blanket over you and your baby to keep her warm) will help her stay awake and encourage sucking. If she is very sleepy, gently massage the back and top of her head in a circular motion, as this may encourage her to wake up and suck. Or try rubbing the palm of her hand or the soles of her feet – this will stimulate natural newborn reflexes that encourage sucking. (Please don't resort to strategies such as cold face washers to wake her up – I have seen it done!)

You may find sitting up with pillows for support easiest at first, although you can also nurse lying down. If you prefer sitting in a chair, use a foot stool or phone books to help elevate your lap, or place a pillow on your lap so you can hold your baby close. If you use a nursing pillow, check it for size against your own body; some are very firm and thick, and may position your baby too high to latch on properly.

If you have large breasts, you may need to use a rolled-up hand-towel under your breast to support its weight; this way, your breast won't be too heavy on your baby's lower jaw, which can tire her out. There is also a neat sling-style device you can buy, called a Booby Booster, which supports large breasts and makes it easier for your baby to latch on (see boobybooster.com.au).

Holding your baby

There isn't only one way to hold your baby while you are breastfeeding. Every woman has different-sized breasts, a different-shaped body and a unique baby. You will also feel varying levels of comfort depending on the type of birth you experienced. If you have had a caesarean, you may need to hold your baby away from your scar. Or, if your perineum is tender from a vaginal birth, you may be more comfortable lying down to feed. Here are a couple of common holds to practise with a doll or teddy if you haven't yet had your baby. If you have already had your baby, try experimenting until you feel comfortable.

• **Cradle hold**. This is the most comfortable and most natural hold, if you can manage it. If you master the cradle hold, with practice, you will find it easier to feed discreetly, or lying down. And when your baby learns to nurse without you having to support your breast, this hold leaves you with have a free hand to stroke your baby or hold a glass of water, a book or the remote control.

Nestle your baby in your arm so that her neck rests in the bend of your elbow, her back along your forearm and her bottom in your hand (as she gets older and longer, your hand will support her back and shoulders). Turn her whole body so that she is facing you chest-to-chest (remember the rhyme 'chest to chest, chin to breast'). Your baby shouldn't have to turn her head or strain her neck to reach your nipple (try drinking a glass of water while looking over your shoulder!). Support the weight of your breast in a 'C' shape (with your fingers underneath and your thumb on top). Place your hand so that your fingers are clear of the areola; this way, your baby has plenty of space to latch on.

- **Football (or 'clutch') hold**. This hold may work better than the cradle hold for babies who squirm a lot or arch their backs and slip off the breast easily. This position can also be used to relieve pressure on a sore nipple or a caesarean scar and is a good hold for twins (with one baby on each side).

  Sit up and place your baby under your arm along the same side as the breast you are using. Lie your baby on a pillow and support her back, neck and shoulders with your hand, and direct her legs behind you (make sure she isn't pushing her feet against the chair or pillow and arching her back); her eyes should be looking up at you. Then, with your hand supporting your breast in a 'C' shape, pull your baby close to you and pop in the breast.

- **Lying down.** To breastfeed lying down, simply lie on your side with one fairly thick pillow or two thinner ones under your head. With your baby lying beside you, cradle  her in your lower arm or bend your lower arm up so that your hand is tucked under your head, and line her up next to your breast to feed.

Once your baby is in position in the hold that seems to suit you best:

- With your free hand, express a few drops of milk to moisten your nipple. Gently tickle your baby's lips with your moistened nipple. As soon as she opens wide, direct your nipple into her mouth (above the tongue) and quickly pull her close to you.
- Get a large part of the areola into your baby's mouth. Flange her lips outward by lining her nose up with the nipple and touching her top lip to your nipple; she should gape automatically. Put her onto the breast quickly and firmly, chin-first, brushing her bottom lip into a flange with your nipple as you do so.
- If you have flat or inverted nipples, or if your baby has a weak suck, as soon as she starts to suck, compress your breast with your thumb and finger (well behind the areola) – this holds the milk ducts forward so that your baby won't lose her grip so easily.
- If your baby seems to be latched on incorrectly, and especially if nursing is painful, gently break the suction before removing her from the breast. To do this, insert your finger into the corner of her mouth and gently lift her lips and gums off the nipple. Then try again.

No teats!

In the first four to six weeks, as your baby learns to breastfeed, it is important to avoid the use of dummies, teats and infant formula unless you are advised to use them by a medical professional. As well as the obvious fact that there are no calories in a dummy (so sucking on an empty teat could affect your baby's weight gains), dummy and bottle nipples require a different sucking action to breastfeeding. By offering dummies and bottles (even with expressed breast milk), your baby may develop what is known as 'nipple confusion' and not feed as effectively at the breast, or he may even refuse to breastfeed (see **Baby on strike!**, page 142).

When your milk comes in

For the first few days, your newborn's feeds will be colostrum. Although you produce only small amounts of colostrum, it provides all the nourishment your baby needs as she learns to coordinate sucking, swallowing and breathing. It is much easier for a tiny baby to learn to feed without also having to contend with a large volume of milk.

Sometime between the second and sixth day after your baby's birth, your milk will come in. For some women, this is a gradual process with relatively little discomfort, but for many it can feel very sudden and surprisingly painful – you can feel as though your breasts are literally bursting. This fullness is a result of additional blood flow to your breasts and accompanying swelling of the tissues as your body prepares to nourish your baby. Perhaps a bigger cleavage is something you have long aspired to! But rock-hard, engorged breasts can be quite frightening and you might wonder: Is this what breastfeeding is like? The good news is that this feeling of extreme fullness usually subsides naturally in a few days. Meanwhile, your discomfort can be relieved by good breastfeeding management and simple treatment (see also **Engorgement**, page 116).

It is common for babies to be unsettled as your milk comes in. Although your baby may want to feed and feed on the glorious flow of milk, her suddenly-full tummy might feel quite uncomfortable. When she is unsettled after a feed, your partner – who doesn't smell like milk – can help by carrying her in a sling or simply walking with her in an upright position against his shoulder (a 'feeding' position might confuse your baby). The 'colic carry' (lie your baby face-down across your forearm, her cheek at your elbow and her legs straddled across your arm) can help relieve discomfort.

Milk let-down

Each time you begin to feed your baby, his sucking action will stimulate the nerve endings in your nipple, sending a message to your brain and causing the hormone oxytocin to be released. The oxytocin causes the cells around the milk glands to contract and squeeze out the milk. When this 'let-down' or 'milk-ejection' reflex occurs, you might feel a tingly 'pins and needles' sensation in your breasts, your breasts may become firm, you may notice milk leaking from the breast your baby isn't feeding from, or your baby may suddenly start gulping as your milk flow speeds up.

Your let-down reflex can be inhibited by pain or stress – for instance, if you feel worried about whether you have enough milk, if you are sitting in an uncomfortable position, or perhaps if you feel you are being 'watched' by others. You can aid your let-down by relaxing; taking slow, deep breaths; listening to soothing music; or stroking your baby's body as you begin to nurse. As the let-down is a conditioned reflex, you may also find that it helps to have a drink of water at each feed time; as you sip your water and relax, your milk is likely to flow naturally.

Hungry or thirsty?

Whether he is wanting to feed because he is hungry or simply thirsty, your baby will be able to regulate the type of milk he needs, if you allow him to set the pace. The composition of breast milk changes throughout the course of a feeding. The first (fore) milk, is rather like skim milk, which quenches your baby's thirst. (This is why he will often have very short, frequent feeds on hot days. If you feed your baby according to his needs, he won't need bottles of water.) As the feed progresses, the milk's fat content increases and more closely resembles whole milk. Hunger will be satisfied by longer sucking periods, when your baby gets the fatty hind milk (like a rich, creamy dessert) that is squeezed down into your ducts by the let-down reflex. Your baby needs to finish (empty) the first breast before he moves on to the second, in order to get the hind milk. If he chooses to drop off your breast after feeding from only one side, try burping him and/

or having a little play and a nappy change, then offering him the other side before you put him back to bed. This way, he is likely to sleep longer before waking for another feed. If he is truly satisfied after only one side, you may need to express a little from the second breast, for your own comfort.

How does your baby feed?

One indicator of how well a baby is feeding is his sucking action. Think about how you suck from a straw: as you suck in a mouthful, your chin drops down for as long as you are ingesting fluid. Similarly, as your baby sucks at the breast, it will look as though he is pausing (with his chin down) between 'chomps', as he sucks in milk. The longer this pause, the bigger the mouthful he will be getting and the more milk he will be drinking. A baby who is sucking effectively (as opposed to 'nibbling') may finish a feed quite quickly, so be guided by your baby's sucking action rather than by how long he feeds at the breast.

Watch your baby, not the clock

Trying to impose a strict feeding schedule, rather than watching your baby's cues, is not only likely to result in unnecessary crying, but may be a risk to her health. When you compare a baby's needs to those of an adult (who is generally not trying to gain weight – at least, not to double or triple their current size!), it is easy to understand that expecting a baby to eat according to a strict regime, which restricts the duration and quantity of feeds, is not only unrealistic and unkind, but can also contribute to a failure to thrive. Consider how often you eat, drink, nibble, snack or sip through an average day. Did you know that you would be having a cup of coffee at four o'clock this afternoon, or did you just feel like one? Did you tell your work colleagues you wouldn't be able to have lunch with them at midday because you are not scheduled to eat until one o'clock? Doesn't your hunger and thirst change according to the weather and your activity level? As adults, we eat and drink according to our own body signals, not a predetermined schedule – and so should babies. In fact, the average baby needs to breastfeed 8–10 times a day, and up to 12–14 times a day during growth spurts!

If your baby suddenly seems to be hungrier than usual, follow his lead. His hunger may be due to a growth spurt or another factor such as an impending illness. (Babies who are coming down with a bug tend to increase feeds; they seem to know, instinctively, that they need a boost of protective antibodies.) If you respond to your baby's hunger cues, your milk supply will catch up with your baby's increased demand. Take it easy for a few days, offer skin-to-skin cuddles (which will help boost your breastfeeding hormones), allow unlimited access to your breasts and, if you can, take baby and a good book to bed with you. Remember, the more your baby sucks, the more milk you will make. Soon, your baby will settle down into a more predictable rhythm again.

Engorgement

Although engorgement (tight, painful breasts) isn't always entirely preventable, it can be minimised by feeding your baby frequently from birth so that your milk comes in more gradually. Although your baby's first sleep after birth may be a long one, after this sleep and for the first two days, gently wake him to feed if he hasn't woken after five hours. From the third day, don't let him sleep longer than four hours. (This applies to a healthy, normal-weight, full-term baby. If your baby has a low birth weight or has any medical issues, you may be advised to feed more frequently. Please follow your doctor's orders.) Feeding frequently from birth will bring your milk in more quickly and will also ensure that your baby gets more of the powerful immune-boosting colostrum.

If your breasts become engorged, it is important to continue to breastfeed frequently – every two hours is ideal. However, engorged breasts can make it difficult for your baby to attach and feed because your nipples become flat as your breasts stretch – a bit like a fully blown-up balloon losing its 'pointy bit'. Try the following techniques to reduce discomfort and make feeding easier.

✳ CHECKLIST : ENGORGED BREASTS

Before feeds . . .

- Have a warm shower or apply warm face washers to your breasts before feeds – this will help reduce discomfort and get your milk flowing.
- Gently massage your breasts towards your nipples, especially if swelling is mainly in one area. Massaging is most effective while in a warm shower.

After feeds . . .

- If your breasts are still hard or lumpy after feeds, gently massage the lumps and express a little milk until your breasts feel soft and comfortable, as blocked milk ducts can predispose you to mastitis (see page 138). Some women worry that expressing even a small amount of milk will stimulate their breasts to overproduce. However, although your milk supply does depend on a balance of supply and demand, removing milk when you are engorged will help relieve congestion and discomfort.
- Apply cool-packs between feeds to reduce swelling. (If your nipples become white and sting when you apply ice, tell your health carers, as this may indicate a condition called vasospasm, which is aggravated by cold – see **When breastfeeding hurts**, page 134.)
- Apply cold cabbage leaves to your breasts: rinse leaves, cut a hole for your nipple (or arrange the leaves so that your nipple is uncovered – this is in case of pesticide exposure and a good reason to use organic cabbages), and tuck cabbage leaves into your bra directly against your skin. As the leaves wilt, reapply fresh ones. Although we don't actually know what properties cabbage leaves have that relieve discomfort from engorgement, they have been used for many years and mothers swear by them for relief!

'Along with a girlfriend, I called in to see my new baby grandson. My son-in-law was worried about my daughter, who had been teary all afternoon. Her milk had come in 'with gusto'. Her breasts were swollen like rock-hard watermelons from her chin to her armpits. This discomfort, plus changing hormones (causing 'baby blues'), as well as a baby with a bellyache (common as newborns adapt to an overwhelming milk supply), was all too much for her.

'While my friend and I took the baby and bathed him, my son-in-law made my daughter a drink, and she had a warm shower and expressed some milk for comfort. When she was settled, I took the baby back to her, telling my friend there was a cabbage in the fridge. Not having had a baby of her own, she looked puzzled. I explained; my son-in-law looked at me as though I was the ultimate witch doctor. My friend asked, "Do I need to wash the cabbage?" I replied that it was organic and should be fine. After some teasing about cabbages and my passion for organics, my friend came in with some leaves. As my daughter applied the leaves to her breasts, she looked up through her tear-swollen eyes and began to laugh. "I think you need to wash them," she said. There was a wiggly green caterpillar making its way across the leaf on my daughter's breast!'

Pinky

Fluctuating milk supply

Babies regulate the volume and composition of your milk by their sucking and by how often they feed. As your baby sucks at your breast, he stimulates milk production. The more milk you remove from your breasts, the more they will make. And as an empty breast makes milk more quickly than a full breast, milk production speeds up or slows down according to your baby's hunger levels. (This is particularly important to remember when your baby has a growth spurt and wants to feed more often for a few days to keep up with his needs. Although it is fairly common for babies to have growth spurts and corresponding appetite increases at two weeks, six weeks and three months, these can happen at any time.) If you are worried that your baby is hungry, offer the breast again, even a few minutes after the last feed. Offering a bottle as a top-up is not a good idea, as your baby won't suck the whole amount of milk from your breasts and they won't get the message to increase the supply. So, next time, your baby will be hungry again, you will offer another bottle, and so on, until the decreased sucking causes your milk supply to dwindle and you find that your baby is weaned.

Is my baby getting enough milk?

If your baby is solely breastfed (i.e. no other foods or fluids are given), you can be confident that she is getting enough milk if she is gaining weight, has a growing length and head circumference, and is having at least six to eight pale wet cloth nappies, or at least five full/heavy disposable nappies, every day. (Dark urine, which tends to be concentrated, or scarce amounts of urine, are a sigh of dehydration and means your baby needs more breast milk).

If your baby gains weight slowly, consider whether you are comparing her weight gains with non-breastfed babies. An article published in *Essence*, the Australian Breastfeeding Association magazine (Volume 42, Number 6, 2006) summarising the World Health Organization Child Growth Standards, explains: 'Breastfed babies have different metabolic rates and different sleeping patterns. Artificially fed babies on average have higher intakes of energy and as a result are heavier.'

One study (Dewey, 1998) explains some of the differences between breastfed and artificially fed infants. The average weight gain of breastfed babies is lower, even after complementary foods are introduced. The length gain is also less, in some studies. Growth in head circumference does not differ by feeding mode. Breastfed infants are generally leaner at twelve months of age. Evidence suggests that there are no adverse effects to the slower weight gain of breastfed infants; they do not differ in activity level, and they experience less illness and have enhanced cognitive development.

If you are concerned about your breastfed baby's size, it would be helpful to check out the World Health Organization Child Growth Standards (who.int/childgrowth/en/), as these standards, released in April 2006, are based on breastfed babies as the biological norm.

Also, whether your baby is large or small, it is worth considering whether her size could be influenced by genetics. Ask your mum and your mother-in-law for your own and your partner's baby books – these could provide reassurance that your child is simply following a family pattern.

'Our first baby was born with a heart defect and, apart from a breastfeed at birth, she was fed through a tube in hospital. She had to reach a goal weight before she could have surgery, and they wanted her to have the surgery before she was five months old.

'Right from the start, I had doctors – and even a dietician – trying to convince me to bottle-feed because she would gain weight so much faster. [But] I was determined to breastfeed her to help her through surgery. Because of her heart condition, she gained weight very slowly and, at one stage, a cardiologist made me get scales and test-weigh every feed at home. That was so demoralising. Thankfully, I had a fantastic paediatrician who went in to bat for me. He called the cardiologist and told him, "This baby is not going to be weighed. She was little at birth and she is doing well." I did supplement her with a supply line and some special protein formula for a while, but we kept breastfeeding and she healed very quickly after the operation. She has started school and she is still tiny, but she is very healthy.'

Mandy

Low milk supply

True low milk supply, where mothers are unable to produce adequate milk despite good breastfeeding management, is rare but often treatable. Reasons can include retained placenta, excessive loss of blood during the birth, hypothyroidism or polycystic ovarian syndrome. Very rarely, inadequate breast tissue can also result in low supply. If you have had breast surgery, such as a breast reduction or implants, your ability to produce milk may be affected; this will vary with individual cases and how or how recently surgery was performed. Although many mothers breastfeed well with implants, the reason for these (such as having very little breast tissue) can impact how easy it is to breastfeed.

Baby-related reasons for low milk supply include poor attachment or insufficient time at the breast. This can be the result of a sleepy baby, strictly scheduled feeds, supplementing with formula, overuse of dummies or anatomical issues such as tongue-tie (see page 134). Thankfully, these issues can be overcome with proper management and support. An excellent book to read if you have low milk supply is *The Breastfeeding Mother's Guide to Making More Milk* (see makingmoremilk.com) by US International Board Certified Lactation Consultants Diana West and Lisa Marasco (see **Further reading**).

Is it a growth spurt?

Now and again, most babies will have a 'frequency day' (or several), when they need to feed more often to temporarily boost your milk supply. This may also be called a 'growth spurt', which neatly explains your baby's appetite increase. This doesn't mean that you are running out of milk. If you follow your baby's lead and let him suck more often for a few days, your breasts will catch up with the increased demand and things will settle down again. Take it easy and remember that the more your baby sucks, the more milk you will make. Conversely, if you offer a top-up bottle, your baby won't need to empty your breasts and they won't get the message to increase milk production.

It can be reassuring to know that although your baby will have appetite increases, where he will need a bit more milk for several days, your breasts are not going to have to produce an ever-increasing volume of milk as your baby grows. In fact, your milk volume will stay about the same (around 750–800 ml per day) from the end of the first month until your baby begins on solid foods. This is partly because of changes in milk composition as your baby grows and also because his rate of growth slows down by around 50 per cent by four to six months.

Feeding to make more milk

To boost your milk supply, your baby needs to be well attached (get an expert to check) and nursing efficiently. Offer both breasts at each feed. As he slows his sucking, encourage him to drain the breast (and stimulate more milk) by compressing your breast so that milk is expressed into his mouth. To do this, place one hand around your breast, with your thumb on top and fingers below, or your thumb on one side and fingers on the other, high up on your breast (not near the nipple), and compress your breast. This action (*press, compress, release*) will help squeeze and drain more milk from the breast. As the milk flow increases, you will notice your baby swallowing more deeply. You can also try 'switch feeding': let your baby suck on one breast until he slows his swallowing, then switch sides, switching several times during a feed.

Do I need to express?

When trying to increase their milk supply, many mums are advised to adopt a regime of feeding and expressing. Although this is sound advice when we consider the physiology of lactation (i.e. that an empty breast makes milk more quickly), in reality, this method often leads to feeding, settling and expressing, then finding it's time to start all over again. Apart from the fact that a baby who sucks effectively will empty your breasts far more efficiently than any pump, the resulting exhaustion can be counter-productive. If your baby isn't sucking effectively, or you are worried about needing to give your baby a top-up, see the expressing checklist on page 129 for some tips.

Medications to make milk

Some mothers swear by herbal teas to increase their milk supply. You could try raspberry-leaf tea, fenugreek tea or a commercially blended nursing tea. Tablets are also available – try fenugreek or blessed thistle. However, please use herbs with caution, as in some cases they have been linked to allergic reactions or fussiness in babies. As well as herbal teas/tablets, you could check out coffee substitutes such as Caro, which are based on barley, a grain that is lactogenic (i.e. enhances milk production). These coffee substitutes usually also contain chicory or dandelion, plus malt – ingredients that are all lactogenic. Many nursing mothers are advised to drink Milo. However, as Milo contains chocolate and dairy milk, it may result in a cranky baby.

Foods such as oats and fresh garlic are also reputed to boost milk supply, and are good for you in any case, so worth adding to your diet. If you aren't used to eating fresh garlic, start slowly with one to two fresh cloves a day and watch how your baby reacts: does he seem to enjoy the taste (many babies reputedly enjoy garlic-flavoured milk) or does it seem to cause some tummy discomfort? The most effective way to eat garlic is to crush some cloves and add to food after the food has been cooked. Try it in vegetables, rice, grains, pulses, salad sauce, spaghetti sauce, or other sauce.

A useful book that details a history of foods and herbs used in different cultures to promote milk supply and mothers' health is *Mother Food for Breastfeeding Mothers* by Hilary Jacobsen, a holistic lactation consultant (see Further Reading or mother-food.com).

If you are experiencing a low milk supply and measures such as skin-to-skin contact, rest and more frequent feeding aren't helping, you can ask your doctor for a prescription medication such as Motilium to increase milk production. This is best done as early as possible, rather than waiting until you become disheartened and desperate.

Lactation Cookies

These cookies contain a number of ingredients that are considered lactogenic. If you have a generous friend or relative who likes cooking, perhaps you could give them the recipe and request a batch. This recipe has been passed around breastfeeding mothers for years, so I have no idea who to credit the original to, and I am sure each mother will adapt this to her own taste by adding extras such as spices or dried fruits.

Makes around 48 cookies, depending on size

Ingredients

2 tbsp flaxseed meal (available from health-food stores)

4 tbsp water

1 cup butter or margarine

1 cup white sugar

1 cup brown sugar

2 large eggs

1 tsp vanilla

2 cups wholemeal flour

1 tsp baking soda

1 tsp salt

3 cups rolled oats

2 generous tbsp brewer's (NOT baker's) yeast (available at health-food stores)

Optional: raisins/sultanas/ carob chips (chocolate isn't recommended as it can make babies very cranky and squirmy, leading to difficult feeds)

Method

Preheat oven to 180°C. Mix the flaxseed meal with the water and set aside for 3–5 minutes. Cream (beat well) butter and both sugars. Add eggs one at a time, mixing well. Stir flaxseed mixture and add, with vanilla, to butter mixture. Beat until blended. Sift together flour, soda and salt, and add to butter mixture. Stir in oats then fruit/carob (if using). Scoop or drop teaspoonsful of the mixture onto a baking sheet (preferably lined with baking paper). The dough is a little crumbly so it helps to use a scoop.

Bake 8–12 minutes, depending on size of cookies.

Dosage: Around four cookies a day should help, though start slowly, in case they work too well!

Wet nappies

What comes out must have gone in! Your baby is getting enough milk if she is having six to eight pale wet cloth nappies, or five heavy disposables, every day and is only drinking breast milk. To gauge what a wet or heavy nappy feels like, grab a clean nappy and pour 30 ml of water onto it (45 ml if your baby weighs more than 4 kg). You can also tear a used disposable nappy to check wetness, or place a cotton ball inside the nappy so that it's easier to tell when your newborn has done a wee.

It is also important to count your baby's poos in the early weeks – some babies may drink enough to pass urine but not enough to gain weight or have bowel movements. From around day four and for the first four to six weeks, a baby who is feeding enough will have at least three stools per day that are bigger than 2.5 cm. After this, although bowel movements may be less frequent, they are usually larger in volume; if your baby is older than six weeks and doing one 'doozey poo' every few days, chances are that everything is just fine.

If your baby's nappies aren't really wet or she isn't gaining weight, you need to have her checked by your doctor or child-health nurse and also seek breastfeeding help from a lactation consultant.

Supplement feeds

The first consideration at any time for a hungry baby must be to feed him, and some babies will need supplements. These can be top-ups of your own expressed breast milk, donor breast milk from a milk bank such as the Mothers Milk Bank (see mothersmilkbank.com.au) or, if this isn't an option, infant formula.

If you do need to supplement, consider using a feeding system such as a supply line (where milk flows through fine tubing into your baby's mouth as he nurses at the breast) so that your supply is stimulated and your baby is encouraged to suck at the breast. However, you may not have the time or resources to organise this, or you may already be topping up your baby by the time you read this. If this is the case, use the checklist below to ensure good supplementary feeding.

✳ **CHECKLIST : SUPPLEMENTING**

• To supplement, you can use a bottle, 'finger feed' (using a syringe to squirt milk into your baby's mouth as he sucks your clean finger, nail-side down against his tongue) or offer milk in a cup (there are specially designed cups for this or, in an emergency you can try a shot glass – even very small babies will 'lap' from a cup).

- If you use a bottle, choose a teat with a slow flow (a 'newborn' teat or one that is specifically labelled 'slow flow') so that you baby has to make an effort to obtain milk. Bottle teats require a different sucking action from breastfeeding and, without a slow-flow teat, babies can quickly become accustomed to the constant flow of milk from a bottle. Lactation consultants Diana West and Lisa Marasco (authors of *The Breastfeeding Mother's Guide to Making More Milk* – see Further Reading) also advise choosing a teat that encourages your baby to latch deeply, extend his tongue and cup it around the teat with relaxed lips. Ultrasound studies show that round teats with a broad base encourage these motions, while flattened-tip orthodontic teats encourage babies to retract their tongues – the opposite of what should happen when breastfeeding.

- Lactation consultant Dr Christina Smillie suggests a 'finish at the breast' method of supplementing with bottles. It might seem sensible to offer the breast first, so that your baby removes the most milk, but a hungry baby may become frustrated if you have a low supply and he knows the bottle will come. Soon, he will be taking more and more from the bottle and your supply will dwindle even further. Instead, allow your baby to quench his initial thirst with a limited amount of milk (this will take some experimenting, but try about 7–15 ml less in the bottle than your baby usually takes) and then, when he looks relaxed or finishes the bottle, switch to the breast. If he sucks well at the breast, more milk is removed and breast milk production will increase. If he fusses again after breastfeeding, offer more supplement then switch again so that he still finishes at the breast. This way, your baby learns to associate his full tummy with the breast – and it is also a much nicer feeling for you to have your baby doze contentedly at the breast than the demoralising experience of watching him gulp down a bottle after he pulls off your breast, dissatisfied. As your milk supply increases, you will gradually be able to offer less milk in the bottle. Be guided by your baby's behaviour and weight gains, and your healthcare provider's advice regarding your baby's wellbeing.

Too much milk

Too much milk – gushing breasts, a baby covered in milk and spluttering with the force of the flow, and breasts that are uncomfortably full again soon after a feed – can be just as problematic as a low milk supply, although this problem isn't often acknowledged. I have had clients who have felt highly stressed as a result of oversupply, and yet have simply been dismissed by health professionals as 'lucky' or been told to 'space out feeds'.

If your baby is finding it difficult to contend with a fast milk flow (hence the spluttering), try expressing a little milk until your initial flow slows before attaching your baby, and also remove him from the breast as you have subsequent let-downs during the feed (let the milk flow into a nappy or a cup – don't express the let-down as you will stimulate more milk). Try positioning your baby so he is more upright as he feeds – perhaps lying on his tummy on top of you as you recline; this will give him more control over the fast milk flow. One effective way to attach a baby who may be finding a fast flow frustrating is to stand up and hold him almost vertically upright against your body. This will take practice, but will help him manage the flow and stay attached.

To help regulate your milk supply, try 'block feeding': feed your baby from one breast only, over a period of three to four hours. If he wants to feed again within that time, return to the 'used' breast. At first, you will need to express just enough from the other breast to be comfortable, but don't overdo this, as you don't want to overstimulate your supply. As well as regulating your milk supply, block feeding ensures that your baby gets more of the fattier hind milk, which will help to keep him satisfied for longer periods of time (and may reduce gas and tummy pains).

If you are desperate, you could try drinking a cup of sage tea, which is believed to inhibit milk production, but do take this carefully to see how your body reacts.

Expressing milk

Expressing means squeezing milk from your breasts either by hand or using a breast-pump. There are a number of reasons you may want to express milk:

- to help your baby attach more easily if your breasts are very full (express just a little before you offer the breast to your baby)
- to relieve an uncomfortable breast and clear blocked areas if you feel 'lumpy' after your baby has fed
- to rest a sore nipple and allow it to heal (although, if positioning is corrected, this may not be the best option – be guided by your carer)
- to stimulate your milk supply if you have low supply or if your baby isn't sucking effectively
- because you have to be separated from your baby if you or he is unwell and hospitalised
- to leave milk for your baby to drink if you leave him with a carer.

Breast-pumps are useful if you need to express longer term – a good electric breast-pump will stimulate and maintain your milk supply more efficiently over time if you have a premature or sick baby or are returning to work. But learning to express milk by hand is useful for all breastfeeding women and, in the first few days after birth, when you are producing a small amount of colostrum, you should express by hand.

Amount doesn't count

When you express milk for your baby, please don't worry if you don't seem to be expressing very much. Whether you use a breast-pump or hand express, your baby's sucking action will be far more effective at taking milk from your breasts – he will almost always get more milk by feeding directly at the breast than you will when you express. The quantity you express is less important than the stimulation of regular expressing to increase and/or maintain your milk supply.

Expressing by hand

1. Always wash your hands before expressing and use a sterile container to collect your milk.

2. Encourage your milk to start flowing by gently massaging your breasts towards the nipple and rolling your nipples between your fingers (see also **Milk let-down**, page 114).

3. Grasp your areola about 4–5 cm back from the base of the nipple, with your thumb on top and your index finger underneath. (If you visualise your breast as a clock, you would have your thumb at twelve o'clock and your index finger at six o'clock.)

4. Push your fingers back into the chest wall and, as you do this, gently compress your breast with your thumb and index finger. Press for about two seconds, then release – the action is *press, compress, release*. Don't squeeze the nipple or slide your fingers towards the nipple at all).

5. Compress your fingers rhythmically until the milk stops spraying. Then work your fingers around your breast (to two and eight o'clock, then four and ten o'clock, for instance), until the milk stops flowing from that breast.

6. When the flow in that breast slows to drops, change to the other breast.

7. Massage both breasts again and repeat the process. By switching sides two or three times, you will gradually increase your milk supply. Expressing will probably take about 20–30 minutes altogether.

✳ CHECKLIST : EXPRESSING

- Try to work out a happy medium so that you do not find yourself in an exhausting cycle of feeding, settling and expressing. So, express for short periods of, say, 20 minutes several times a day (this may vary from a few times a day to every three hours – be advised by your lactation consultant), with perhaps one longer expressing session when it works best for you, such as after your baby is in bed at night and you are feeling more relaxed.

- A good rule of thumb when considering how often to express is to keep one feed ahead of your baby's needs so that you balance rest, feeding yourself and feeding your baby, and have some expressed milk in the fridge as insurance if your baby needs a top-up (your own milk is better than formula for both your baby and your supply).

• If your breasts aren't soft (drained), express after feeds; otherwise, express between feeds to keep your breasts as empty as possible so that milk production speeds up.

Hands-on pumping

In my lactation practice, I have found that the most effective way to increase a mother's milk supply (provided there are no medical reasons for low supply) is to encourage skin-to-skin contact between mother and baby, along with 'hands-on pumping' with a double-system electric breast-pump (that pumps both breasts at once).

A Stanford University study (Morton, 2009) found that the suction of an electric pump could not reliably remove a significant portion of colostrum and milk, and that hand-massaging and compressing those areas of the breast that felt firm improved milk removal. In this research, mothers were taught to use their hands to express colostrum (early milk) during the first three postpartum days. Once milk volume increased, they were instructed to use a technique called 'hands-on pumping', using both an electric pump and hand compression as they pumped and massaged firm areas and, after the flow of milk slowed, to revert to hand-expressing. Mothers of babies born before thirty weeks of gestation who hand-expressed colostrum more than five times a day in addition to pumping, and then used hands-on-pumping for eight weeks, produced an average of almost double the amount of milk than mothers who pumped only. The hands-on mothers were even able to express less frequently, and by eight weeks postpartum, could sleep longer at night.

✳ CHECKLIST : **HANDS-ON PUMPING**

• Begin hand-expressing or breast-pumping within six hours of delivery.
• Use a hospital-grade breast-pump with a double-pump kit (so you are expressing both breasts at once) eight times or more every twenty-four hours.

- You don't need to pump on a regular schedule; express whenever it's convenient.
- Make sure the pump flanges (the part that fits over your nipple) are the appropriate size so they are comfortable and not pinching or hurting.
- It can be helpful to wear a bra or singlet with holes cut around the nipples to hold the flanges in place while you are pumping and massaging.
- Start with slow massage to stimulate a let-down (milk flow). When you massage, pay special attention to the outer areas of your breasts – massaging and compressing high up on the breasts.
- Apply the breast pump and use the maximum suction level that is comfortable, not painful. Pumping shouldn't be painful.
- Watch the sprays of milk and adjust your hand position to where milk flows the most easily.
- When the sprays of milk subside, switch to single pumping so you can be more vigorous with the massage. When the sprays of milk subside again, turn off the pump and hand-massage into the pump flange. Some mothers can double their output this way. This is hind milk – the richest milk for your baby – and is especially beneficial for a premature baby in need of calories.
- Empty your breasts so there are no lumpy areas.
- Watch the video at http://newborns.stanford.edu/Breastfeeding/MaxProduction.html

Storing expressed milk

The guidelines for storing your milk might vary slightly, depending on why you are expressing.

❋ CHECKLIST : MILK STORAGE

- Fresh milk will, of course, have the maximum immunity components – some of these are destroyed by freezing.
- Glass or hard plastic containers are best to store breast milk.

- If you are expressing for a premature baby, store each collection in a separate bottle and label each container with your baby's name, the date and time of pumping, as well as any medications that you are taking. If you aren't taking your milk to the hospital for your baby within twenty-four hours, you will need to freeze it. Plastic storage bags aren't recommended for storing milk for premature babies because they can alter some of the nutrients and there is the risk of leakage.
- If you are expressing to leave an occasional bottle for a healthy full-term or older baby, you can add breast milk to expressed milk in the fridge – but, as breast milk is obviously warm when it is expressed, it needs to be chilled before you add it to previously expressed and chilled milk.
- Do not add freshly expressed milk to milk that has already been frozen.
- Expressed milk for a healthy, full-term baby can be stored in the fridge for 3–5 days. Keep it at the back of the fridge, where it is coldest. Breast milk can be stored for up to two weeks in the freezer compartment inside the fridge, up to three months in a freezer section with a separate door, and for 6–12 months in a deep-freeze (-18°C or lower).
- Always note the date and time on containers so that you use the oldest milk first. And, as with any other foods that may not be fresh, please remember the motto: 'If in doubt, throw it out.' Discard any leftover, previously frozen expressed milk after a feed.
- To thaw frozen milk, place the container in a bowl of warm water, run it under warm tap water or defrost it in the refrigerator overnight. Don't use the microwave for defrosting or warming – it kills the nutrients in breast milk. And don't ever save partially drunk portions for later use – throw out any milk that is left in your baby's bottle.

Expressing for a premature or unwell baby

Your milk will probably come in more slowly after a difficult birth such as a caesarean and/or separation from your baby, but please be reassured that your baby will only need a small amount of milk at first and every drop (collect it in a syringe if you don't have enough to squirt into a bottle) is precious to your baby's immune system. It is important to express frequently in these early days, while your post-birth hormone levels support optimal milk production. If you are aiming to breastfeed exclusively, plan to express eight to ten times daily until you get a good supply that is ahead of your baby's needs. Then, if there is a setback or your baby needs extra milk, you will not have to feel stressed about the amount of milk you can produce.

To boost your milk supply while you are expressing, it can be helpful to express while you are next to your baby or to express just after you have cuddled your baby. Ask whether 'kangaroo care' (snuggling skin-to-skin) is permitted at the hospital, as studies show that this ongoing close contact with your baby has a significant effect on milk production. If you are expressing at home while your baby remains in hospital, you could take an article of your baby's clothing home and smell it, and/or look at a photo of your baby and visualise him growing strong and healthy, as you express.

Breast massage before expressing, and using a breast-pump that can express both breasts at once, will also help increase supply (see **Hands-on pumping**, page 130). It is important to take care of yourself and rest as much as possible, so it is okay to express more often during the day and sleep a stretch of 5–6 hours at night. You can also ask your doctor about prescribing medication to help increase milk supply (see page 123) – the sooner you start this the better, so that you can get a head start before your baby begins to need larger quantities.

Expressing when returning to work

As well as keeping your baby healthy, and saving you from having to use up your sick leave to care for her, one very important factor for choosing to breastfeed when you return to work is the special connection you will maintain with your little one. However competent her carers are, breastfeeding is the one thing only you can do for your baby. For specific information about breastfeeding, expressing and employment, see **Breastfeeding and returning to work**, page 152.

When breastfeeding hurts

Some nipple tenderness is normal in the early days, but breastfeeding shouldn't be painful. If it is, get an expert to watch you feed, as the problem may be the result of incorrect positioning or a problem with your baby's suck – for instance, a baby with a high palate or tongue-tie may make your nipples sore.

Tongue-tie

In some babies, the little membrane called the frenulum, which joins the middle of the tongue to the floor of the mouth, is too tight and 'ties' the tongue down so that the baby has difficulty poking her tongue out. She will be unable to feed effectively because she can't bring her tongue forward enough to latch well onto the breast.

Tongue-tie is often hereditary – if either you or your partner have or had (you may have had your frenulum snipped when you were a baby) a tongue-tie, there is a higher chance that your baby will also have this condition.

To check for tongue-tie, run your finger under your baby's tongue; if you can't slide smoothly across his mouth, a tongue-tie may be present. If you are unsure and breastfeeding is painful (your nipples and areola will be pinched with each suck and you may have a graze or crack across the top of your nipples), get a professional to check. A tongue-tie can be easily remedied by seeing a doctor, who will snip the frenulum (the younger the baby, the easier it is). You will be able to feed your baby straightaway and you may be surprised at how much more easily he feeds after this simple procedure.

Nipple soreness can also be related to dryness and cracking from inappropriate treatment (such as using soap), a lack of skin suppleness or nipples that are not especially stretchy! Many experts recommend massaging your nipples with pure lanolin before the birth, to increase their suppleness.

However, after your baby is born, it is better to avoid creams, film and hydrogel dressings as these can keep nipples moist and may encourage the growth of *Candida albicans* (thrush) or bacteria. Instead, try applying a warm wet face washer after feeds to help relieve pain. To keep nipples healthy, squeeze out a small amount of hind milk after feeds and massage it into your nipples, then let them dry naturally.

Vitamin supplements – a good multivitamin containing zinc and vitamin E, as well as evening primrose oil and 1000 mg of vitamin C daily – will help sore nipples to heal and increase your energy levels.

Other reasons for nipple pain include:

- **Nipple vasospasm**. This condition is caused by poor peripheral circulation. You may notice that your nipples look white after a feed, when they are exposed to cool air after a shower, or if you treat sore breasts with cool-packs. They may also turn purple before they return to their normal colour. As you feed, vasospasm will cause a stinging, stabbing pain, and as circulation returns to your breasts and they regain their normal colour, you will feel an intense burning feeling.

  Some asthma medications, decongestants, caffeine, cigarette smoking (even two cigarettes daily can affect your circulation), a condition called Raynaud's phenomenon or poor attachment at the breast may be contributing factors to vasospasm.

  Vasospasm can be avoided or treated by:
  - exercising to increase circulation
  - keeping yourself warm (for example, breastfeeding in a warm room)
  - applying heat-packs to your breasts before and after feeds (cool-packs are not appropriate if you have vasospasm)
  - taking supplements of magnesium and a six-week course of evening primrose or fish oil – discuss this with your doctor or lactation consultant.
- **Milk blister or 'white spot'**. You may notice a small painful white lump or blister on the tip of your nipple. This tends to occur when skin grows over one of the nipple pores, causing milk to block up behind the skin and thicken. These spots often open and clear during a feed, but if not,

you can help the blister open and clear by soaking your nipple area in warm water or applying a warm wet compress before feeding. If this doesn't work, you will need to open the nipple pore with a sterile needle (if you aren't comfortable doing this yourself, seek professional help from your doctor). It can often be easier to do this after your baby has sucked a little. Once you have opened the blister, remove the thickened milk by expressing or continuing to feed your baby.

- **Thrush.** This is a fungal infection (*Candida albicans*) described by most women as excruciating. It is most likely to occur if you or your baby are treated with antibiotics (which kill the natural gut bacteria), during summer and in hot, humid climates (which encourage yeast growth). Nipple thrush may also occur if you have vaginal thrush or if you or your partner has tinea.

   Symptoms of nipple thrush are red and stinging nipples (check baby's mouth for white spots if this occurs), and/or a burning pain deep in your breast during feeds. If your baby is affected, he may suddenly have difficulty latching on or fuss unusually while breastfeeding. Look inside your baby's mouth: thrush produces a white, cheesy substance on the insides of his cheeks and/or tongue and you won't be able to wipe it away. In the early stages, thrush may not be obvious in your baby's mouth – your first warning may be excruciating, shiny red nipples, and your baby may develop a red, angry-looking nappy rash.

   If you suspect thrush, see your healthcare provider as soon as possible Your doctor can make a diagnosis (symptoms of nipple thrush can be similar to symptoms of a bacterial infection) and will prescribe medication and an antifungal cream. (Just to be sure, it may be wise to ask about a cream such as Kenacomb, which is antifungal *and* antibacterial.) You will need to treat your baby's mouth, too, as infection will pass from your nipples to baby's mouth and vice versa, so take your baby with you to the doctor and have him checked too.

   Meanwhile, there are some environmental precautions you can take to reduce/alleviate thrush:

- To prevent reinfection, apply antifungal cream to your nipples, wash your bras frequently, use disposable nursing pads and boil all dummies, teats and toys that come into contact with your baby's mouth. Insist that everybody who handles your baby washes their hands first.
- Reduce thrush in your body by eliminating refined sugar, alcohol and yeast from your diet (use yeast-free breads and avoid products such as Vegemite). Increase your intake of plain yoghurt containing live cultures or take acidophilus tablets (the potent ones are kept in the refrigerator at the chemist or health-food shop) to increase the 'good' bacteria that control yeast in your gut.
- Keep your nipples dry (avoid creams other than those advised for the treatment of thrush), and expose them to sunshine when possible.
- Make sure any family members who have a fungal infection such as tinea are also treated; they will need to adhere to the diet, too.
- **Blocked duct**. You wake up and, out of the blue, you have a sore, red, lumpy patch on one breast. This soreness may be the result of a blocked duct and should be treated quickly in order to prevent mastitis (an inflammation of the breast, which may or may not also be infected).

As the name suggests, a blocked duct is an area of the breast that hasn't been properly drained of milk. When this happens, fat globules can clump together, causing milk to bank up behind the blockage and inflame the breast tissue. If you have a blocked duct, your milk may taste salty, so your baby may not feed well on that side. A tip from lactation consultant Sue Cox is to eat freshly crushed garlic. The garlic taste will mask the salty taste and, because babies like garlic-flavoured milk (yum!), your baby will drain your breast, which is exactly what you want. Also, as garlic contains allicin, a natural antibacterial agent, it could help reduce infection.

You can also massage any lumps towards the nipple to encourage drainage – try massaging under a warm shower and applying warm a wet face washer before feeding your baby, then massaging as your baby sucks. (If it is too difficult for you to do this, ask your partner to massage.)

- **Mastitis**. Feeling 'fluey' is a warning sign that you could be coming down with mastitis. Symptoms of mastitis can hit suddenly and hard: one minute you feel fine, and the next you feel shattered and aching all over with chills and a fever. Sometimes, flu-like symptoms come on even before you get a fever or notice breast tenderness. Mastitis can affect you emotionally, too – it is common to feel 'just awful' and teary.

  Another sign that mastitis may be rearing its ugly head is an intensely painful breast. Your whole breast may feel tender and 'tight', and be swollen, red and hot, or you may present with a red, sore, lumpy patch on just one area of your breast. A sore, lumpy breast may also be caused by a blocked duct or, in the early days of breastfeeding, can be due to engorgement (full breasts). A blocked duct or mastitis without infection will start to feel better with simple measures such as rest and emptying the breast, but if you feel increasingly unwell, you need to seek medical treatment – the sooner the better!

✳ CHECKLIST : MASTITIS

Prevention

- Watch your baby, not the clock. Avoid overly full breasts and feed long enough to drain your breasts. If you feel tender or full after a feed, express a little milk for comfort.
- If your breasts feel very full (perhaps because your baby has slept for a long stretch), offer your baby a feed – chances are he will nurse enough to relieve your fullness even if he is sleepy. Try not to miss feeds: if you go on a long car trip, stop to feed your baby, and if you express milk for him before going out, don't forget that you will probably need to find somewhere to express while you are away from him.
- If you feel any lumpiness, massage your breast gently towards the nipple under a warm shower (or apply a warm face washer if water restrictions are an issue) and express for comfort.

- Avoid under-wire or tight bras that may compress milk ducts. Also, take care when you are sleeping that you don't sleep in a position that may squash your breasts – such as lying on your stomach.
- If you have cracked nipples, seek help early. Correct positioning (get a lactation consultant, your health nurse or midwife to check that your baby is correctly positioned at the breast) often solves this problem. Cracked nipples can set you up for mastitis because the broken skin leaves the breasts vulnerable to infection.
- Above all, take care of yourself. Mastitis is often a result of lifestyle stresses that lead to exhaustion. Rest, a nutritious diet and relaxing activities that make you feel good will reduce the effects of stress and boost your immune system. Remember: 'Warmth, rest and empty your breast.'

Treatment

- If you suspect mastitis, consult your doctor early. Mastitis is a medical illness and should be taken seriously. Take sick leave from all duties except feeding your baby. The good news is that if you start treatment early, you can often get on top of mastitis before you become very ill.
- Have a warm shower or apply a warm face washer to your sore breast. (You can even use a disposable nappy dipped in warm water; this will stay warm longer than a face washer but test carefully first to make sure that it isn't too hot). Alternate hot and cold packs on your breast for comfort – hot before a feed to stimulate circulation and mobilise infection fighters in the breast, and cold afterwards to relieve pain.
- Take pain relief such as Panadol or Nurofen half an hour before feeding.
- Feed your baby on the sore side first. If your affected breast feels too sore to nurse on, feed first on the least sore side for a few minutes, then switch sides when your milk lets down. It's important to keep feeding even if your nipples are sore (you may need to try shorter, more frequent feeds); feeding less doesn't usually help sore nipples because a hungrier baby will suck harder, only aggravating the problem.

- Vary feeding positions to empty all ducts.
- Drink plenty of fluids – fever and infection will increase your need for fluids.
- Weaning isn't wise while you are treating mastitis because this will increase your chances of developing an abscess that needs to be surgically drained.
- If you are prescribed antibiotics, be sure to take the full course.

What if I have 'flat' nipples?

One of the most common reasons for using a nipple shield (see next section) is that the mother has 'flat' or 'short' nipples – but, in many cases, this isn't justification for resorting to a nipple shield. If you do have flat nipples, you may be able to help your baby attach directly onto the breast (without a nipple shield) by compressing your breast into a 'sandwich' (rather like you would squash a sandwich that is too thick to fit into your mouth). As this 'breast sandwich' fills your baby's mouth, it will elicit the sucking reflex and encourage your baby to stay attached as he feeds. To use this technique, hold your fingers and thumb well behind the milk ducts where your baby's jaws and lips will be. The shape of the 'sandwich' needs to match the position of your baby's mouth. You will probably need to support your breast throughout feeds – you can use your free hand or a rolled-up hand towel under your breast if you have large breasts – until your baby learns to feed well by himself. Remember, it isn't easy for a baby with a tiny mouth to stay attached to a heavy breast and learn to suck while he also coordinates breathing and swallowing, without some help. If supporting your breasts results in any lumpiness after feeds, you can relieve this by massaging your breast.

Nipple shields

A nipple shield can be a boon or a bane, depending on your situation. For a desperate mum with flat nipples who is struggling to attach her baby to the breast, a baby who is struggling to manage an extremely fast milk flow, or a mum with excruciatingly sore nipples, nipple shields might be a temporary solution. Or not. Many mothers who have tried to hold a nipple shield in place as they grapple with a baby who is having attachment problems will tell you that it isn't as simple as it may sound. Also, many experienced breastfeeding specialists will tell you that although nipple shields may help breastfeeding to continue in some special cases, they can also convey the illusion of solving a breastfeeding problem without really addressing the cause and, used incorrectly, can potentially create problems such as a reduced milk supply.

Using a nipple shield

If you are advised by a health professional to try using a nipple shield, or if you simply can't get your baby to attach and would like to try using one, it is important to use it correctly. A good way to comfortably apply a nipple shield is to warm it in water for a few minutes to make it moist inside (this will help to maintain a seal once the shield is in place) and more pliable. Then, turn the shield half inside-out – so that the brim looks like a turned-up hat – and roll it over your nipple, peeling it back over your areola to create a tight fit. The cut-out space should be where the baby's chin is. Expressing some milk into the shield before you attach your baby will encourage him to latch and start sucking. You can also get your partner to drizzle a little expressed milk over the outside of the shield to encourage your baby to lick and latch on if he is a bit hesitant. As your baby sucks, your nipple will be drawn more deeply into the shield, allowing his jaws to compress the milk ducts and feed effectively.

Just as when feeding directly from the breast, it is important to make sure your baby is latched on properly when you use a nipple shield: your baby's jaws should be closing on the breast as he sucks, not back on the shaft of the shield. If your baby isn't properly positioned, you are likely to experience increased nipple pain and damage, your baby won't get sufficient milk, and the breast stimulation necessary for milk production will be reduced.

While using a nipple shield, you need to monitor wees and poos to make sure your baby is getting enough milk and that your milk supply isn't being adversely affected. See your child-health nurse regularly to check your baby's weight gain. You may also need to express after feeds to maintain your milk supply.

Weaning from the shield

To wean your baby from a nipple shield, try removing the shield after he has been sucking for a little while, so that your nipple is drawn out and easy for him to grasp. If he becomes upset, allow him to feed with the shield and try again later or at another feed time, so that he doesn't associate feeding with feeling stressed. One way to encourage your baby to feed directly on the breast is to plan a day or two at home, snuggling skin-to-skin and feeding often. Try to view each attempt to feed as 'practice' rather than becoming obsessed about 'success'. Remind yourself that your baby is getting your milk and your cuddles, and be reassured that some mothers have happily breastfed for months using a nipple shield. And remember, help is always available from a lactation consultant or an Australian Breast-feeding Association or La Leche League counsellor (see **Resources**).

Baby on strike!

If your baby 'refuses' the breast, he isn't simply being stubborn. Generally, a baby who won't breastfeed simply can't, for some reason. A baby's reasons for refusing the breast aren't always obvious – and, after the early days, even babies who have been feeding beautifully can suddenly refuse to breastfeed or seem to struggle at the breast – but some of the more common reasons are listed below.

✳ **CHECKLIST : REASONS FOR BREAST REFUSAL**

- Newborns might have trouble feeding if they are affected by drugs that you have taken during labour – latching on and coordinating sucking, swallowing and breathing isn't easy when your central nervous system is 'hung over' by drugs such as pethidine, which have passed through the placenta to your baby and remain in his body for several days or longer. Some drugs given by epidural have been found to affect breastfeeding for up to four weeks.

- If you had a difficult birth, early feeding attempts might be difficult for your baby. For example, babies who have had a forceps delivery may have some pain when they feed; others could be in pain in particular positions if, for instance, they have a sore shoulder or clavicle after birth. These babies often benefit from some gentle adjustments by a paediatric osteopath or chiropractor (it is important that any practitioner is specifically trained to treat infants).
- Some babies' oral anatomy – such as a high palate (which can be helped by careful breastfeeding positioning) or a tongue-tie (see page 134) – can make it difficult for them to latch on, so you may need to experiment to find the best position for your baby.
- If your baby is pushed against your breast and 'forced' to breastfeed – for example, by a zealous midwife – then his natural reflex is to resist. It is important never to push your baby's head forwards and, if a midwife grabs your breast in one hand and your baby in the other, put your own hand up in a 'stop' sign and state firmly but politely, 'I would like to do this myself. Please can you just guide me?' There really is no need for anybody to grab your breast.
- If your baby was given bottles in the early days, she might be experiencing nipple confusion because bottles and dummies require a completely different sucking action to the breast (see **No teats!**, page 112). If your newborn is having difficulty feeding at the breast, it is better to offer supplements by spoon or a syringe, or you could use a 'nursing supplementer' or supply line (a device with fine tubing that slides into your baby's mouth so that she gets milk while she is at the breast). If you do have to offer some feeds from bottles temporarily, please don't feel that this is the end of your ability to breastfeed. It may take a few weeks, but with patience and persistence, it is possible to gradually encourage your baby to breastfeed again. Babies who have received regular bottles might seem to prefer drinking

from a bottle – they get used to the fast flow. See the checklist on supplementing (page 125) for techniques to manage this.

- A baby who has oral thrush (see page 136) may find it uncomfortable to breastfeed.

- A baby who has gastric reflux (see page 234) might squirm and pull off the breast if feeding is causing discomfort. A baby with reflux may find it more comfortable to feed sitting up – perhaps straddled across your leg.

- Babies with allergies can also seem restless during feeds or may reject the breast (see **Food intolerance or allergy**, page 231). Although your baby is never allergic to your milk, he may be sensitive to something in your own diet, and a bit of detective work to eliminate the offending food can make all the difference. If this is a concern, a lactation consultant or a paediatric dietician can advise you on how to vary your diet.

- Older babies can seem to be rejecting the breast as they become more efficient feeders because they feed more quickly. These babies are often getting enough milk in a short time; as long as they are having plenty of wet nappies and soft yellow poos (some breastfed babies only poo once every few days – this is fine), then they are getting enough.

- Some older babies are easily distracted and unable to focus on feeding. If this is the case, feed your baby in a quiet space for at least some feeds or try feeding him while he is still drowsy, just as he is waking from sleep.

- Painful teething can cause babies to go 'on strike'. Try to relieve teething pain by giving your little one a cool teether or damp face washer to chew on (pop the teether or washer in the freezer for a short while first). Or you might consider offering him some breast-milk icy poles to suck on. Again, he may feed better if he is drowsy.

'My first boy weaned suddenly at around eight months. For around ten days, he would only bite. I think it was because I had started giving him a bottle of formula at night in the hope that he would sleep through. I think he was impatient for my slow let-down. He was also a big solids eater; I thought I had to give him solids first then offer the breast. So, in hindsight, I brought it on myself, but I was shocked at the time. I ended up joining the Australian Breastfeeding Assocation and they were so supportive. I cried through my first ABA group discussion. I am planning on feeding my second boy for much longer. No bottles for him!'

Jennifer

Whatever the reasons for your baby refusing to breastfeed, the most important thing to do is to feed your baby (please don't ever try to 'starve' him into taking the breast), and to maintain your milk supply by expressing so that when your baby does attempt to feed, his efforts will be rewarded by good milk flow. Here are some other things you can do:

- Offer lots of skin-to-skin contact – wear clothes with quick access to the breast and leave your top off to cuddle your baby, allowing him to fall asleep on you. Wear, cuddle and carry your baby lots and sleep with or close to him so that you can offer the breast at his very first hunger cues.
- Try feeding in different positions and at different times – lying down, walking, in the bath. Try offering the breast as your baby is just waking up, as he is falling asleep and when he is asleep but stirring slightly.
- Don't pressure your baby to feed. Stay calm (not always easy!) and avoid making your baby frustrated. If he is becoming stressed, feed him in whatever way you have been doing, and try the breast again later. If your baby is having bottles, he may try the breast after he has had a little bottle-feed first, rather than when he is very hungry.
- Be patient. It can take time for babies to learn to feed effectively, but expert help from a breastfeeding counsellor or lactation consultant can speed up the process.

Night-time feeding

During the early weeks, it is important to feed your baby during the night. His tiny tummy will need frequent refills and your breasts will also need the stimulation of night feeds to establish a good milk supply. Since you produce more prolactin (the milk-production hormone) at night, night-time feeds will increase and maintain high levels of this important hormone – and a plentiful milk supply.

To make night feeds easy, keep the lights dim so that neither you or your baby is stimulated to a fully awake state. Also, avoid disturbing your little one unnecessarily by changing nappies (unless they are very wet, or soiled). If you do change nappies during the night, change your baby half-way through the feed, then let him snuggle and relax as he finishes his feed, rather than disturbing him after his feed, when he is all full and drowsy.

When will my baby give up night feeds?

Your baby will give up night feeds when he is ready – anytime from a few months old to much older. Some babies give up night feeds relatively early but start to wake again after a few months and are comforted by a night-time suckle as they go through a growth spurt or experience a developmental leap (such as learning to crawl) that means they're too busy to feed enough during the day. (If your baby seems easily distracted during the day, it can help to feed him in a quiet room with minimal stimulation.) Babies who are teething or experiencing separation anxiety (a natural developmental stage) will be comforted by nursing, and little ones who are in childcare during the day may get into a reverse-cycle feeding pattern and sleep long periods during the day but feed more at night. Try offering these little 'reverse cyclists' cluster feeds (several feeds close together – see page 57) during the evening so that they at least sleep longer for one spell during the night, when you can sleep. Some mothers find that a quick breastfeed is an easy way to settle a baby or toddler (whatever the reason they may be waking) and if this works for you, it isn't a problem – so don't be put off by those who might criticise you for it or suggest that you are creating 'bad habits'.

'When I had Josh, the question everyone asked me was, "Does he sleep through the night?", implying that a "good" baby is one who sleeps through the night from as early on as possible. So I felt triumphant when Josh was sleeping eight hours at four weeks old, and then eleven hours at nine weeks old. However, then he started to lose weight, and my milk supply began to decrease – so much so that we ended up back in hospital for five days to work on his weight and to build up my milk supply again.

'After this experience, I realised that Josh was simply too young to be sleeping through the night, and was just a sleepy baby who needed to be woken during the night to be fed. I didn't have to feel that I had a "difficult" baby because I was feeding him during the night! Next time, I will make sure that my baby is fed through the night until I am confident that he/she does not actually need it any more.'

Angelina

Is she really hungry?

When your baby is a few months old, you can, if you like, wait a minute or two when she wakes during the night to see whether she is just stirring between sleep cycles or whether she is going to wake fully and need a cuddle or a feed. Some babies make noises as they stir but don't wake fully. By picking them up too soon, you may inadvertently disturb a baby who would otherwise snuggle back to sleep by herself. On the other hand, waiting even a few moments may mean that some babies become more awake and so more difficult to resettle – so do whatever works best for you and your baby.

Feeding to sleep

Although you may like to use other sleep cues as well as breastfeeding, advice that includes warnings to never, ever allow a baby to fall asleep at the breast is unrealistic and impractical: it is the most natural thing in the world for a relaxed baby and mother to snuggle and doze together as they breastfeed.

The soporific effect of breastfeeding is hormonally induced. As well as hormones known as endocannabinoids (yes, as the name suggests, they do have a blissful effect on your baby and we could say that when your baby comes off the breast, he isn't drunk on milk, he is actually stoned!), breast milk contains cholecystokinin (CCK), a hormone released in both mother and baby during breastfeeding. CCK has a sedating effect on both of you. In babies, sucking-induced CCK peaks at the end of a feed, drops to almost baseline after ten minutes and is high again 30–40 minutes after a feed. It is thought that this second peak is induced by fats in the breast milk, so this is another reason to watch your baby, not the clock, as you breastfeed, and allow your baby to nurse long enough to fill up on the rich fatty hind milk.

It makes no sense to resist this naturally sedating and bonding process, or to wake your baby who has fallen asleep, cocooned against your warm body, only to try some other settling technique or plug him up with a dummy to get him to sleep again. Please be reassured, any fears you may have that a baby who falls asleep at the breast will never learn to sleep by himself are unfounded.

It is true that if breastfeeding to sleep is your baby's primary sleep association, when she wakes during the night, she will probably expect to be soothed back to sleep with a breastfeed. If you are enjoying the closeness and convenience of nursing her to sleep, then this isn't a problem. But if it is an issue for you, once your baby is at least four months old, you can gently teach her to go to sleep without the breast. Rather than resort to a cold-turkey approach where you let her 'cry it out', it is kinder for your baby (and you) to make this change in baby steps:

1. For a week, feed her a little earlier in the evening and then rock her to sleep in your arms (or your partner's). Throughout this transition, feed her back to sleep as usual when she wakes at night.
2. Once you have broken the association between feeding and bedtime, you can shorten the rocking period and try putting your baby into bed when she is calm but still awake. You may find that some calming music will help her to settle and drift off more easily.

3. Once your baby learns to go to sleep without a feed, she will naturally
    be able to fall asleep again by herself if she wakes during the night, and
    you will also be able to put her to bed in the daytime without feeding
    her to sleep. Remember, though, that hunger and thirst are affected by
    factors such as the weather, your baby's activity levels, growth spurts
    and impending illness, so please be flexible. Any changes like these are
    best made gradually, with love, to avoid confusion and stress to your
    baby – she doesn't understand why you have chosen to change the
    rules. It is also wise to consider that resistance (in the form of crying
    and becoming distressed) may be an indication of a strong need that is
    not being met. Be sensitive to your baby's responses.

Out and about with your nursing baby

One of the huge benefits of breastfeeding is the convenience of having your
baby's food literally on-tap. As long as you have a spare nappy or two in
your bag, you can spontaneously change plans and accept an invitation to
have lunch with friends. You can go on holidays (even camping) without
stressing about packing feeding equipment and, if facilities are question-
able, you can relax because you know your baby will be protected from
germs by the ultimate mum-made food, available at the perfect temperature, anywhere, anytime.

   However, just as it takes a little while for most mums to get used to
breastfeeding comfortably, it can take some time to pluck up the confidence to breastfeed while you're out and about. Wearing clothing that
doesn't make you feel exposed is one way to make this step easier.

The breastfeeding cover-up

Although there are some fabulous nursing clothes designed to make
breastfeeding more discreet, you can feed unobtrusively (apart from baby-
sucking noises!) by simply wearing tops that are loose enough to pull up
from your waist, rather than unbuttoning shirts from the top down or pulling tops off your shoulder. If you wear a nursing bra that can be opened

easily with one hand and allows easy access for your baby to feed, you can hold your baby so he is covering your tummy (many mums are more concerned about exposing wobbly 'mummy tummies' than their breasts) – not a bare nipple or stretch mark in sight!

If you have a baby who is likely to pull off and look around during a feed, try to find a quiet space or drape a wrap over your shoulder and your baby to block out stimulation so that he focusses on his feed. This will also offer a little extra cover for you, if it helps you feel more at ease.

In most countries, it is your legal right to breastfeed anywhere. This, however, doesn't mean that others will always feel comfortable in the presence of a nursing mother. In an extreme case of ignorance, somebody may even ask you to feed your baby in a restroom. Try not to feel stressed in such a situation. Other people's discomfort is their problem; you aren't responsible for their feelings and your baby deserves to be fed when he is hungry, not made to accommodate adult hang-ups. Besides, by breastfeeding out and about, you are helping break down barriers for all breastfeeding mothers and babies. The more commonplace breastfeeding in public becomes, the more this absolutely normal and natural event will be accepted and, hopefully, supported.

Getting out on time

Perhaps one of the most challenging things about going out with your baby is managing outings around feed times, especially if you have an appointment at a specific time. Also, rushing out can mean that your baby may not feed as well as when you can offer a relaxed, leisurely feed. Rather than becoming stressed about when she is due for a feed, try getting yourself ready to go, then offering a top-up just before you leave. Of course, there is always the chance that your baby may not want to feed, but it's worth a try – and even if she does get hungry while you're out, you have the goods right there.

Are we there yet?

Another potential challenge of being on the move with your baby is having him screaming for a feed while you are driving. It can be enormously stressful to drive with a screaming baby, whatever the reason, and it is important to find a safe place to pull over and settle your baby (don't ever take him out of his car restraint while the car is moving). This is another benefit of breastfeeding – you can stop and settle your baby with a feed, or just give him a top-up and finish feeding when you arrive at your destination, if it's a reasonably short distance.

Breastfeeding and alcohol

The Australian National Health and Medical Research Council safe-drinking guidelines recommend that the safest option for breastfeeding mothers is not to drink alcohol at all. This is because, in light of worldwide research, a safe limit of alcohol consumption during pregnancy and breastfeeding can't be determined – there are potential risks to babies whose immature livers aren't able to process the alcohol transmitted through the placenta or their mother's milk. The guidelines particularly advise against drinking any alcohol during your baby's first month and then limiting alcohol consumption while you are breastfeeding to no more than two standard drinks a day.

Daily consumption of alcohol by breastfeeding mothers has been shown to have the following adverse effects:

- the baby's sleep patterns are interrupted (with babies falling asleep more quickly but waking more often)
- the baby's risk of slow weight gain is increased
- the baby's gross motor development is slowed
- the mother's milk let-down is inhibited (despite the fact that people might tell you that a glass of alcohol will increase your milk supply)
- the taste of the breast milk can be altered, meaning that the baby might not like the taste and so not drain the breast, potentially leading to a reduction in milk supply and/or mastitis.

Also, remember that alcohol will affect your responsiveness to your baby so, whether you are breastfeeding or not, if you drink, it is wise to have a 'designated parent' (i.e. one parent who stays sober and in charge of the baby), just as you would have a designated driver. Also, please remember the safe co-sleeping guidelines (see checklist, page 177): if either you or your partner has been drinking – even a single drink – it is unsafe to sleep with your baby.

Alcohol levels in your milk

If you do choose to drink while you are breastfeeding, it is important to be aware that alcohol passes into your milk very easily – as your blood-alcohol level rises, so does the level of alcohol in your breast milk. (Similarly, as your blood-alcohol level drops, so does the level of alcohol in your milk.)

Alcohol peaks in your blood approximately half an hour to an hour after drinking (this varies among individuals, depending on factors such as how much food was eaten in the same time period, and your body weight and percentage of body fat). It takes approximately two hours for your body to break down one standard drink and your blood-alcohol level to drop to zero (two standard drinks will take four hours).

If you plan to drink while you are breastfeeding, wait until your baby is at least one month old and then either express before drinking and feed your baby alcohol-free milk, or have a drink after a feed and wait until your blood-alcohol level is safe again before you breastfeed. Expressing after you drink will not reduce the alcohol level in your milk, and could actually increase the transfer of alcohol from your bloodstream to your milk

Breastfeeding and returning to work

Breastfeeding has been going well; your baby is thriving and happy. But now you are returning to work and feel sad at the prospect of weaning your baby. Take heart – returning to paid work doesn't mean you have to stop breastfeeding. Your baby can continue to enjoy the health and nutritional benefits of breastfeeding, and you can maintain that unique connection through the one thing that only you can do for him – snuggling him close as he drinks your milk.

Another big advantage of continuing to breastfeed (or feed your baby breast milk) after you return to paid work is the immunity provided by breast milk (see page 95). When you return to work, you will inevitably come into contact with bugs, and if your baby is at childcare, he will be sharing space and toys with other children who may have coughs, colds and infections. But your amazing breast milk will contain antibodies to these bugs, your baby will receive these antibodies when he feeds, and this boost to his immunity will mean fewer sick days for you both.

Choosing a carer

It is important to choose a carer whom you trust implicitly. However, to make breastfeeding and working possible from a practical perspective, you will need to choose a carer who is also breastfeeding-friendly – they must be motivated to follow your instructions to store, thaw and feed your milk to your baby. And they must understand how breastfeeding works and be adaptable enough to fit in around your work/feeding schedule; there is nothing worse, for instance, than arriving with full breasts to pick up your baby only to find that he has just been fed. If your baby is hungry not long before you are due to collect him, your carer can either help your baby wait (as long as he isn't upset) or offer a small amount of milk, rather than a full feed, to tide him over. This will require close communication on your part – perhaps a call as you leave work with an estimated arrival time.

Expressing and returning to work

Read the checklist below for some tips on what to do if you're planning on returning to work and need to express milk for your baby.

✳ CHECKLIST : EXPRESSING FOR WORK

- If you know from the early weeks that you will be returning to work before your baby will be old enough to drink from a cup (some babies of six to nine months can manage with a cup, but most babies can't manage until they're closer to twelve months), and you won't be able to have your baby brought to you to feed during your work day, it would be wise to try offering an occasional bottle of expressed milk (once a week is fine) from around eight to ten weeks, as long as breastfeeding is well established. This will make the transition easier for him when you do need to leave him with a bottle. Some really good breastfeeders won't take even expressed breast milk from a bottle unless it is introduced early. This can make leaving your baby quite stressful for you both; you never want to 'starve' your baby into taking a bottle.

- Start expressing once or twice a day about two weeks before you return to work. This will allow you to become efficient at expressing and to store some milk in case you have some low-supply days when you are back at work. (Don't worry if you do have some low-supply days as a result of your change of routine; breastfeeding according to your baby's cues on your days off will boost your supply again.)

- To maintain your milk supply when you return to work, it might be worth buying or hiring a good-quality electric pump, depending on how much you are working. A pump that expresses both breasts at once will shorten the time required to express and also stimulate milk production more effectively (see **Hands-on pumping**, page 130).

- At work, you will need a private space to express, a fridge or esky with ice-packs, and milk-storage containers (clearly labelled if the fridge is a shared one!). If your co-workers object to human milk in the office fridge (it has happened), store your milk inside a lunchbox with your name on it – they will be none the wiser.

- At work, it can help to look at a picture of your baby or smell an article of his clothing as you express.

- Besides expressing at work, other options to help maintain a good milk supply include asking for some flexibility – perhaps you could work from home one day mid-week (and breastfeed as your baby needs). Or, if it's practical, you could either go to your baby or have him brought to you by his carer for a feed during your lunch break.

- After a weekend of more frequent feeding, take care to express for comfort to avoid engorgement and the possibility of developing mastitis.

- Although legally your right to breastfeed or express at work may be protected by law, an understanding employer and co-workers will make things a lot easier. If you feel less than assertive about requesting support at work, you can tell your employer that your paediatrician has prescribed breastfeeding for health reasons or to prevent allergic reactions (this isn't necessarily untrue – your baby may develop health problems or allergies if he is fed formula).

How much milk does my baby need?

The research shows that from one to six months, breastfed babies take in an average of 750–800 ml a day (after the first six weeks, intake of breast milk doesn't increase with age or size as it does with formula). This will, of course, vary between individual babies, but most babies would consume somewhere between 570 ml and 900 ml a day.

To estimate how much milk your baby will need each feed while you are at work, count how many feeds your baby has in twenty-four hours then divide 800 ml by that number. For instance, if your baby has six feeds a day, you would make up feeds of 150 ml (800 divided by 6 equals 133; add a little to be sure to equal 150).

It is wise to leave some smaller amounts (30–50 ml) with your carer, to offer as a top-up if your baby is extra hungry or it is almost time for you to pick her up. Then, she will still feed when you arrive and, also, your carer won't waste precious expressed milk by starting another full bottle if your baby is a bit hungrier than usual.

> **Q:** I have just returned to work full-time and I still want to breastfeed my six-month-old son. I have been feeding him in the morning, evening and middle of the night, but not during the day. Will I still be able to feed him full-time on the weekends? Or will my milk adjust to just feeding in the morning and at night? I have been expressing once during the day at work, but would prefer not to continue as I am finding it stressful. Do I have to continue to express at work to keep my milk supply up for the weekends?

A: Ideally, it would be best to continue expressing during the day so that you have breast milk for your baby to drink while you are at work, until he is eating a variety of other foods. (See the checklist on page 153 for some tips on expressing at work.) Although your milk supply will reflect the amount of milk your baby drinks (or how much you express), if your baby nurses several times during the evening and at night, you should be able to breastfeed as often as you like during the weekend; it is rather like your baby stepping up feeds when he is feeling unwell and, with some extra feeds, your supply adjusts quite quickly.

'He's too big for that!'

How long you continue to breastfeed is a matter between you and your baby. Although breastfeeding a toddler isn't everybody's drink of milk, if you choose to nurse beyond babyhood (the definition of 'baby' is relative to the culture we live in), you can expect some disapproval. At various times while I was breastfeeding, I was told:

- 'You will make him gay.' (Interestingly, no one ever suggested that I would make my daughters gay, but it certainly made them all happy!)
- 'You will be going to school to give him lunch.' (*Only if I'm on tuckshop duty.*)
- 'He will be wanting a breast at his twenty-first birthday.' (*He might, but it won't be mine.*)
- 'It is taking too much out of you.' (*Mostly just milk.*)

When I breastfed our first two babies, I wasn't aware of the nutritional benefits of breastfeeding older babies and toddlers; I simply kept nursing them because it felt right. In fact, with each of our children, breastfeeding has been an integral part of my relationship with them and not just a matter of sustenance. As newborns, breastfeeding gave them a gentle beginning, and as toddlers, it soothed life's little knocks, easing the discomfort of swollen teething gums and picking them up when they fell (or fell apart emotionally). Breastfeeding provided a quiet space in the day if they (or I) felt overwhelmed, no matter where we were. Even a few minutes 'touching base' at the breast seemed to nourish our toddlers at a deep, soulful level, reassuring them if they felt challenged. When he was three, my last baby told me, 'Mummy, booby makes me feel brave when I get scared.' And breastfeeding not only soothed my little ones but calmed me as well. Once, when our youngest was little and I was dealing less than coolly with one of our teenagers, the youth in question looked at me with a grin and suggested, 'Why don't you go and feed the baby!' I'm convinced that if prolactin could be bottled, pharmaceutical shares would skyrocket.

Although extended breastfeeding raises eyebrows in our culture, the world average age for weaning is 4.2 years. The World Health Organization recommends exclusive breastfeeding (that is, no fluids or food other than breast milk) for the first six months of life and that infants continue to be breastfed for up to two years of age and beyond. Mothers, too, benefit from extended breastfeeding; it reduces their risk of developing breast cancer and osteoporosis (see **How long should I breastfeed?**, page 98). Women who breastfeed for a lifetime total of two years have a reduced risk of developing breast cancer. The risk among mothers who breastfeed for a total of six years or more is reduced by two-thirds, and because maternal bone density increases with each child who is nursed, breastfeeding mothers experience less osteoporosis in later life.

Because brain development is incomplete for several years, there is particular interest in the role of breast milk and children's intelligence levels. One study in New Zealand (Horwood & Fergusen, 1998) demonstrated that children who were breastfed as babies performed better in school and scored higher on standardised maths and reading tests – and that the longer they had been breastfed, the higher they scored.

Although research into the effects of extended breastfeeding on psychological development is scarce, another New Zealand study (Fergusen et al), which dealt specifically with babies nursed longer than a year, showed fewer behavioural problems in children aged six to eight years. According to the test results, the longer the children had been breastfed, the better they tended to behave. However, when you decide to wean your baby isn't simply about immunity, health and intelligence; it is also about comfort, pleasure and communication for both mother and baby.

If you sense disapproval from friends and relatives about how (or how long) you feed your baby, remember that you don't owe them an explanation of your child-rearing philosophy any more than they owe you their support (and an explanation offered by you may be taken by them as criticism of their parenting style). If you simply state the obvious (positively, not apologetically, and with a smile) – 'Yes, I am still breastfeeding,' or, 'No, I'm not breastfeeding,' – you'll usually find that they back off. If you are really under pressure to wean, try responding with, 'Our [GP/paediatrician/lactation consultant] has advised us to continue breastfeeding'. Or, if they are really rude, put it back on them with, 'I'm sorry you can't appreciate the beauty of it.'

Weaning – gradually, with love

Weaning may be mother-led or child-led. Ideally, it shouldn't be the sudden end of a relationship, but rather a gentle transition to the next stage. For this reason, the best way to wean is gradually, and with love: throwing out bottles or painting foul-tasting substances onto nipples (yes, it does happen!) is a sad way to deprive a little one of comfort and security. Although your baby might not be a toddler yet and you may not have even considered what it will be like to parent a toddler, I have outlined some variations of weaning in the checklist below, so that you can see how this can be a natural process if you decide to breastfeed past the first year.

'I have grown accustomed to her breastfeeding and to the special bond and connection it creates. Weaning is the end of a relationship. Now she is weaned, our routine is different. Now we have to help her find something else to comfort her and interpret her needs for her because she can't quite say what she wants yet.'

Graeme, father of a 20-month-old

✳ CHECKLIST : WEANING

- If you are weaning a baby under twelve months old, gradually drop one feed at a time. Make the transition as gentle as possible – and avoid engorgement of your breasts – by eliminating no more than one feed a week. Many mothers wean off several feeds over a month or so, but hang on to an early-morning or bedtime feed, or both, for weeks or months longer.
- Wean gradually and not by desertion (such as going on holiday without your baby).
- If you are encouraging a toddler to wean, adopt the 'Don't offer but don't refuse' approach. But be flexible: even a toddler may need to refuel at the breast from time to time, for emotional and/or nutritional sustenance.
- Whether you are weaning from breast or bottle, develop creative alternatives to comforting. A story, a game or a walk to the park may avert a toddler from nursing out of boredom. Try to observe your child carefully and stay one step ahead. If you want to drop the early-morning feed, for instance, get up before your child and have a drink and a distraction ready, rather than putting her in a refusal/rejection situation. Carry snacks and drinks with you when you go out, and if you aren't prepared to nurse your little one for comfort, try not to overextend her so that she feels stressed.
- Night-time or nap-time feeds are usually the last to go. One simple approach is to gradually substitute them with story time: read the same story at each bedtime feed, so that it becomes the 'bedtime story'. Later on, you can read different stories, but familiarity helps give littlies a sense of security. Alternatively, have your partner take over the bedtime comforting, or overlap the bedtime feed with another sleep cue: for instance, begin playing a gentle piece of music as you give that feed, then gradually drop the feed and just play the music.
- If you prefer a child-led approach, simply let the child decide and go with the flow. Toddlers will naturally breastfeed less as they become

busy and more able to entertain themselves, and your milk supply will drop accordingly. Your decreasing milk supply will mean that your child will start to prefer a drink of water in a cup, and although he may keep up one feed a day – perhaps early-morning or at bedtime – it won't be long before you suddenly realise that he has self-weaned.

Bottle-feeding

Although I have devoted a large amount of space to breastfeeding, I am in no way trying to neglect or diminish the importance of responsive bottle-feeding. I do find, though, that many women end up bottle-feeding because they have had inappropriate advice about breastfeeding. My wish would be that any woman who wants to breastfeed will find enough advice here to overcome most common difficulties and that she will seek help before any problems become insurmountable.

If you are bottle-feeding, please be reassured that this by no means rules out being a responsive mother. Read the checklist below to give your baby the very best start you possibly can.

✳ **CHECKLIST : BOTTLE-FEEDING**

- Carefully follow all mixing instructions on the formula package, using level measures, not heaped measures (an over-concentrated mixture can put an extra load on your baby's tiny kidneys).
- *Always* hold your baby when you feed; never prop a bottle against them. Apart from a propped bottle being a choking hazard, your baby deserves loving interactions – cuddles, eye contact and encouraging conversations – while he is being fed. Feeding is never about just the milk.
- Be respectful of your baby's appetite; never try to force him to drink a whole bottle if he signals he has had enough.
- Change sides as you feed your baby just as you would if you were breastfeeding; this will help both his eyes to develop equally and will

stimulate both sides of his body. Also, as your baby sucks, you will notice that he opens and shuts his hands. By changing sides as you feed him, both sides of his brain will receive stimulation as he grasps your clothing and touches you with each of his hands in turn.

- Offer your baby lots of skin-to-skin contact through cuddles and massage; this will release bonding hormones in you both and it may help you overcome any feelings of disappointment if breastfeeding didn't work out because of difficulties that couldn't be resolved.

'Baby massage helped me come to terms with not being able to breast-feed. I now have a beautiful emotional connection with my baby and I have been able to let go of my sense of failure.'

Stephanie

Starting solid foods

Around the middle of your baby's first year, that is at about six months, your baby will start showing signs that he is ready for family foods: he will be able to sit up in a highchair or on your lap; he will have lost the tongue-thrust reflex (that protects him against choking in the early months, but also means food gets thrust out of his mouth, rather than swallowed); he will be watching you closely as you eat and probably reaching for your food and he may seem suddenly hungrier but not satisfied by extra milk feeds.

You can start your baby on solid foods by gradually introducing a teaspoon of a low-allergenic food such as baby rice cereal, which is gluten-free, low in protein and high in carbohydrates. Mix the cereal to a runny consistency with breast milk if you are breastfeeding or formula if your baby is already weaned; then, as your baby becomes used to eating, you can reduce the amount of liquid and give him a thicker consistency. Your breastfed baby may enjoy a small amount of ripe mashed banana, as this will be sweet like the milk he is used to – you may want to add some breast milk to this, too. You can offer him food from a spoon or place a bit of food in his mouth with a clean finger. Watch your baby's reaction and see how he enjoys this new experience.

Gradually over several days, increase the amount of food you offer by around one teaspoon per day until your baby is enjoying up to around half a cup of food per meal. You can introduce each new food in this way – a single food at a time in increasing proportions so that you can see how it affects your baby. If he experiences any adverse reactions with a new food, such as tummy discomfort, vomiting or rashes, it is best to stop that food.

Another style of introducing family foods is simply to offer your baby whole pieces of food from your own menu, rather than pureeing or mashing 'baby' foods, and allow him to choose how much to eat. This style has been labelled 'baby-led weaning' because your baby will naturally set the pace at which he is ready to proceed with eating.

The main principle to keep in mind with baby-led weaning is that you offer food to your baby by either allowing him to take it from your hand (or not, as he chooses), or you simply place food such as soft fruits or cooked vegetables on his highchair tray and allow him to feed himself. There are no purees and no spoon-feeding. The baby leads.

Proponents of baby-led weaning claim the following as advantages of this style of feeding:

- Babies get to explore taste, texture, colour and smell of foods naturally
- It encourages independent eating
- It helps develop hand-eye coordination
- It makes fussy eating and food-fights less likely because you avoid stress resulting from pressure to 'eat it all up' or encouraging your child to eat when he may not want to.

Don't start solids too soon

You may be told or hear that you should start your baby on solids earlier than six months. Unless this advice comes from a medical practitioner who is caring for your baby, this isn't a sensible decision. There is absolutely no advantage to starting solid foods earlier than around six months – there is no evidence that solid foods will help your baby sleep longer, for instance.

Starting solids early poses a number of risks, such as premature weaning and malnutrition if your baby eats too many solids and these displace milk feeds (milk will continue to form the bulk of your baby's diet for the first year). Or you could increase the risk of allergies by exposing your baby to potential allergens that his tiny gut isn't equipped to deal with. Between four and seven months, a baby's intestinal lining goes through a developmental growth spurt called closure. This means that the intestinal lining becomes more selective about what to let through. This is due to increased secretion of IgA, a protein immunoglobulin that acts as a protective coating in the intestines, preventing harmful allergens from passing through the gut wall. In the early months, IgA secretion is low (although breast milk is high in IgA), allowing allergens to pass easily through the gut wall and enter the bloodstream. As these particles enter the bloodstream, antibodies may be produced to them, causing an allergic reaction. These are all good reasons to see introducing solid foods as just that – an 'introduction' rather than a meal – and to wait until your baby is developmentally ready.

Why won't my baby eat?

Please don't worry if your baby seems disinterested in eating with gusto for several months after you introduce his first tastes of solid foods. It is important to be respectful and trust that your child knows his own body signals for food. Remember the mantra: 'It is your responsibility to provide healthy food and it is your baby's choice whether he eats or not.' He will never starve himself as long as he has access to healthy nutritious foods. If your baby is a 'late starter' and still seems disinterested in eating family foods at 8–10 months, you can ask your doctor for a blood test to check your baby's iron levels. Chances are, if he received all his cord blood at birth, if you are breastfeeding and eat a healthy diet yourself, if he is active (a baby with low iron levels will probably be lethargic) and his growth and development is on track, you can relax. Just expose him to family mealtimes so he can socialise, and model your own enjoyment of food; he will join in when he is ready.

8

Sleeping

💙

'I spent so much time trying to teach my first baby to sleep; I wish I had spent it enjoying him.'

Megan, mother of two

People who say they 'sleep like a baby' probably don't have one. It's easy to imagine a baby either smiling or sleeping (alone, in a frilly cradle) – until you have one at your place. Then, reality strikes and you become utterly exhausted, your thinking becomes cloudy, and you can become convinced that either you or your child are faulty.

'I had just dozed off (at least, that's what it seemed like), when he woke. Again. I staggered towards the cot. It was a beautiful antique cot made of wrought iron. We had lovingly restored it, sanding and painting, polishing the old brass knobs until they glowed, and searching until we found an elderly craftsman who could make us a matching knob to replace one that was missing. We had talked and daydreamed about the child we were expecting as we smoothed every rough patch off the old iron railings. I had crocheted little blankets and shawls from soft, pure wool to wrap our baby in and keep him snug. They looked so pretty on his cot as we waited for him to be born.

'As I reached into the cot, in the middle of that cold night, a thought crossed my mind: how easy it would be to pick up that crying bundle and simply put him out the window. If I just slid the window open and dropped him over the ledge, the crying would stop.

'I wasn't thinking of hurting my baby. I didn't even consider him falling to the footpath two storeys below. Maybe he would just fly away. I just wanted the crying to stop. He would take that damn awful noise with him wherever he went to. And I could sleep.

'I scooped the baby up out of his cot and took him back to our bed. I offered him a breast, but still he didn't settle. I looked across at his daddy, sound asleep next to us. I reached over and told the daddy, "Here, take him, or I will put him out the window."

'The daddy didn't get cross. He didn't tell me I was a hopeless mother (although I felt hopeless and very, very tired). The truth is, he probably didn't even hear what I said. He just opened his arms and snuggled our baby onto his bare chest. The crying stopped. We all slept. I woke with bursting breasts. The sun was shining. For a moment, I couldn't remember where I had put my baby. There was no crying. Not even a whimper. The daddy and the baby were still asleep, snuggled together.'

Lily, mother of a one-year-old

Images of the angelically sleeping baby are not only perpetuated but promoted as entirely possible if you follow the latest 'expert' and their particular method of 'teaching' your baby to sleep. This promotion has turned sleep into the new milestone, as parents brag about how well their baby sleeps – the longer the better. The truth is that being able to fall asleep is not a learned skill like playing the piano or riding a bike; instead, it is a complex brain process that depends on your child's neurological maturity, not your consistency with any particular sleep 'program' or your child's brilliance. And, just like every adult, every baby needs a different amount of sleep. Whatever your baby's sleep needs, it would be far nicer to delight in all the exciting things he does when he is awake, rather than beating up on yourself and feeling resentment towards your littlie because other people's babies sleep more than yours.

Most children go through stages of disturbed sleep during their first three years of life or even longer. It's normal for babies (even those who have slept soundly for weeks or months) to begin waking at night as they reach new developmental milestones; it is normal for a toddler to wake at 1 a.m. and want to play; and (hard luck if you are not a morning person) it is normal for little kids to wake up at 5 a.m. ready to start their day. It is also normal for parents to have less than pretty feelings about disturbed sleep. It's likely that your feelings have more to do with concerns about *your* lack of sleep than a concern about whether your child is getting sufficient shut-eye: chances are, she has loads of energy. It is the big people who wonder whether they can survive this stage. However, simply knowing that sleep is a natural process and that you aren't an incompetent parent if your baby doesn't sleep according to the textbook won't help you feel less exhausted. So, let's look at how you can create an environment to encourage sound sleep – for you and your baby.

There is a range of options to help you create a positive sleep environment and the responsibility for deciding which options best suit your child and your family is yours. But I would urge you to ask yourselves three questions as you make your decisions regarding your child's sleep environment: Is it safe? Are we being respectful? What are we teaching?

✳ CHECKLIST : SLEEP ENVIRONMENT

1. **Is it safe?** Your child's safety is the number-one prerequisite in any choice about sleeping practices. From choosing a sleeping environment to implementing a bed-time routine, you will always need to assess whether your choice is safe for your baby at every level. Although you are certain to get various suggestions about leaving your baby to cry for a prescribed length of time, nobody has actually researched how long this is safe, if at all. Babies can become overheated when left to cry leading to a risk of febrile convulsions or choking on saliva or mucus. Even if these bigger risks don't eventuate, leaving your baby to cry poses risks to their mental

health; crying is your baby's language and a communication that he needs something or someone to help him feel safe and secure. Your baby's own sense of safety is important, too – he is biologically programmed to feel safe when he is in proximity with his carers. This is a deep and legitimate need. If a Stone-Age baby were left alone in a cave to sleep, he would be at risk from predators. As a result, our Space-Age babies are programmed to cry out when they are left alone. Even though our baby is generally safe from predators, he doesn't know he is in a safety standards–approved cot in a room inside a house with a monitor on the wall so that his carers can hear his every cry. To him, feeling safe is knowing that somebody is nearby, and he will only know this through his senses of smell, touch, sight and hearing. If he needs help to settle or he feels unsafe, he will let you know through his cries.

2. **Are we being respectful?** We do many things to small children and babies without even considering how intrusive or disrespectful it might feel to them. For instance, can you imagine being woken from a sound sleep and having food stuck into your mouth, regardless of whether you are hungry or not, just because somebody else decided it was convenient for them to feed you now? Or having your legs whipped up in the air and your pants pulled down without even a please or thank you? And yet this is often how we approach everyday tasks such as changing a baby's nappy. Instead, talk to your baby about what you are planning to do, whether this is dressing, bathing, or implementing a bedtime routine. And please remember, you are the grown-up here; your baby is a small, vulnerable person whose most important task in the first year is learning to trust. This is a prerequisite for future relationships, and he needs love and respect to develop this trust in you (see also **A little respect, please**, page 91).

3. **What are we teaching?** It may be difficult when you are utterly exhausted, but try to think about the bigger picture and consider what messages you want to send to your child. Will you be teaching your child that sleep is a lovely, nurturing space where he is safe to

go, and that he can trust you to soothe his fears and mend his hurts whatever the time of day or night? If you can do this, you will not only be investing in sound sleep, but you will be creating a precious bond with your child that will outlast these early sleepless nights.

'My partner and I used different sleeping arrangements with different children at different stages. They all spent various amounts of time sleeping in our bed when they were little. Some started off in their own beds and came into ours when they woke for a feed. Those who fed as I was going to bed simply stayed there (I was often asleep before they were!). They all moved into their own beds willingly when they were ready. Some returned for visits (once, one of them told us: 'There is no sleep in my bed'). But there was never any need to force them to sleep and none were ever frightened of the dark, perhaps because they had no reason to associate night-time with fear or loneliness. Indeed, perhaps because being sent to bed or their room was never used as a punishment, our kids' beds have always been a warm and comforting place for them to retreat to. As teenagers, they would occasionally go and lie on our bed (by themselves) to read or rest, if they were finding the going a bit rough. When this happened, we knew they needed some extra nurturing or time to talk; it was as though the place where they came for cuddles and stories when they were little was inviting them back to restore their spirits.'

Pinky

Understanding how babies sleep

The first step in helping your baby to sleep is understanding how babies sleep. Quite simply, babies don't sleep like adults. Not only do babies take longer to fall asleep in the first place, but they arouse more easily.

Like us, babies' sleep is divided into light (rapid eye movement or REM) sleep and deep (non-REM) sleep. However, adults have several levels of deep sleep in comparison to babies, and researchers classify newborn sleep as either 'active' or 'quiet' sleep. If you do some baby-watching, you will find that the label 'active' sleep is very appropriate: you may notice your baby's eyes dart from side to side under his eyelids, he may frown or wriggle his arms and legs, his breathing will probably be irregular and he may even cry or whimper – all without waking. In contrast, during 'quiet' sleep, although your baby may have an occasional startle response or make sucking movements with his mouth, he is generally very still, with quiet, regular breathing.

The greatest difference between infant and adult sleep is that newborns and adults have different sleep cycles. While adults have a 90-minute sleep cycle and spend about 75 per cent of their sleep time in quiet (non-REM) sleep and about 25 per cent in active (REM) sleep, babies have much a shorter sleep cycle of about 45 minutes and spend twice as much time in active sleep than an adult. Your baby's sleep cycle will be divided into about 20–25 minutes each of active and quiet sleep, and for the first 3–4 months, she will enter quiet sleep through an active sleep state. This is why newborns usually need help to fall asleep – it's not easy to reach a deep sleep when your brain is active and your body is having difficulty being still.

Babies also arouse frequently. Arousals are related to the maturity of your baby – the younger the baby, the more arousals. Premature babies, for instance, tend to spend more time in active sleep and may wake more frequently at night than full-term babies for the first few months or even longer. (Then again, some premature babies sleep a lot and need to be woken to feed, at least in the early weeks.) According to researchers such as Professor James McKenna, these frequent arousals are part of an infant's inbuilt survival mechanism and may play a protective role against SIDS. Babies need to arouse if there is a breathing obstruction, if they are too hot or too cold (both SIDS risk factors), and, of course – in the early weeks, at least – to breastfeed in order to maintain an adequate supply of milk.

It may be easier to accept your baby's light sleep if you see it as 'smart sleep' that plays an important role in brain development. During active infant sleep, there is an increase in the production of certain nerve proteins – the building blocks of the brain – and blood flow to the brain is nearly double that during deep sleep. It is also thought that the brain uses active sleep to process information. This may explain why it is common for babies who have been sleeping well for weeks or months to become wakeful as they enter new developmental stages and 'practise' their new skills, such as crawling or standing up. It must be rather like the difficulty we have trying to sleep after a busy day, a big night out or perhaps as we start a new job.

There is a range of factors that can affect your baby or toddler's sleep – see the checklist below.

✳ CHECKLIST : SLEEP DISTURBANCES

- **Developmental stages.** Babies tend to wake as they reach significant milestones (these can be physical, emotional or neurological).
- **Diet** (your child's or your own if you are breastfeeding). Food allergy or intolerance, or sensitivity to stimulants such as caffeine, can cause restlessness, which may affect your baby's sleep patterns. Dietary deficiencies (such as low levels of DHA, an omega-3 fatty acid), are also being shown to affect infant sleep patterns.
- **Activity.** Different children need different activity levels during the day to optimise their sleep. While some babies and small children can become easily overstimulated, more physical activity and time outdoors will help others to sleep more soundly. Although a younger baby may tend to 'catnap', as babies become physically active and start crawling, they tend to sleep for longer stretches during the day. Of course, this is a general observation because just like adults, infant sleep requirements can vary depending on the individual baby. However, an activity such as a good physical play, an outing to the park, swimming with your baby or a massage will encourage a longer sleep.
- **Sleep environment.** See the checklist on page 166.

It is also worth noting that most baby sleep requirement charts were compiled in the 1950s or '60s, when the technology first became available to measure sleep patterns. Although babies haven't changed, these charts are a reflection of infant feeding practices, which have changed: most babies at this time were bottle-fed cows' milk or cows' milk–based formula. Also, these charts are based on 'averages' – some babies would have been below the average and others above these sleep requirements. Because formula is more difficult to digest, it is common for bottle-fed babies to sleep longer than their breastfed peers. This isn't, though, a reason to reach for the bottle, because if your baby is susceptible to allergies or becomes unwell due to missing the immunological properties of mother's milk, you will be up at night with a wakeful baby anyway.

Despite advice suggesting that 'all night' for the 'ideal baby' is from 7 p.m. to 7 a.m., infant sleep studies define 'all night' as five hours. So, if you are asked, 'Does he sleep all night?' you can confidently respond 'Yes' if your baby sleeps for a five-hour stretch. You can also request a definition of 'all night' from the smug women at mothers' group who claim, 'My baby sleeps all night.'

Realistically, 'sleeping like a baby' can mean interruptions by little night howls for several months or longer: according to long-term research at Bristol University (the *Avon Longitudinal Study of Parents and Children*), at 6–8 months, only 16 per cent of babies sleep straight through (remember, 'straight through' is actually five hours), over half wake occasionally, 9 per cent do so on most nights, and 17 per cent wake more than once every night (between two and nine times!).

I often find that babies who don't seem to need a large amount of sleep (and are contented) seem to be following a genetic blueprint – their parents also seem to function well on lower than average amounts of sleep. Many are either athletes or work in high-energy occupations, such as hospitality. This can, of course, be difficult if the other partner needs more sleep, so some sharing of baby care will need to be negotiated, with the person who needs less sleep taking on some extra duties and allowing the other to have some 'catch-up' sleep.

Even if you are a lucky mama whose baby does sleep a longer stretch from an early age, things could change as he reaches new developmental milestones. For example, babies from 6–8 months are notorious for waking even after they have slept long stretches for weeks. But consider the intensity of their development at this stage: neurologically (beginning to perceive distance); emotionally (realising that their mother is a separate person – separation anxiety); physically (teething, becoming mobile, and 'practising' new skills in lighter sleep phases, as well as experiencing different tummy sensations as they begin eating solid foods). Knowing this, it is much easier to understand why your baby is waking and then to address the issues at hand.

A safe sleep space

The best place for any baby to sleep is where she sleeps best and this will depend on your individual family situation. Having said this, I would like to qualify that wherever your baby sleeps, it is paramount to maintain a safe sleeping environment. It is especially important to bear in mind that when we are exhausted, it is easy to lose perspective and do whatever 'works' without taking the time to do safety checks; this is when accidents can happen. For instance, leaving a baby asleep on a sofa, or sleeping with your baby on a sofa, is not a safe sleeping environment because babies can fall onto the floor, become wedged in crevices or wriggle under cushions that may impede their breathing. Your baby's bed can be as elaborate as an heirloom cradle (although you should check that it meets current safety standards – see productsafety.gov.au or babysafety.com.au – and that it can be locked into a non-rocking position, as babies can become stuck in unsafe positions when unsupervised) or as simple as a small patch of space alongside you in your own bed, but please, always do a safety check of your baby's bedding and the surrounding space, and eliminate potential hazards such as:

- cracks and crevices between mattresses and bed frames (your baby could roll into these and get stuck and/or be unable to breathe)
- blind cords (these can be a strangling hazard)

- pictures or mobiles that could fall into your baby's bed
- toys that your baby could climb on and use to get out of the cot.

Reducing the risk of SIDS

One of the greatest fears for parents is the possibility of SIDS (sudden infant death syndrome, also known as 'cot death'). SIDS is defined as the sudden, unexpected death of a baby or child for no apparent reason. There is no single cause of SIDS, but experts have identified risk factors and found safe sleeping practices that dramatically reduce its incidence.

✳ **CHECKLIST : REDUCING THE RISK OF SIDS**

- **Put your baby on her back to sleep** – this is the safest sleeping position. If a baby's face is nuzzled into bedding, her breathing can be hindered. Babies wake naturally if their oxygen level decreases, but it is unclear whether the SIDS risk factor is the challenge to the baby's breathing or the baby's response to this. For this reason, do not put your baby to sleep on a soft surface such as a couch, beanbag or waterbed. Lying face-down with her face pressed into the mattress may also increase your baby's contact with bugs that thrive in the warm, moist environment of a bed. If your doctor advises you to put your baby to sleep on her tummy or side to alleviate a particular medical condition, they will explain what precautions to take. If you are advised to put your baby to sleep on her side, keep her lower arm well forward to stop her rolling onto her tummy – or you might like to use a product such as a Baby Wedge (babywedge.com.au) or a Safe T Sleep Sleepwrap (safetysleep.com), which are specifically designed to maintain a safe sleeping position. As your baby grows beyond five or six months, she will be able to move around the cot and roll herself over. At this stage, settle her to sleep on her back but then let her find the sleep position she feels most comfortable in. If you notice that your baby is developing a misshapen head, it may help to change her position to avoid the development of positional plagiocephaly (the medical term for an asymmetrical head). Often, newborns have funny-shaped heads as a result of their position in the womb or some 'moulding' as they came through the birth canal, but by about six weeks after birth, your baby's head will have regained a lovely round shape. However, because the bones in her head are thin and flexible, if your baby lies with her head in the same position for too long, her head can develop a flat spot. To avoid this, each time you put your baby to bed on her back, gently turn her head so it's on the alternate side. Moving her cot around so that she turns her head to look at her surroundings will also encourage her to change positions. And when she is awake, rather than leaving her to play on the floor on her back for long periods, or keeping her restricted in an infant restraint or car seat that will press against her tiny head, it is important to encourage tummy time (see page 201).

- **Use a firm, clean, well-fitting mattress.** Research carried out at De Montfort University (Sherburn & Jenkins, 2004) has identified a link between SIDS and bacteria that breeds in babies' mattresses. The study suggests that bacteria may be implicated in up to 50 per cent of SIDS cases. The bacteria seemed to thrive on moisture (from vomit or urine) in water-soluble material in polyurethane foam filling, and concentrations were a hundred-fold higher if the baby had been fed formula rather than breast milk. The research confirmed that the abundance of bacteria rose with the number of babies that had used the mattress, which may explain why SIDS is more common among second and subsequent babies, who may be using a hand-me-down mattress. To ensure that your baby's mattress is safe, use a washable mattress cover. Wash the mattress with soap and water (not chemical cleaners), check for nicks in the covering that could allow moisture to enter the mattress filling, and air your baby's mattress regularly (the same goes for pram mattresses).
- **Keep your baby's head uncovered.** Overheating poses a risk to babies. Excess heat is lost through the scalp, so don't put a hat on your baby for sleep. It is also vital to keep your baby's face uncovered during

sleep. Use natural-fibre bedding that can 'breathe', and tuck bed coverings in securely so that your baby can't slide under them. In a cot, prevent your baby from sliding down under bedclothes by placing him 'feet-to-foot' (with his feet at the bottom end of the cot) – you only need to make up the bottom half of the bed.

- **No pillows**. Do not use quilts, doonas, pillows or cot bumpers for babies under twelve months old, and do not place soft toys where your baby sleeps. If your baby has a snuffly nose and needs to be propped up to make breathing easier, or is teething and needs to have her head elevated to relieve pressure, place a folded towel under the mattress, prop up the head of the cot on phone books or use a Baby Wedge (see babywedge.com.au).

- **No butts**. Keep your baby smoke-free before and after birth; the risk of SIDS is increased if the mother smokes during pregnancy or after the birth. There is also evidence to suggest that a father smoking during his partner's pregnancy increases the risk of SIDS, and if both parents smoke, the risk is doubled. In fact, it's preferable not to let anyone smoke near your baby, especially inside the house or in a car.

- **Share your room**. Although results vary, several studies have shown that when a committed caregiver sleeps in the same room (but not the same bed) as their baby, the chance of the baby dying from SIDS can be 50 per cent less than for a baby sleeping in a separate bedroom (solitary sleeping). A comprehensive New Zealand study (Mitchell & Thompson, 1995) showed that the risk of SIDS for sleeping infants sharing the room with non-smoking adults was one-fifth that of babies sleeping in a separate room, and a UK analysis of a large case-control study (Fleming & Blair, 1998) demonstrated a ten-fold increase risk associated with solitary sleep.

SIDS and Kids, the Australian organisation for SIDS prevention, recommends sleeping with your baby in a cot next to your bed for the first 6–12 months of life. The SIDS and Kids room-sharing recommendation (see sidsandkids.org/safe-sleeping) explains that room-sharing facilitates a rapid response to a baby's needs, more convenient settling and comforting of babies, and closer mother–baby contact and communication.

- **Avoid medicating your baby.** No matter how desperate you are for sleep, please don't be tempted to dose your baby to get her to sleep. Even over-the-counter medicines such as Panadol or Nurofen may have sedative ingredients that could send her into a deep sleep from which she may not be able to arouse easily. Although this may be exactly the effect you were hoping for, it is potentially dangerous because your baby may not wake if she needs to. Research has, for example, linked use of the antihistamine Phenergan with SIDS, especially for infants with colds, possibly because Phenergan (which has a sedative effect) decreases the swallowing and arousal reflexes that prevent choking. Phenergan should not be given to children under six months and some researchers recommend a minimum age of two years. Also, excessive or prolonged dosage of such medications may be harmful to your baby's immature liver and kidneys, and sedating your baby will deprive her of active sleep, which she needs for growth, memory and learning. In any case, it is unwise to give a baby (or anybody else, for that matter) medicine if you aren't certain of what the problem is. A wakeful baby is safer than a sedated baby.
- **Check with your health-care provider** if you suspect your baby's waking is the result of a medical condition such as reflux, which may be helped by appropriate medication, or if you suspect your baby may be unwell, please check with your health-care provider.
- **Encourage 'tummy time'** when your baby is awake. Tummy time (see page 201) will strengthen her neck and shoulder muscles so that, eventually, she'll be able to lift her head and roll away if she finds herself in a position where breathing is difficult.

Three is not always a crowd

Co-sleeping is defined as having your baby sleep 'within arm's reach'. There are many different co-sleeping style that will allow you to comfort your baby easily: you may use a hammock or crib next to your bed; you may choose to put your baby in a cot until you go to bed or until she wakes for her first feed during the night; she may sleep in her cot most of the night, until you bring her into your bed for an early-morning snuggle (and sleep-in); or you may prefer to embrace a whole new concept in bedroom decor by pushing the cot against your bed with one side down (make sure neither the cot nor your bed can roll, leaving a gap) so you can reach out and comfort your baby easily. (There are specially designed cots that attach to your bed safely – see the Resources section.)

Whatever your sleeping arrangements, it is paramount to provide a safe sleeping environment for your baby. If you choose to sleep with your baby, both parents should feel comfortable with the decision and accept equal responsibility. For some parents, co-sleeping will not be appropriate, particularly if either of you has been drinking or if one of you is on medication that affects your awareness, is a heavy snorer or has sleep apnoea, or if you have an extremely restless baby. Since adult beds are not designed with infant safety in mind, it is sensible to take some basic precautions – see checklist below.

✳ CHECKLIST : SAFE CO-SLEEPING

- Do not sleep with your baby if you or your partner is under the influence of any substance such as alcohol or drugs (prescription or otherwise) that may induce a deeper sleep and inhibit awareness of your baby.
- Do not co-sleep if either you or your partner is a smoker. Smoking poses serious health risks to babies and young children, regardless of where they sleep, so now would be a good time to consider quitting. (Call Quitline or see your GP or pharmacist for advice.)
- If you have long hair, tie it back. Also, remove jewellery and avoid clothes with string ties that might get caught around your baby's neck.
- If you are obese or large-breasted, consider that you may not be able to feel exactly where your infant is. I doubt there is an 'unsafe' weight per se, but the safety of your baby depends on your own body awareness.

- Take precautions to prevent your baby from rolling out of bed – for example, place the bed against a wall (make sure it can't move, leaving a gap) or use guardrails.
- Don't leave a baby on an adult bed unattended. (This doesn't mean you have to go to bed at the same time as your baby every night. You can settle her in a cot until you go to bed or until she wakes, then transfer her into your bed.)
- Ensure that the sleeping surface is clean and firm (waterbeds and sofas are unsafe), and that the mattress tightly intersects the bed frame so that there are no gaps where your baby could get stuck.
- Use sheets and blankets rather than a doona or quilt, as they are less of a risk factor for SIDS (especially for babies under fourteen weeks old), and ensure that your baby's head is never covered.

'Co-sleeping was a pleasure I didn't allow myself with my first baby. I was desperate to maintain some sense of order and control so I was very structured in how I went about feeding her: I got out of bed, sat in the rocking chair, fed twenty-five minutes from each breast, changed her, rocked her to sleep and put her back in her bassinet. Every three hours for six weeks. It nearly killed me.

'I was expecting to have to do the same with my second baby, as my husband's blood type almost guarantees a jaundiced baby. However, the very afternoon of Will's birth, I lay in the hospital bed with him nuzzled against my breast and it was one of the most beautiful experiences of my life. I can't say it turned me into a co-sleeper but I am much more relaxed about co-sleeping and don't hesitate to bring Will into bed with me and 'dream feed' all night if he's unsettled. We have kept the dreaded jaundice at bay, together with the feeding regimes and mastitis, and I treasure the time cuddled up to him, drinking in his newborn smell. I'm in no rush for a big cot in a different room to come between me and my early-morning cuddles with Will!'

Julianne

'I feel a sort of sadness that while I am snuggled up to one of the men I love, the other (our baby son), is sleeping by himself in his own room, so I have an afternoon rest with him. I love him snuggling into my neck as he sleeps.'

Janine, mother of a one-year-old

If you choose to co-sleep, it will probably take you a while to get used to sharing a bed with your baby. Even sharing a room with your baby will probably be quite a new experience – at first, you will be aware of every little sniffle and grunt. Nobody ever mentions how noisy a newborn can be!

If your baby is in your bed, you will, at first, be very aware of her presence; but, as you get used to sharing sleep, you will stop worrying about what she is doing as she sleeps. In case this sounds a little scary, ask yourself when you last fell out of bed. Or lost your pillow. Just as you know exactly where the edge of the bed is when you sleep, you will be aware of your baby, too, provided you are healthy, sober and unmedicated.

Although you will find your own way to sleep safely and comfortably with your baby snuggled next to you, if you bed-share, I would suggest tucking your baby into the crook of your elbow, with her head resting on your arm. I felt safe this way because I couldn't roll over an outstretched arm and I was aware of where my baby was, rather than having her 'loose' in the bed between me and my partner, or on the edge of the bed. This way, my babies and I slept facing each other (which is notably safer), and breastfeeding was easier – after the early months, a baby can usually 'help herself' and you won't be woken from a deep sleep as your baby stirs, or find yourself wide awake and unable to get back to sleep after you have fed her.

During the night, you don't need to worry too much which breast your baby fed from last. You will find yourself rolling your baby across you onto your other arm as you change sides for sleeping comfort, so she will probably get both breasts if she wakes to feed. And if you are a bit lopsided in the morning, give her the big breast for breakfast!

'At the conclusion of each day, I feed my son to sleep and place him in the cot. When he wakes for the first (of many!) feeds of the night, I bring him into bed with us. We have adopted a position where we curl our bodies into each other, like a cocoon. He feeds when he needs to throughout the night and I often don't even wake. Co-sleeping allows me to have a full night in bed. Besides, when we wake in the morning, the first thing my son sees is me, which I believe provides reassurance and love. And the first thing I see is a big smile from my precious child. I couldn't imagine starting the day any other way!'

Jane

A bed of their own

If you choose to co-sleep, don't be concerned about creating 'bad habits', and ignore comments like, 'You'll never get that kid out of your bed.' There are ways to make a baby or toddler's transition to a bed of their own fairly smooth, at whatever age you feel that you and they are ready to make changes. As you make any changes to your child's routine or environment, it is wise to remember the mantra 'gradually, with love', and to make each change in baby steps. If you take each step as you and your child are ready, then change is likely to be more permanent, although it is natural for little backward steps at times of stress or sickness. If you pressure your baby or toddler into making changes that he isn't ready for, the trade-off could be whiny, clingy behaviour or broken sleep.

Here are some tips for transitioning from co-sleeping to solitary sleeping:

- Over several weeks, move your baby from your bed to a cot next to your bed, then move the cot to the other side of your room, then into the baby's room.
- Try slipping your own soft, unwashed t-shirt over your baby's mattress. Although this isn't exactly a substitute for you, she will be comforted by your familiar smell as she sleeps.

- At around 4–6 months, introduce a Baby Wedge (see page 173) into your bed, letting your baby sleep on it there so that the wedge gets to smell more like her familiar sleeping space. Then, after a few days, placed her in the cot on the Baby Wedge. This lovely gentle transition could also be achieved by using the Baby Wedge as a feeding pillow so that it acquires the familiar scent of you, your milk and your baby, before you put your baby to sleep on it.
- Encourage your baby or toddler to have day sleeps in her cot or bed. Then, as she feels secure and associates her own bed with sleep times, she could start having night sleeps there, too. Or, if you prefer to co-sleep until your little one is a toddler, you might move your child from your bed straight into a single bed, depending on her age at the time of transition. Toddlers who are old enough to talk (around two or older) tend to love the fuss of shopping for a new doona and sleeping in their own 'big-person' bed.

'Our kids all slept with us from the beginning until they were about three. They still come and hop into bed with us in the mornings at the weekend. We have had some of our best 'deep and meaningful' talks with them at these times.

'My sister, who is thirty-something and single, loves it when she comes to stay. The kids all go and get into bed with her in the mornings and talk to her. We'll be sitting having breakfast on our own, thinking that this feels really strange. I think it is so natural for me because when we were kids, we could go into Mum and Dad's bed, and we used to go camping and all sleep together then.'

Suzanne, mother of three

Helping your baby to sleep

For all babies, reaching the point where they 'sleep through' is a developmental process – just like being ready to eat solid foods, walking or learning to use the toilet. And, just like these processes, it cannot be rushed. In fact, also like these processes, being able to sleep 'all night' (remember, that's defined as five hours!) can be delayed by worry or pressure, and older babies and toddlers can especially be affected by your own anxiety around bedtime and sleep. Although babies vary in temperament and their pace of development, they all do eventually sleep right through until the sun comes up. However, sleep deprivation can be pretty grim for parents, especially if you have more than one child. Maternal exhaustion may also mean that you are less able to wake up yourself and attend to your baby. (For some tips on alleviating exhaustion, see **Keeping burnout at bay**, page 252.) If this is the case, I discuss some gentle strategies below that you can use to help your baby – and you – sleep better. (For more comprehensive information on helping your baby sleep, see my book, *Sleeping Like a Baby* – details in **Further reading**).

Follow a bedtime routine

Bedtime routines and rituals can become cues that help even tiny babies wind down and become conditioned to fall asleep. They can also help create a positive sleeping environment, so that wherever you are or whatever the age of your child, you can help your littlie relax without anxiety or battles. Over years of observation, I have noticed that children who are parented to sleep (i.e. a parent either stays with their baby until she is asleep or stays long enough to help her settle and feel calm before they leave the room) as babies and toddlers are far more likely to view sleep as a warm and comforting experience and to actually enjoy bedtime. By making the effort with your baby now, you are creating a positive sleep environment for the future.

Falling asleep, especially at night-time, is a major transition for little ones. If they sleep alone, they are 'leaving you' temporarily. At various ages and developmental stages, this may be confusing to your baby or toddler, so she will cling to the security of the person she loves the most in the whole wide world – you! This is why implementing a predictable bedtime rhythm can help babies and small children feel secure, and then they are likely to cooperate and relax into sleep more easily.

There are, of course, nights when you would just love your baby to be safely tucked up, sound asleep – but the moment they sense this longing, they seem to resist slumber. For this reason, it is usually worth taking a few extra minutes in the first place to follow their normal bedtime routine in a relaxed way. And try to avoid conflict: gentle, peaceful bedtimes gain everyone the best sleep. (See also **Make bedtime positive**, page 187.)

'One of the most important ways we nurture our children's souls is with rhythm, routine and warmth. Little children thrive in a gentle environment. For the under-sevens, in particular, we need to create an environment where they don't waste energy worrying about what is happening next.

'In the morning, I go in, open the curtains and get their clothes ready. Even though they are growing older, we have a pretty similar routine. When they go to bed, we sing songs, then we light a candle and have a story. At mealtimes, we light a candle and say a blessing. Rituals help them learn that the world is a good, safe, protective place.'

Louise, mother of four (aged between six months and ten years)

Connect at bedtime

You may be warned against helping your baby fall asleep because you will develop 'bad habits' or 'negative sleep associations'. The term 'sleep associations' refers to the cues or conditions that your child associates with going to sleep and assumes that he will require the same cues to help him return to sleep if he wakes during the night. Some people say that by allowing babies to develop an association with any particular cue or object, you are setting yourself up for sleep problems. The theory goes that if you place your baby in his bed in a safe sleeping position and leave him to cry long enough, he will 'learn' to self-settle without any props. As far as I am concerned, the notion of 'teaching' your baby to self-settle and sleep all night long (because a 'good' or 'clever' baby will know how to return himself to sleep without assistance) is about as appropriate as trying to teach a three-month-old to ride a bicycle.

In reality, at around four months, some babies will simply lie there, perhaps watching their little hands, and fall asleep without much help. Other babies will be older before they're able to self-settle. And all babies will find it easier at some times than others. For example, when they're going through a developmental change, such as when separation anxiety kicks in (usually between six and nine months), your baby may need you to be present at bedtime to help him calm down and drift off. Even toddlers and older children may need help to feel relaxed and calm at bedtime, just as we might need our own form of comfort after an especially busy or stressful day, when our minds are racing or we are worried about something.

Sadly, this pressure to avoid developing habits creates an enormous amount of angst for parents, as most babies and small children don't simply lie down and go to sleep without any help. (Nor do most parents, for that matter – do you have a warm drink, read a book or cuddle your partner before you fall asleep?) In fact, even parents who claim that their babies 'self-settle' often tell me that their babies have some sort of prop – such as a dummy, 'blanky' or 'lovey' – that acts as a 'mummy substitute'. This is not intended to be a judgement or criticism, just an observation that it is the rare baby who falls asleep easily without support. Perhaps the number of articles about 'bedtime battles' is a reflection of small children expressing their need for comfort. The real 'battle' is that children's needs often conflict with parents' needs for convenience.

Rather than seeing the process of settling your baby as negative, it can help to appreciate the long-term benefits of sharing this precious time. Later, when your child becomes a toddler or preschooler, a bedtime routine can include stories and talks about your child's day. The trust that builds as your child confides in you is not something to be dismissed as an inconvenience to your busy life, but a foundation for your ongoing relationship with your child. The goal is to impart the skills your child needs to fall asleep without you (most of the time) but there is no hurry and, in fact, if your baby or toddler senses your stress and goes to sleep anxious or cries himself to sleep, he is unlikely to sleep well because his little body and brain will be affected by elevated stress hormones, causing him to wake more during the night, or he may express feelings of insecurity by becoming clingy during the day. On the other hand, a child who feels secure is likely to become more independent in the long term. So, it seems logical to calm and connect with your little one at bedtime and to make an effort to set up a positive sleep environment rather than creating bedtime battles that may last beyond infancy.

'My husband and I have often had long and emotional discussions about how to parent Jesse. In the early days, it was how best to get an infant to settle, and it quickly evolved that in the daytime, my husband (working from the home office) would "wear" Jesse in a sling and the little cherub would quickly fall asleep and easily transfer into the bassinet in the living room for his daily naps. Later, after Jesse was five or so months old, we struggled with the dilemma of him either feeding to sleep or needing to be cuddled to sleep. Well, it wasn't really a dilemma, but when other mums – old and young – frowned at me because I was "spoiling" my baby, it did make me quite self-conscious at times. But Jesse made the transition to putting himself to sleep when he was ready. I am not even sure when it happened. One night after his bath, books, booby and lullabies, my toddler looked up into my eyes and said "cot". So we calmly walked up the passage and I tucked him into his cot, gave him a kiss and said goodnight. Since then, if he doesn't fall asleep quickly in my arms, I simply ask him if he's ready for his cot. If he's a bit too awake when I put him in his cot, he sometimes finds it hard to settle to sleep and will call out. On these occasions, I just wander into his room and ask him if he wants a little cuddle; we lie on the bed together until he falls asleep and I put him back into the cot asleep – this takes less than fifteen minutes. Now Jesse is two-and-a-half and I feel very happy that there are never any tears at bedtime.'

Marcelle

Teach her day from night

A study at Fukushima University (Fukuda & Ishihara, 1997) asked mothers to track their babies' sleep behaviour for six months. The study found that in the first few weeks, babies were as likely to be awake in the dark as in daylight hours. At seven weeks, almost all the babies shifted to sleeping more at night than during the day. By twelve weeks, most (though not all) had consolidated their daytime sleep into naps and rarely woke for long periods at night, although many still woke to feed.

You can't force your baby to learn the difference between day and night. However, many parents find that emphasising the differences can help alter their baby's rhythm so she learns that night is for sleeping. This doesn't mean not attending to your baby at night; it simply means being more 'boring' by keeping the lights dim for night feeds and saving playtime and noise for daylight hours.

Some parents also find it helpful to leave the curtains open both day and night so that their baby's circadian rhythm (the internal body clock that tells us when to wake and sleep) can adjust. Spending time outdoors during the day also helps night-time sleep, and although grandma will swear it is the fresh air that makes the difference, it is likely that exposure to sunlight helps babies tune in to the difference between day and night. Putting your baby to bed at the same time each night will also help your baby's internal clock to adapt, and help her fall asleep more easily.

As your baby grows, another way of discouraging her from waking up completely during night feeds is to avoid changing her nappy during the feed unless it is really necessary. If she does need a change, it is better to do it before or halfway through the feed rather than disturbing her when she is content and groggily full. However, please don't be too hard on yourself if you find yourself enjoying some midnight goo-ing and gaa-ing with your little one; you have a right to enjoy any smiles your baby gives you. And be patient: whatever you do, her internal body clock won't be fully developed until at least six weeks and, more likely, not until around 12–15 weeks.

Remove your clock

A positive mindset, so that feelings of resentment don't affect the amount of sleep possible, can make a big difference. Simply knowing how long you are awake can be enough to make you too tense to get back to sleep, or it may encourage you to rush your baby and make him feel anxious. So, before you go to bed, either remove clocks from the bedroom or turn them to face the wall. Viewing your baby's waking as a genuine need, rather than as 'bad behaviour' that is inconveniently keeping you awake, will help you to enjoy this precious cuddle time: feel the softness of his skin, breathe in his delicious smell, and snuggle! And remember the 'mummy mantra' for when the going gets tough: *This too shall pass.* It will, all too soon – I promise!

Make bedtime positive

Keep your baby or child's bedtime routine fairly simple so that it can be managed by a babysitter or by you when you are away from home. Try to carry out the routine in the same order every night (as long as it is working), to convey a sense of security and predictability

You can adapt your child's bedtime routine as he grows. For instance, a massage *and* a bath will be too stimulating for a newborn, so it may work better to give your baby his bath during the day and massage him before bed, or vice versa. Whatever your bedtime routine, if it has a predictable sequence each night, most little ones respond and relax contentedly into sleep.

Your routine might include:

• **Wrapping**. The startle reflex, a primitive survival reflex that produces spontaneous, jerky movements, even in sleep, can be disturbing (literally). Provide a sense of security by wrapping your newborn firmly in a gauze or muslin sheet (in summer) or a soft shawl or bunny rug (in winter) – see page 226 for how to wrap. As well as helping your newborn feel secure, wrapping or swaddling can become a sleep association – but this is one that will need to be changed before your baby becomes mobile and can get tangled in her wrap. From around three months, you can transition from a wrap to a sleeping bag that is the right size for your baby; just like the wrap, a sleeping bag can signal to your little one that it is time for bed.

- **Patting**. You can pat your baby's bottom as you hold her against your shoulder, or while you hold her on her side in her cot. Although you probably won't consciously count the beat, the odds are that you will be replicating the rhythm of your heartbeat as you pat your baby's bottom. Most babies have their bottoms closest to your heart when they are heading down ready for birth, so perhaps this patting is a familiar rhythm. If you pat while she is in her cot, when she falls asleep or becomes drowsy, gently roll her onto her back.

- **Stroking**. Stroking your baby's face can feel soothing and induce drowsiness. In the early days, there is a particular 'magic touch' that sends some babies into dreamland: if you stroke your little one's forehead down the bridge of his nose, you will trigger an early reflex that induces sleepiness. Although this reflex wears off at about two months, the sleep association may be set, so it is worth using this gentle stroke if it seems to be working.

- **Rock-a-bye baby**. Rocking reminds tiny babies of the movement they experienced in the womb so it will comfort and lull most babies to sleep. See the checklist on page 230 for more on rocking and movement.

  The knee jiggle, a variation on rocking, also utilises movement to mesmerise tiny babies to sleep. Wrap your baby firmly and lay her on your knees, facing you, with her head well supported in your hands and her feet towards you. Now, keeping your toes on the floor, jiggle your knees up and down one at a time, in a peddling motion. Also try keeping your knees and ankles together as you move both your legs from side to side, taking care that you aren't jolting your baby. This is a useful tool if you are unable to get up and walk or simply want to remain sitting.

  Rocking is another sleep association that is sure to earn you critical comments along the lines of: 'How do you think you will be able to rock him when he's two, or if you have another baby?' But, like any other sleep association, you can wean your baby from rocking when you and he are ready, gradually and with love. As your baby grows – often by around three to four months, although this varies quite a bit – you will be able to wean her off rocking by playing gentle music and rocking less, and popping her into her cot drowsy but awake. Later, if you want to, you can gradually reduce the volume of her 'sleepy music'. And, as you stop rocking your baby to sleep, consider other ways to meet her need for movement in all directions during her awake times. If you have a baby who seems to need rocking or is easily soothed to sleep by movement, consider a baby hammock (see page 44), or try cuddling her as you sit together in a rocking chair. Instead of seeing rocking as a negative, it can help to understand how it benefits your baby's development, and why some babies seem to need it.

- **Soothing sounds**. The calming, repetitive sounds of traditional lullabies recall the 'womb music' your baby heard before birth (your heartbeat, and fluids whooshing through the placenta). Baby music that incorporates elements such as three-quarter time (like a waltz), the rhythm of the maternal heartbeat or 'white noise' has remarkably soothing effects, especially if played continuously through the night. (A beautiful CD that incorporates these elements is *Music for Dreaming* – see soundimpressions.com.au.) A more portable way to provide 'sleepy sounds' for your baby is to sing or hum. (Humming will help you feel calmer because you have to focus on your breathing a little more than usual, and it is also less stimulating to your baby's brain than singing. It can be very helpful if you are feeling stressed about your wakeful baby.)

  If you are pregnant while you read this, you could choose a settling song now and familiarise your baby with the tune before he is even born, since studies show that babies remember and are soothed by music they have heard in the womb. My own first baby spent time in hospital in the early weeks and, later, we travelled with him. I used to sing a traditional Maori song, 'Pokarekare Ana', to settle him and, despite my complete lack of singing talent, it worked wherever we went.

- **Massage**. Silent nights could be at your fingertips! Research by Dr Tiffany Field from Miami University (1995) showed that infants and toddlers who were massaged daily for fifteen minutes prior to bedtime fell asleep more easily by the end of the month-long study. Massage releases hormones that help to calm your baby (and you!), and this naturally helps her fall into a deeper sleep.

Introduce massage gradually and when your baby is calm so that she associates it with relaxed and happy feelings; then, later, you will be able to create a conditioned relaxation response with a few simple strokes. At first, your baby will only want a short period of massage, but you'll be able to build up to longer sessions as she gets used to your soothing touch. It is wise to massage babies less than three months old separately from bath-time (because a bath and a massage could be too stimulating). If your baby tolerates a bath and massage in succession without becoming overstimulated, it is best to massage before the bath to prevent her from getting cold. An older child might prefer a more informal massage – simply stroking her forehead or rubbing her hands or back when she is lying in bed can help her to wind down and relax.

Remember to always ask your child's permission to massage her and respect her response, whatever her age – even babies a few weeks old will give clear signals to show whether they are ready to accept a massage or not. This way, you are teaching your littlie that her body is her own and she has a right to refuse any unwanted touching. For more about baby massage, see page 82.

- **Bath-time**. The relaxing effects of a bath work at a psychological level as well as a physiological one. One of the triggers for sleep is a slight drop in core body temperature. A warm bath temporarily increases our core body temperature; then, as this temperature lowers after a bath, we feel drowsy – and babies feel the same. This is why timing matters for the bedtime bath. For example, it is best to have a quiet play before your child's bath, then bath her before dressing her warmly and taking her to bed, drowsy from the bath, for the remainder of her bedtime routine.

  To give your baby a relaxation bath, rather than swishing her in shallow water in a baby bath, run a warm, deep bath in the adult bathtub. (If you are concerned about water usage, recycle the water onto your garden or bath with your baby to make the most of the water.) The water needs to be deep enough for your baby to float and should be as comfortably warm as you would have it yourself (check the temperature with your wrist before you pop your baby in). Hold your baby so she is floating on her tummy by supporting her under her shoulders and chin. If you don't feel confident about holding her this way, floating her on her back will still help her to relax. Remember *never* to leave her alone in the bath, even once she is much older.

Aromatherapy products aren't recommended for babies under six months old, but for older babies and toddlers, a few drops of lavender mixed with vegetable oil or milk (so concentrated droplets of essential oil don't float about and irritate your baby's skin) can be added to the bathwater for extra soothing effects. Please be careful, though, about using bubble-bath products because many of these are not made from natural ingredients and can cause skin and genital tract irritation; rather than relaxation, they may cause itchiness and sleeplessness.

Bathing with your baby can be a relaxing and bonding time for you both, or, if you and your baby prefer, you could take a shower together.

- **Special words or sounds**. A word, sound or phrase used each time you put your baby to bed can be a positive sleep association and is wonderfully transferable. Start using your special words whenever you put your baby into bed, whether or not you are also using other cues such as music, rocking or breastfeeding. Eventually, you will be able to wean him off some of the other cues and just use a cuddle and your special words.

- **Books or stories**. Snuggling together for storytime is one of the nicest ways I can think of to wind down, for both parents and children of any age. You can start reading to your baby as soon as you like (some parents even introduce a story or two while their baby is still in the womb). Books with a strong rhythm or with rhyming words, such as those by Dr Seuss, are especially engaging.

The calming effects of reading together are increased if you cuddle as you read. While a story helps to engage the frontal lobe of your child's brain (inhibiting motor impulses), body contact encourages your child to release sleep-inducing hormones. Also, dim lighting such as that from a bedside lamp (rather than a bright overhead light) will stimulate the release of melatonin, the sleep-inducing hormone.

Reading is an enjoyable and stimulating activity at any time of day and I would recommend that you spend many happy hours reading to your children. However, for babies and toddlers, it is good to keep a small number of specific books for bedtime only. There are some lovely 'going to bed' stories. One I recommend is *Time for Bed* by Mem Fox.

Can I feed to encourage longer sleep?

Although the best way to feed your baby is to respect and respond to his hunger cues, you will no doubt come across a plethora of information that advises you to implement some sort of 'proven' feeding routine, with a promise that this will guarantee you a full night of sleep. But, as I have discussed, implementing rigid routines can have adverse effects on your baby's health and development. However, if you do feel you want to tweak feed times to try to encourage a sleep pattern that may give you some relief, there are some gentle things you can try that don't require you to leave your baby to cry in order to 'train' him.

- **Encourage daytime feeds**. Because your baby will need a certain amount of food in a 24-hour period, it makes sense that if you try to space out his daytime feeds too much, he is more likely to wake at night to make sure he gets his required amount of food. It also makes sense that because tiny tummies need frequent refills, your baby will feed fre-quently at first – day and night! But within a few weeks, your baby will start sleeping at least one longer stretch between feeds. Although you should never force your baby to wake from a sleep, if he sleeps more than four hours between feeds during the day, it is reasonable to gently unwrap him, allow him to stretch and wake, then offer a feed; this way, he might save his longer sleep for night-time. However, please be patient if he is not ready to alter his pattern; he will, in his own time.
- **Try a 'dream' feed**. Whatever time your baby was last fed, gently offer a

feed just before you go to bed yourself. You don't need to wake him – he will suck in his sleep (this is why these feeds are often called 'roll-over' or 'dream' feeds) – and, with luck, his longer sleep may coincide with yours. Of course, not every baby will accept a feed at this time and some will take this feed and still wake again a couple of hours later, as though to say, 'Bonus – thanks, Mama!'

Some families see this late feed as an opportunity for mum to go to bed a little earlier while dad gives the baby expressed milk in a bottle. Personally, I would encourage fathers to bond through activities such as bathing with their baby or giving a massage (which encourages lovely interaction as well as relaxation), rather than giving bottles; the hormonal response that enhances bonding will not work as effectively while you bottle-feed as it will when you share a bath or massage with your baby, and it may be creating more work in the long run for a tired mother (who is likely to be the one washing and sterilising bottles and pumps). But if you do choose to do this, it is important to express at around 9 p.m. (if the dream feed is at 10 p.m.) so that your milk supply isn't compromised and you don't risk blocked ducts or mastitis.

Also, if you are breastfeeding, please make this feed breast milk, not formula, or you could risk your milk supply and compromise your baby's health (see **Why breast is best**, page 95). Besides, although you may hear that your baby will sleep longer if you top him up with formula before bed, research shows that this isn't the case. A recent US study of parents with three-month-old babies who were breastfed in the evening and/or at night slept an average of forty-five minutes longer than babies who were fed formula in the evening (Doan et al, 2007). Parents' sleep was measured both objectively using wrist actigraphy and subjectively using diaries. Parents of infants given formula at night also reported (in their diaries) more sleep disturbance than parents of babies who were exclusively breastfed at night.

If you are offering a bottle at this time, please hold your baby; this contact will also encourage peaceful sleep.

Warm Fuzzies

Up,
  down,
Up,
  down,
I rock
On Daddy's chest.
Warm and fuzzy,
Skin on skin,
Big arms holding me
Snug and safe,
I listen to his heart.
Up,
  down,
Up,
  down,
I rock
On Daddy's chest
To sleep.

9

Playing

♥

We often hear the saying, 'Play is a child's work.' And while you may think this applies to toddlers who can walk and talk and initiate their own games, play is also critically important for babies; it helps them to develop, to learn and to form strong bonds with the important people in their lives. But you might find yourself wondering: How do I play with a baby? What 'games' are appropriate?

You are your child's best toy

While neuroscience tells us that play is critical in helping babies' brains to develop, you can relax and simply enjoy your baby without seeing play as an academic exercise or becoming stressed that you might not be doing it 'right'. Studies show that with every interaction between you and your baby, you both experience elevated levels of beta-endorphin – the hormone of pleasure and reward – in your brains. This naturally enhances and encourages playfulness and responsive interactions with your baby. In other words, the more you interact with your baby, the happier you both feel, so the more you want to play and the more you are helping your baby wire her tiny brain for learning. How easy is that? You are your baby's best toy, his best teacher and the rock of his world!

In terms of what sort of play to engage in, your baby will be your best guide to the activities he enjoys, how long he wants to play and when he wants a break. Your goal is to have fun with your baby; if you do things with him as though they are a worthy chore, he will sense your lack of enthusiasm. And if developmental advancement of your child is your main motivation, you are likely to be overly serious and focussed on your goals, rather than simply enjoying the moment. If you can have fun by reconnecting with your own inner child and being spontaneous, your baby will develop naturally, at his own pace. If you don't find spontaneous, animated play comes naturally to you (you may simply be a quieter person by nature or it may have been a while since you actually 'played' without inhibitions), you might have to 'fake it till you make it'. It may help to attend a few baby classes with your little one such as Gymbaroo or a baby music group. These can be a bit like a little 'in-service', where parents learn lovely baby games and songs, and any good instructor will make you feel at ease as she models playing with your baby. Very soon, you will find yourself letting go and bursting into song or chuckling joyfully back at your baby!

The benefits of baby play

Babies are born with a natural urge to learn and you can enhance their development very simply – through touch, movement and play, along with optimum nutrition and an appropriately stimulating environment that includes music, colour, things to touch, and normal household activity and conversation – with minimal expense or stress to either of you.

New research shows that the most critical factor in helping your baby's brain to develop is loving, responsive interactions between you and your child. The loving interaction and sensory experience of your cuddles, touch, eye contact, movement and conversations that are all part of playing with your baby are hardwiring your little one's immature brain for emotional and neurological development (see also **Bonding and attachment**, page 67). As you touch and talk to your baby and share eye contact, you stimulate the development of connections between nerve cells in his brain that will form foundations for thinking, feeling and learning. This means that as well as preparing your baby's brain for academic learning, by simply 'tuning in' and enjoying your baby, you will also be supporting the development of structures that will help him to respond sensitively to others and read social cues, to manage strong emotions such as anger, and to be able to plan and make choices, so that as he grows, he will have the capacity for problem solving, self-awareness, generosity, kindness and empathy as well as curiosity, creativity and joy.

Appropriate toys

Millions of dollars are spent on advertising 'essential' toys for babies. But really, your baby doesn't need a squillion toys. (Have you noticed how many toys are plastic fantastic, anyway? All these toys smell, taste and feel the same!). Mostly, he needs people to interact with and a few quality toys, along with interesting household objects and, importantly, the freedom to move and explore on a clean, safe floor.

Although your baby will have the most fun playing with an expressive, interested person, you will no doubt want to add a few toys to encourage other kinds of play. Here are a few toys that are appropriate at different stages:

0–3 months

- **Mobiles** (hanging, not phones!). Your newborn can see the contrast of simple black-and-white more easily than shades of colour so a mobile made of black-and-white shapes will help stimulate his vision. At first, your newborn will turn his head to one side, so he will see a mobile better if it's hung beside where he is lying, rather than directly above. By two months, he will enjoy a coloured mobile or even a musical mobile above the change table.
- **Coloured scarves**. Gently wave these within his vision range to help him track with his eyes. Gently stroking his body as you wave the scarves will also give him a new sensory experience and help create body awareness.

- **Books**. While your newborn won't 'understand' what you are reading, he will love snuggling in your arms, and listening to the rise and fall of your voice, so choose books with plenty of rhythm. Books by Dr Seuss and books of nursery rhymes are especially good. You can also show him board books and cloth books, especially those with pictures of people's faces.
- **Rattles**. At around two months, encourage your little one to reach for a rattle – he won't 'shake' it yet but he will enjoy a little game with you.
- **An activity gym.** Short periods watching colourful objects suspended above him will encourage your baby to kick his legs and track with his eyes. A frame that allows you to change the objects will help him stay interested. Remember, though, not to leave him on his back for too long – he needs tummy time as well (see page 201).
- **Musical toys**. Bracelet bells (small elastic bracelets with musical bells securely attached – you can buy these ready-made) will help your baby get used to how his hands move, and various rattles and maracas can be fun to grasp, watch and listen to, especially once he realises he is making the noise. You can also sew bells securely onto your baby's socks.

3–6 months

- **A music box**. Your baby will love watching and listening to a music box (some wonderful old-fashioned clocks have a musical dancer inside them – check with grandma!) and this will also encourage him to enjoy lying on his tummy. Of course, you will need to supervise and keep the box just out of reach if it is fragile or has small pieces that could break off.
- **A play blanket.** You can buy or make your own play blanket with pockets and flaps made from various fabric textures (leather, wool, velvet, satin etc.) and colourful shapes sewn onto a heavy washable fabric for backing. Use loops to safely attach rattles, soft squeaky toys, teething rings and other objects to explore; this can be your own portable play space that encourages movement and physical exploration.
- **A mirror.** A safe mirror made especially for your baby to gaze at himself

(check toyshops – Lamaze makes a good one) as he lies on the floor will fascinate him and encourage tummy play.

6–12 months

There is a huge variation in the skill levels of babies at this stage. Watch your baby for signs that he may be ready to try new experiences, but please don't push him – for instance, don't offer him toys to encourage standing or walking, such as trolleys or activity centres that require him to stand, before he is adept at crawling and is pulling himself up and cruising. Your baby needs to crawl to develop brain pathways for later academic learning such as reading and maths.

- **Stacking or nesting toys**. Before your baby can stack, he will love knocking over the stacks that you make. He will also love pulling rings off a stacking toy with a pole in the centre and, as he gets a bit more dexterous, he will try putting the rings on by himself – this is great for hand–eye coordination.
- **Push-along toys**. Move these along in front of your baby at first and praise him with excitement when he tries to reach them. These are great for encouraging crawling and also for hand–eye coordination.
- **A xylophone**. Show your baby how to bang and make music. A spoon and a mixing bowl or metal colander is just as good as a xylophone for letting him know that he can cause things to happen through his actions.
- **A collapsible fabric tunnel or a large cardboard box with open ends**. This will encourage crawling and is fun to 'hide' in.
- **Bath toys**. Use simple plastic cups to pour water onto your baby's body or specific baby bath toys such as watering cans, boats, squeakers and squirters. He will love tipping and pouring as well as squeezing sponges.
- **Homemade toys**. Plastic bottles half-filled with coloured water and small floating toys, or with tinsel and bells, are an attractive home-made toy – but do make sure the lids are secure.

- **Bubbles**. Get a bubble wand or a small bubble-making machine, blow bubbles and watch your baby's delight! This is a great way to encourage eye-tracking skills.
- **Books**. Look for animal themes and make the noises of various animals as you read. He will love books with textured pages to feel and picture books with stories and rhymes.
- **Balls**. Your baby will love watching as you gently throw a colourful beach ball above him and catch it just before it lands on him. A soft felt ball will be lovely for him to squeeze and feel, and a ball with a bell inside will be intriguing to shake or chase as he crawls. (Check pet shops for safe, suitable toys such as cat balls with bells inside – they are often interesting and less expensive than toys made specifically for babies, but make sure they are too big to be a choking hazard.)
- **Noise-makers**. These can be musical instruments like maracas or a xylophone, squeaky toys or anything else that makes an interesting noise. Show your baby how to shake, bang and squeeze. To make your own noise-makers, fill plastic containers with objects that make a noise when your baby rolls or shakes them – rice, pasta, pebbles, a teaspoon, a couple of blocks or some jar lids (but nothing small enough to choke on if he manages to open the container).
- **Role-play toys**. A toy telephone, some hats to try on in front of a mirror and, when your baby is standing and cruising, a toy stove with a few small pots and pans can be lots of fun (this is a great first birthday present!).

When your baby is standing and cruising

Once your baby has reached this stage, you can offer him a trolley to push and activity centres where he can stand and play – these will help him to develop strength, and often have lots of noises and flashing lights that will give him a sense of power as he plays and learns about cause and effect.

Rotate toys

Although it can be tempting to give your baby a stack of toys, he will only be able to hold one toy at a time and having too many things around him at once can confuse or frustrate him. One way to make the most of toys is to rotate them. Choose a few different ones each day and put the others out of sight. Then, when boredom strikes, you can bring out a 'new' toy (this works for toddlers and older children, too). Another suggestion is to check out your local toy library: this way, you get to see what your baby really enjoys before you go wasting big bucks on the latest fad, and you have a constant range of new and interesting toys.

Tummy time

You've likely heard that 'tummy time' is important for babies to strengthen their neck muscles, to learn to push up onto their knees and, eventually, to crawl. Until several years ago, most babies were placed to sleep on their stomachs. This meant a baby was not only accustomed to this position, but had ample opportunity to learn to lift her head and prop on her arms while on her tummy. The more recent recommendation to put babies to sleep on their backs has greatly reduced the incidence of SIDS or cot death, but now parents seem to be fearful about putting their babies on their tummies at all.

Because babies are used to sleeping on their backs, they often feel most comfortable in this position and protest loudly when placed on their tummies. However, tummy time is beneficial for many reasons:

• **Muscle development**. Tummy time helps your baby strengthen her neck, shoulder, arm and torso muscles. This strength will prepare her for crawling as well as getting her ready to push up, roll over and, eventually, to stand.
• **Skull development**. With babies spending more time on their backs, paediatricians have noted an increase in flat or misshapen heads (see page 173). Babies' skulls are still quite soft and constantly lying on their backs can cause a flattening of the back of a baby's head.

- **Gross-motor development**. Tummy time during waking hours allows your baby to gain head and body control. Motor skill develops in a cephalocaudal fashion, meaning that a baby first gains control of her head, then her shoulders, then her abdomen and so on down to her feet. Developing head control first allows your baby to visually explore everything around her.

- **Fine-motor development**. Tummy time gives your baby a chance to develop her fine-motor skills in a number of ways – for example, as she grasps at your clothing while you hold her across your legs or on your chest, or at a blanket she is lying on as she balances on one arm to reach for toys. Pushing her hands against the floor to lift herself up a little also develops her hand and finger muscles; as she gets older, these muscles are required to pick up small objects, hold a crayon, feed herself and so on.

When to start tummy time

You can start tummy time from birth – with your newborn lying skin-to-skin on your chest. From there, small amounts of tummy time throughout the day are sufficient – even if only for a minute or two. Gradually increase the time, as long as your baby is comfortable.

Early on, it is important to restrict tummy time to periods when your baby is calm, and to respect her responses so that she doesn't associate this new experience with feeling stressed. Make sure she isn't tired or hungry, but don't place her tummy-down on a full belly of milk either, as this could be uncomfortable. If she becomes unsettled while on her tummy, try to coax her a bit longer by talking with her or playing with her. But if she has clearly had enough, pick her up and try again later.

To encourage tummy time, place your baby on her tummy on a firm, flat surface (a rug on the floor is best, as a soft or padded surface makes it too hard for her to move) with her arms forwards. To begin with, your baby will tire quickly because moving on her tummy is hard work. So, keep tummy time short but frequent as she gradually builds up her strength and learns to move more efficiently.

If your baby cries when you put her on her tummy, help her to become more confident by using some of the ideas in the checklist below.

✳ **CHECKLIST : TUMMY-TIME IDEAS**

- While you are lying on your back or reclining on the sofa, lie your baby on your tummy so that she will be encouraged to lift up and look at your face. Try gently rocking her from side to side as you hold her.
- Roll your baby over onto her tummy for a short while after every nappy change. It's easy to remember to do this and your baby is likely to enjoy the view if she's up on a changing table. But do hold on to her securely so that she doesn't roll or push off.
- Lie down on the floor facing your baby and talk or sing to her.
- Hold a rattle or a squeaky toy, wave a colourful silky scarf or place a mirror in front of your baby for her to look at.
- Sit on the floor and hold your baby on her tummy across your lap or thighs. Stroke gently and rhythmically down her back, making circular motions between her shoulder-blades.
- Lie her on different textures: a (treated) lambskin or a 'feelie blanket' made of squares of contrasting fabrics such as soft velvet and corduroy, coarse hessian, shiny satin, and woollen, fleecy or fluffy fabrics. Curtain shops often sell sample squares of suitable fabrics in inexpensive bundles.
- Place a toy within her reach – perhaps a coloured ball or a plastic container with some bells or marbles and tinsel in it (make sure the lid is tightly secured and always supervise). As your baby gets older and more mobile, you could place the toy just outside her reach to encourage her to stretch and move.
- Swish her through the air to music, supporting her with your arms and hands under her body and chest.
- Lie her across a beach ball or exercise ball, or a rolled up sleeping-bag, and rock her gently to and fro and sideways; this will also stimulate her vestibular (balance) system and help her get used to being in different positions.

- Lie your baby on your bed, near the edge, and sit on the floor with your face next to hers. She might appreciate the softer surface for a change, and you can talk and sing to her in this position.
- If your baby can't support her weight on her forearms, support her on a rolled-up towel placed beneath her arms (with her arms forwards), so she can practise mini push-ups or play with a toy. When she can get up on her forearms independently, remove the towel and let her work on her motor skills without it.
- Once your baby has sufficient head control (usually at around four months), you can play aeroplanes. Lie on the floor and bend your legs. Put your baby's tummy against your shins, with her head at your knees – she will be facing you – as you hold her with your hands under her arms. Now, keeping your feet on the floor, bend your legs up and down while holding on to her firmly. As she gets bigger and feels comfortable, you can lift your feet off the floor so that she 'flies' as you move your legs up and down. She'll probably love the new view!

How do I play?

At first, playing with your baby will involve short periods of gentle interaction such as talking, rocking, eye contact and singing. It's important to be respectful of your newborn's short attention span and not to overstimulate him. If he gets restless or turns away, it's time to give your baby a break. As your littlie grows, it won't be long before you'll be encouraged by chuckles of glee as he begs for more vigorous play that involves bouncing, rolling and 'peekaboo'. As he becomes more mobile and gains a heightened sense exploration, you will need to child-proof toys and play spaces (see the checklist on page 208).

Here are some games to try at various stages:

0–3 months

- Hold your baby on your lap, facing you. Support her head as you gaze into her eyes and talk or sing to her, gently rocking her from side to side.

Hold her in your arms and sing as you dance to music.

- Look into her eyes and experiment with facial expressions as you talk; even a newborn might try to copy you as you poke your tongue out (this is a game that siblings can play with their baby brother or sister).

- Soft silky scarves provide both a visual and a tactile experience. Place your baby on her back and gently wave a colourful scarf across her line of vision as you talk or sing. Bring it close and move it away, wave it from side to side, and gently stroke your baby's bare tummy with the scarf. Play 'peekaboo' as you pull a scarf backwards and forwards through a cardboard tube (it disappears inside the tube then 'pops' out again).

- Carry your baby in a sling or soft carrier where she can enjoy the delights of movement and feel the textures of your clothing, skin and hair as well as the security of your heartbeat, voice and familiar smell.

3–6 months

- Show your baby her reflection (and yours) in a mirror. Talk to her about the baby and the mummy or daddy she can see. Let her lie on her tummy to watch herself in a mirror (a portable make-up mirror with a stand is ideal); this will encourage tummy time. Hold one of her little hands or feet against the mirror and watch her fascination.

- Blow on a pinwheel or blow bubbles and watch her visual tracking skills develop.

- As she plays on her tummy, put some interesting toys just out of reach to encourage her to stretch and develop strength for crawling.

- A small colourful felt ball or a soft knitted ball makes for a lovely tactile experience.

- Hold your baby under her armpits and chant: *Tick tock, tick tock* [dance your baby from side to side] *I'm a little cuckoo clock Tick tock, tick tock Now I'm striking one o'clock* [lift your baby up to the sky once for one o'clock, twice for two o'clock etc.]

6–12 months

- At this age, your baby will love making his own 'music' by banging on pots and pans with wooden or plastic spoons.
- A variety of balls, large and small (but not small enough to fit into your baby's mouth, of course) will facilitate all sorts of games: roll a ball for your baby to chase along the floor; sit opposite your baby and roll the ball to her, encouraging her to try rolling it back; or hide the ball under a bucket or box to play 'peekaboo!' by lifting the cover to show her where the ball is hiding.
- Bath toys are great fun now. In particular, she will love filling and emptying containers in the bath – raid your kitchen cupboard for different-sized containers.
- A bottle of bubble mix and some different-sized wands will provide instant amusement as you and your baby try to catch shiny, shimmery bubbles. Blow a cascade of bubbles as a diversion when you change nappies and at bath-time; let them float in the wind outside; or blow some around your baby while she's on the carpet, where they will last a bit longer and give crawlers a chance to catch them.
- Play clapping and tapping songs and bounce your baby on your lap or legs as you sing.
- Make a cushion 'mountain' to crawl over. Encourage her climbing skills (and coordination and balance) by playing 'peekaboo' or placing a favourite toy on top of the 'mountain'.
- A baby-sized collapsible cloth tunnel (you can buy these inexpensively at IKEA and some toy shops) or some large cardboard boxes with open ends are fun to crawl through. Roll a ball through the tunnel and encourage your baby to chase it.
- Stacking toys will amuse your baby at this stage, especially if you stack them up and give her the chance to knock them over! Make your own stacks with plastic cups, bowls and boxes of varying sizes.
- Delegate one low cupboard as your baby's space – rotate a few toys or safe household objects (unbreakable bowls, cups, spoons) and let her explore 'her' cupboard.

- Make a magic scarf box. Collect lots of old colourful scarves or squares of soft fabric and knot them together at their corners to make a long 'trail'. Put the trail into an empty ice-cream container, taping the last scarf inside the lid and making a neat hole in the bottom of the container (which will become the top of your magic box). Put the lid on the container, with the scarves squashed loosely inside, then pull the tip of the first scarf through the hole and show your little one how to keep pulling to reveal the next brightly coloured scarf, and the next . . .

Your baby's treasure basket

As your baby learns to sit, assemble a basket of treasures for her to rummage through (under strict supervision, of course). At this stage, babies will explore objects with all of their senses – by sucking, smelling, grasping, mouthing, stroking, banging, rolling, tipping and examining them with great concentration. And as she is playing with her basket, your baby will also be learning to make decisions and choices, to concentrate and to store information. What should you put in your baby's treasure basket? Avoid plastic objects – they lack texture and smell. Instead, choose natural or textured materials such as large smooth shells, a plug on a chain, a soft brush, a small leather purse, a pine cone, a pretty rock, a woollen pompom or a felt ball, a small glass bottle (thick glass, of course), a metal teaspoon, large wooden beads threaded on elastic, a natural sponge, or beanbags made of various fabrics (such as velvet, corduroy, soft cotton) and filled with rice or popping corn. The possibilities are endless, but all the objects should be checked for sharp edges or for pieces that may break off. And you must always be with your baby when she uses the treasure basket, for safety's sake and so that you can help if necessary. As an added precaution, check the contents of the basket before each play session.

✳ CHECKLIST : **CHILD-PROOFING**

The best way to ensure that you have created a safe space for your baby to play is to get down on your hands and knees and look around at things from a baby's perspective: what can he reach, poke, push, pull over, put into his mouth or fall from?

Although nothing will keep your baby as safe as constant supervision, it only takes a moment for a little one to hurt himself. It's important to implement as many precautions as possible so that your baby can play and learn by exploring safely, and so that you are not feeling on edge as you watch him.

- Use safety devices such as switch covers over electrical outlets, corner covers on tables (to prevent knocks and bumps), door stops to prevent little fingers being jammed, and safety latches and locks on cupboard doors.
- If you can't lock cupboard doors, shift dangerous substances (such as cleaning agents) to high cupboards that are well out of reach.
- Use door gates to prevent falls down steps and stairs.
- Keep sharp objects and choking hazards out of reach.
- Check toys for loose parts that could break off or separate and become choking hazards, and be guided by age limits on toy packaging (these limits are more to do with safety than how 'advanced' your child is).
- Keep hot drinks away from babies.
- Keep curtain and blind cords out of reach – these can be strangulation hazards.
- Secure furniture or move it away so it can't be pulled onto a little explorer (this includes television sets).
- Never leave your baby playing alone in a bath – not even for a moment!
- Be vigilant – what may be out of reach today could suddenly be within reach tomorrow.

10
Crying

♥

'Is he a good baby?' they asked me.

'Yes, he's a wonderful baby,' I told them. What did they think I would say: 'No, he's a real dud, but they wouldn't give me a refund'?

Then they asked me, 'Does he sleep all night?' Oops, they had me there. My baby had failed and so had I.

I was an innocent then. He was my firstborn. I hadn't ever related goodness to sleepiness before. Now, I know better. I have learned that we tend to be judged as parents by our child's goodness, or lack of it. 'Goodness' is defined differently according to the child's age, but it is nonetheless equated with convenience or compliance at every stage.

It is easy to succumb to the myth of the 'good' parent. We believe that if we are 'good' parents, we will be rewarded with 'good' kids. Of course we want to be the best parents we can be – and perhaps for the first time in our lives, we might believe we can be perfect. This is our time. Our child. Our family. We desperately want to get it right. And because of the enormous pressure to get it right, we beat up on ourselves and we let others beat up on us when we don't live up to our own or their expectations. If our child fails to live up to our own or society's expectations in some way, we agonise as we ask ourselves, 'Where did I go wrong?' or, 'Why am I such a failure?' (For more on the maternal art of self-flagellation, see chapter 11.)

Real babies

When your proficiency is under scrutiny, it is easy to think traitorous thoughts, to start believing that your child is a feisty little rebel plotting against you. But in fact, there is no such thing as a 'good' baby. There aren't any 'bad' babies either. There are only 'real' babies and, just like real people – you and me – real babies have easy days and days when they need more cuddles. On days when your baby needs more cuddles, it's all too easy to make comparisons (with other parents as well as other babies) and to believe that, 'If I were a "good" mummy or daddy, I'd have a "good" child, too.' And on days like that, it's also easy to feel pressured to live up to other people's expectations and to surrender to advice that promises a quick fix. Occasionally, you do just need a quick fix, to give you time to collect your bearings. But when you come to rely on quick fixes, you can be lulled into a false sense of security. It can become all too easy to start seeing babies as little objects that need to be fixed, and to set up a struggle that lasts well beyond infancy. Then, when the quick fixes don't fit your child and make him 'good', you become increasingly resentful, your con-nection with your child is weakened and you feel less and less competent.

> 'I did get confused with all the advice and found myself trying to get my babies to self-settle (which really meant just leaving them to cry them-selves to sleep). I find it very difficult to listen to my babies cry, and I also find it scary as I seem to deal with it by "switching off" to them and doing something else to occupy myself. Then I feel awful for not being a nurtur-ing mother.'
>
> *Shelley, mum of three-month-old twins*

Baby training?

A baby's cry is his only way of telling you that he needs something – or someone. Yet, increasingly, there is pressure for parents to train babies to 'self-soothe' using techniques that undermine your natural impulse to offer comfort. These techniques are generally in the context of sleep, and are known variously as 'controlled crying', 'controlled comforting', 'modified response' or 'self-settling'.

Under such a 'self-soothing' regime, parents are often advised not to allow even a tiny baby to fall asleep in their arms or on the breast. (Interestingly, it is usually considered okay – even advisable, in some cases – in our culture for a baby to fall asleep sucking a dummy or to seek comfort in an inanimate object like a teddy bear or a 'lovey'.) Imagine you are snuggled up to your partner and you have dozed off in each other's arms. Suddenly, your partner wakes you and pushes you away, saying, 'Wake up! This is a bad habit – get on your own side of the bed and self-settle!' Crazy, isn't it?

When a baby cries, she is saying, 'I don't feel right. Please help me.' Just for a moment, put yourself in your baby's bootees. Imagine you have arrived in a foreign country, you don't speak the language and you are totally dependent on the kindness of the people around you to find food and shelter. What if you are extremely hungry and tired, but nobody around you can understand what you are trying to tell them? How would you feel if all your efforts to communicate pain, discomfort or loneliness were ignored?

What does it mean when you resist or distance yourself from a baby's distress? Is it about trying to protect yourself from more work? Or is it perhaps a coping mechanism you relied on when faced with pain and frustration as a child? Or are rationalisations such as 'Kids are tough, she'll adjust,' 'Crying won't hurt her,' or, 'We don't want to spoil her,' a way to avoid responding to a baby's feelings or needs so that they will develop 'independence'? Surely the point is to teach them that their feelings count, that we will respond to them, and that it is safe for them to be open and expressive – to be interdependent?

'We did controlled crying with our baby. It was the only solution we were offered at the time. He had a rough beginning – in intensive care plugged into machines with a tube in his throat. He had cried and cried then, but his cries couldn't be heard because of the tubes.

'When he was two, he was a very unaffectionate little boy. He didn't come for hugs. With hindsight, I realised that he'd really needed immediate attention to show him this was a safe place. I started to take a nap with him in the daytime, and I went to him if he cried at night. Gradually, he learnt to reach out. Now, he loves it when we cuddle up and read together.'

Annabelle, mother of a four-year-old

Brand new and blue

You may be able to 'train' your baby to be 'good' (read, undemanding) but the trade-off could be a baby who simply 'gives up' and doesn't express his needs. According to paediatrician William Sears (see Resources), these babies may appear to be compliant and 'good', but in fact may be depressed.

Babies can indeed be 'brand new and blue', with a diagnosis of clinical depression. Often, the predisposing conditions for depression in infants are beyond our control, such as trauma due to early hospitalisation and medical treatments. However, it is easy to understand how extremely rigid regimes that avoid important elements of bonding and attachment, such as eye contact and interactions that are responsive to infant cues, as well as leaving the baby to cry without any hope of being soothed, can also be associated with infant depression. Surely this isn't worth risking, especially if your child has already experienced early separation. You too would withdraw and become sad if the people you loved treated you as little more than an inconvenience whose only means of communication was an interruption to their lifestyle.

Wiring tiny brains to manage stress

Leaving a baby to cry alone evokes physiological responses that increase stress hormones. Crying infants experience an increase in heart rate, body temperature and blood pressure. These reactions are likely to result in overheating and, along with vomiting due to extreme distress, could pose a potential risk of SIDS in vulnerable infants.

Babies need our help to learn how to regulate their emotions. When we respond to and soothe their cries, we help them understand that when they are upset, they can calm down. On the other hand, when infants are left alone to cry, they fail to develop the understanding that they can regulate their own emotions. There is also compelling evidence that increased levels of stress hormones may cause permanent changes in the stress responses of infants' developing brains. These changes then affect memory, attention and emotion, and can trigger elevated responses to stress throughout life, including a predisposition to later anxiety and depressive disorders.

English psychotherapist Sue Gerhardt, author of *Why Love Matters: How affection shapes a baby's brain* (see **Further reading**), explains that when a baby isn't responded to appropriately his brain may become flooded with cortisol; as a result, the cortisol receptors in his brain close down. (Cortisol increases the heart rate, raises blood pressure and dampens the immune response in readiness for fight or flight.) This means that your baby's brain will actually develop fewer cortisol receptors, and this can predispose him to lifelong difficulties when it comes to managing stress: as his brain becomes flooded with stress hormones (during stressful or frightening events), he will feel overwhelmed and unable to combat feelings of anxiety and fear because he will not have the receptors to manage the excess stress hormones and switch off his stress response.

The good news is that through responsively nurturing your baby and protecting him from stress now – through your presence, your touch, responsive feeding (as opposed to rigid parent-directed routines) and loving interactions – your baby's brain will respond by developing more cortisol neurons. Then, as your baby grows into a child and an adult, and inevitably experiences stressful events, his brain will be well-stocked with cortisol receptors, and as stress hormones are released, they will have somewhere to go: stress hormones will be 'mopped up' by the receptors and his brain will have the capacity to switch off the stress response more quickly.

'Our first baby was planned and very much wanted. After the first few months, things settled down and she was sleeping through the night. The only help she needed to get to sleep was for us to rock her cot, but this was becoming a 'chore' and I was advised by my maternal and child-health nurse to use controlled crying at six months so she could learn to self-settle. My husband and I really struggled to cope with her screaming but we were told to go against our gut feeling and leave her to cry (we went into the room every two, four, six minutes and so on). Within approximately a week, she learnt to self-settle and slept beautifully from then onwards. However, at this stage, I had signs of PND that were not officially diagnosed until my daughter was around eight months of age. The PND was already causing me to withdraw from my daughter (which is why I was feeling that settling her had become a chore) and resulted in emotional neglect. Sadly, using the controlled crying method with my daughter seriously compounded the lack of attachment in our relationship.

'A few years later, my daughter was displaying clear signs of anxiety and having issues with trust. As young as four years she talked about not wanting to live and how horrible life was for her. This continued and it was only when my husband and I came across a web site on attachment disorders that we realised our daughter was displaying symptoms of a mild attachment disorder. We had to work extremely hard from this time on with therapeutic parenting skills and changing our parenting to more attachment-based approaches. Slowly, our daughter started to learn to trust again. She is nearly a teenager now and still has some mild issues linked back to her poor attachment as an infant. I have many days I wish I could turn back to clock, ignore my child-health nurse's advice and continue to meet my baby's needs instead of seeing it as a 'chore' and an inconvenience. I hope one day she understands that we did not mean to hurt her in this way and that when she comes to have her first baby, she has enough support around her to follow her instincts and to respond to her baby's needs, however challenging they are. We have had two children since our first child and have never used controlled crying again.'

Michelle

Failing sleep school

One of the arguments for using techniques such as controlled crying is that they 'work' — but perhaps the definition of success needs to be examined more closely. In the small number of studies undertaken, while most babies will indeed stop waking when they are left to cry, 'success' varies from an extra hour's sleep each night to little difference between babies who underwent sleep training and those who didn't, eight weeks later. Some studies found that up to one-third of the babies who underwent controlled crying 'failed sleep school'.

A recent Australian newspaper headline boldly claimed: 'Why tears at bedtime are good for babies and mothers, finds study' (Weaver, 2010). The article cited some new research suggesting that controlled crying is not harmful. With all due respect to the researchers, the newspaper's claims need some sifting through. According to the study, after four months of controlled crying, 30 per cent of babies slept better. In my reckoning, this means that not only did 70 per cent of babies not sleep any better, but I would suggest that any improvement would, at least in part, be developmental: babies undergo a lot of development in four months and many babies would simply have a better capacity (larger stomachs, more developed brains and so on) to sleep longer.

The study also said that parents claimed they had better relationships with their child after controlled crying. These babies are now six years old and the research regarding relationships with parents was defined by questionnaires filled out by the parents themselves. I would expect most parents who voluntarily took part in such a trial to answer questions in a socially acceptable way. There are also many variables that affect a child's development and their family relationships.

In other research studies – for instance, regarding the effects of early skin-to-skin contact with babies on the parent–baby relationship – video recordings of parent–child interaction was assessed by independent observers. This would seem a more accurate and objective way to measure such an important aspect of development. (And by the way, these studies showed a positive correlation between the amount of early skin-to-skin contact and the strength of the parent–baby bond.)

I don't believe there is sufficient proof that leaving babies to cry in order to 'teach' them to sleep is not harmful at all and I find it worrying that proponents of leaving babies to cry often claim that they have 'proof' that such practices are 'safe'. However, I should also point out that the babies in the study reported in the newspaper were all over six months old, and that parents were allowed to respond to babies (they were not forced to leave babies for mandatory lengths of time regardless of the babies' distress).

My greatest concern about this kind of media hype is that more and more parents might be pressured by family, friends and onlookers to leave even tiny babies to 'self-settle', which usually means letting them cry themselves to sleep, often for long periods of time.

If your baby needs help to settle, it means that he needs you. If your baby is excessively wakeful (and if this is a problem for *you*), it means that the reasons for waking need investigating, and a one-size-fits-all baby-training program is not the answer. Instead, you might need to have your baby checked by a health professional to eliminate conditions that may be making him uncomfortable; you may need to try changing your baby's diet or your own diet if you are breastfeeding; or you might experiment with 'tweaking' your baby's sleep routines, or altering the sleep environment (see chapter 8). Or, you might simply need to wait for your baby to mature a little: babies and toddlers often become unsettled as they reach new developmental milestones.

Whatever the reasons for your baby waking or not self-settling, it is worth remembering that you are the grown-up here, and that your baby is the small, vulnerable person who can't yet meet his own needs. Do you enjoy a cuddle at bedtime? Do you ever wake from a scary dream and need a little reassurance? Do you find it difficult to wind down and sleep after a busy day? Do you sometimes need a sip of water in the night? Your baby needs your care around the clock – this is the parental 'job spec' and, however unreasonable it might seem at times, he is not an object that you can simply put away when his presence is inconvenient to you.

Having said this, I do want to say, as a mother of five, that I completely understand how seriously exhaustion can affect your perspective, your health and your relationships, so please don't be a martyr. It is important to seek help – whether this is a few hours of practical help a week or some strategies to help you deal with your baby's unsettled behaviour.

It is also important to remain in charge when you do this: check out the background of anybody who is working with your family or giving advice about babies. Is this person a health or early-childhood professional? Will they refer you to appropriate services if the situation is beyond their professional scope? What is their philosophy about babies? Do you like their 'energy' – for instance, do they seem as though they will advise or bully you into anything that makes you feel uncomfortable, or will they help you feel calmer and more confident that you are the expert about your baby?

When the crying gets trying

As you get to know your baby, you'll find that you respond intuitively to her crying without consciously asking yourself, 'What kind of cry is this?' And, as you learn her pre-cry signals, you will be able to avert most crying spells by responding before your little one becomes distressed. However, it helps to be familiar with some of the reasons why babies cry, so that you know it's not a reflection on your skills (or some sort of rejection by your baby) when they do. It's common, for example, for babies to have a crying spell in the evening. In fact, this unsettled behaviour is so universal that it has been labelled (by mothers, of course!) the 'arsenic hour'!

It seems that even in cultures where babies have continual close contact with their mothers and ready access to the breast, and rarely cry during the day, it is quite common for them to cry for long periods in the evening. Babies who have these evening crying bouts may be responding to a busy day, lots of handling by visitors, or frustration as they practise a new skill. Some babies are less able than others to block out stimulation or move smoothly from sleeping to waking (and vice versa). Also, it is very common for babies to 'cluster feed' (have several feeds close together) in the evening, as though they are 'stocking up' before a longer sleep at night or catching up on feeds they missed during the day.

Just like you and me, when babies are upset, they feel better if they're supported – preferably by a pair of loving arms. Your baby's crying may upset you, but it's important to accept and try to interpret it rather than become impatient. Limit stimulation – a quiet environment (turn off the television) is less stressful. Simply walking around while you carry your baby – perhaps with some gentle music playing, or you could hum quietly (this will help you to calm down, too) – may help.

And a word of warning: no matter how frustrated you are by her crying, *never* shake your baby – this can cause brain damage or even death. If you are feeling very tense or angry, put your baby down or get somebody else to hold her for a bit. If you are on your own, wrap her firmly and put her down somewhere safe. Take some deep, slow breaths, call a supportive friend (or a helpline if nobody else is available). It might help to put your baby in a sling or pram and go for a walk – she will probably stop crying as soon as you get out the gate. If it is the middle of the night, try the bumpy-ride trick described later in this chapter (see the checklist on rocking and movement, page 230).

Why do babies cry?

There are many reasons why babies become unsettled – see the checklist below. Of course, if you think your baby is unwell or in pain, contact your healthcare provider (your doctor, maternal and child-health nurse or hospital).

✳ **CHECKLIST : WHY IS MY BABY CRYING?**
- Physical: hunger; discomfort; a wet or dirty nappy; pain
- Emotional: loneliness, exhaustion, boredom, frustration, fear – including separation anxiety
- Environmental: sensitivity to loud noises and bright lighting; excessive stimulation; extremes in temperature
- Developmental: a number of emotional, physical and neurological stages cause upheaval and anxiety in babies

Temperament is also a factor in how much babies cry. Some babies, for example, find it more difficult than others to block out stimulation, or to move smoothly from sleeping to waking (and vice versa). Again, this is not a result of the way you care for your baby. In fact, research suggests that some babies simply cry more than others. A study into foetal movements revealed traits akin to temperament that can predict how much individual babies are likely to cry. Paediatrician William Sears coined the label 'high-needs baby' to emphasise that crying and clingy behaviours are a factor of the baby's temperament and reaction to her environment rather than inappropriate care by the parent. Personally, I prefer the label 'high-interest' baby, as I often find that these babies, who seem to be more expressive about their needs, are very bright, alert little beings who tend to find it difficult to switch off to their environment and seem to know that they deserve responsive care to thrive. I also find the observations of Professor James McKenna (director of the mother–baby sleep laboratory at the University of Notre Dame, Indiana) reassuring: he says that the babies who are most adamant about having their needs met (and who are often the most resistant to 'baby training') are the most well-adapted for survival. This makes sense when we consider the Stone-Age baby who, if left alone to self-soothe (or left alone at all) was in danger of being eaten by predators. Although our modern baby may well have all of the recommended safety equipment such as a standards-approved cot and a monitor on the wall, he isn't any more aware of this than a Stone-Age baby and is hardwired to expect a responsive carer to be nearby to protect him.

Developmental changes

It is fairly commonly accepted by both parents and professionals that babies reach a 'crying peak' at around six weeks of age. A study at the University of London concluded that a developmental process causes most babies to cry more at six weeks. It also found that premature babies get grizzly at about the time they would have been six weeks old and, apparently, even babies in non-western cultures – where mothers are less likely to leave their babies to cry – have a six-week grizzle.

As well as the six-week crying peak, there are several major developmental stages during the first twelve months that may be quite confusing to a baby, even in a calm, gentle environment with responsive carers. Just as babies have physical growth spurts, their brains grow more rapidly during the first year of life than at any other time, doubling in volume and reaching 60 per cent of adult size by the end of that twelve months. Neurological studies have shown that dramatic changes take place in the brains of babies and children at certain points, shortly after which they experience a marked leap forward in cognitive development.

According to Dutch researchers Hetty Van de Rijt and Professor Frans Plooij, all babies go through at least seven of these developmental leaps in the first year of life. Although calmer babies cope with these stages relatively easily, in others, confusion, frustration and anxiety may make them so unsettled that they cling to the only safety and security they know – you!

It may help to photocopy the following list of developmental 'leaps' and post it on your refrigerator as a reminder that your little one's unsettled spells may be the result of normal physiological changes. Always remember, though, that the age at which babies reach these developmental milestones does vary; the point is that there is a lot going on in your baby's inner world that may not be obvious to you.

✳ CHECKLIST : DEVELOPMENTAL LEAPS

- **6 weeks**: Significant sensory and digestive changes take place. Your baby is more awake and alert, breathes more regularly, cries real tears for the first time, and startles and trembles less often. She expresses her likes and dislikes more frequently and is more interested in her surroundings. Babies commonly experience a growth spurt at this time and may require more frequent feeds for a few days.

- **8 weeks**: There are big changes in the way your baby experiences his senses. He sees, hears, smells and tastes in a way that is completely new to him – this can make him feel puzzled, confused and upset. He may be fascinated by patterns and light, listen more keenly to sounds, and discover his hands. He may be more wary of strangers, want you to keep him occupied, sleep badly, lose his appetite, and suck his hands.

- **12 weeks**: Your baby is able to coordinate her movements much more smoothly, is more perceptive about changes taking place in her environment, and notices people's comings and goings. There may be another bout of shyness, sleeping badly, and not wanting to feed but wanting to suck a great deal.
- **19 weeks**: His understanding of the world around him develops. He begins to grasp that the world is made up of objects that continue to exist even when out of his sight. He may become clingy again.
- **26 weeks**: Your baby can perceive distance between objects, and will climb up to reach things. She will also understand about the distance between herself and her mother (previously, she didn't perceive herself as separate from you). She may be more fearful.
- **37 weeks**: Your baby recognises categories of things. He begins to experiment with foods and toys, and wants you to play constantly. Your baby's experimentation at this stage (squishing food, picking up specks of fluff and crumbs from the floor) is the precursor to recognising categories of things such as people, animals and sensations. For instance, as he squishes banana between his fingers and rubs pumpkin into his hair, he will be aware of the differences in texture and tastes, but he will understand that they are both foods. This leap into recognising categories will affect every sense – sight, hearing, smell, taste and touch.
- **46 weeks**: Your baby begins to see things in sequence and is able to string events together. This means that she can now make associations like, 'Here comes the babysitter: that means Mummy will be going out' – so she may cry in anticipation of being left.

So, just as your baby may need more feeds to satisfy an appetite increase or to boost her immunity if she has been exposed to bugs (see chapter 7), she may also, at times, need extra support to help her cope with the frustration and confusion of developmental change. It is logical, too, that babies' patterns of behaviour (read, 'sleeping' and 'feeding') alter to match each new phase.

Separation anxiety

Most babies go through clingy phases. For instance, newborns depend on close contact to adapt to the world outside the womb; carrying your newborn will not only help him feel secure but will regulate his immature heartbeat, rhythmic movements and respiration, balancing irregular waking, and sleeping and feeding rhythms. As they grow, it is common for babies to become clingy at significant developmental stages. Just as babies have physical growth spurts, they also achieve neurological milestones. Studies show marked increases in brain development as babies reach these milestones and, for some babies, this causes confusion, frustration and anxiety. When they are feeling this way, they are likely to cling to the only safety and security they know – you.

A significant developmental milestone usually occurs at around twenty-six weeks, when babies begin to be able to perceive distance. This may result in 'separation anxiety' because your baby is suddenly able to recognise when you – the most important person in the world to him – is moving away from him. This anxiety commonly lasts from the time babies realise you are a separate being until around eighteen months, when they understand that when you disappear, you will come back. It is also normal for toddlers and older children to experience episodes of separation anxiety. The best way to deal with this is to help your little one feel secure by responding to her cries for reassurance. And if you have to leave her with a carer, be honest and say goodbye – it is helpful to have a farewell ritual as well as a return greeting, to help her learn that although you leave her sometimes, you will always come back. She will probably yell as you say goodbye the first few times, but if you sneak away, she will become distrustful and clingy, which means more crying in the long run. Usually, if you have been honest and your baby is familiar with her carers, she will settle quite quickly once you have gone.

'I feel as if my five-month-old is super-glued to me. She screams if anybody else holds her and if I dare to leave the room, she gets hysterical. She is my third baby so, even though there are days when I just want to run from the room screaming, "LEAVE ME ALONE!", I know, "This too shall pass." But I am sick of everyone telling me I am spoiling her or that I should just let her cry and she will get over it.'

Antoinette

If, like Antoinette, you have a 'velcro baby', please be reassured: your baby's clingy behaviour is not your fault, you have simply been responding to the baby you have. Although it can be stressful to contend with a highly sensitive baby who wants to be held constantly, especially if she only wants to be held by you, it can help to see things from your baby's perspective. In her mind, you are a part of her and, at this stage, she feels that things are not right if you are not there. See the checklist below for some tips on coping with a clingy baby.

✳ CHECKLIST : LIFE WITH A CLINGY BABY

- Help your baby feel secure by holding her and carrying her in a sling, where she is protected from poking by strangers.
- Introducing her to other people gradually. At first, hold her as others interact with her; then, as she gets used to family members and close friends, let them hold her for short periods with you close by, eventually increasing the distance and length of separations as she feels comfortable.
- If you need to leave her, give her carer an article of your unwashed clothing (such as your dressing gown or a t-shirt); this is likely to be comforting for her while her carer is holding her.
- When you need to leave her, be honest and say goodbye. It is helpful to have a goodbye ritual and a return greeting so she learns that although you leave sometimes, you do come back.
- If you receive flak about your velcro baby, remember: your baby's needs are more important than your critics' opinions. You are not spoiling your baby; you are teaching her to love and, all too soon, this clingy phase will pass. In just a few short years, she will probably be too embarrassed to even kiss you goodbye!

Hunger

Is your baby hungry? Don't watch the clock; watch (and listen to) your baby. She could be having a growth spurt, in which case she will need to suck more to signal your body to produce more milk. (See chapter 7 for more about feeding your baby.)

Physical discomfort

Does your baby have a wet or dirty nappy? If she seems hot, remove a layer of clothing. Is she cold? Itchy? Pain, fever and rashes may be symptoms of illness, so observe your baby carefully and seek medical advice if you have any concerns. As a rule, try to dress babies and children comfortably, in natural fibres, in an appropriate number of layers for the weather – perhaps add a layer more than you have on in winter, but check your baby's chest or back to see if she is comfortably warm – cold hands are normal, not necessarily a sign that your baby is cold. Use only gentle, natural products for washing skin and clothing, to minimise irritation.

Missing the womb

Consider the enormous sensory changes from 'womb to room' from your baby's perspective. Babies who have had a difficult birth, have been separated from their mother or are unwell may be especially sensitive to these changes.

By offering what I call 'womb service', you can help your baby adapt to being 'on the outside'. Womb service involves re-creating the sensations your baby experienced while he was safely inside you. To help you remember the important aspects, I have called these the five Ws:

- Warmth
- Wrapping
- Wearing your baby and moving
- Water
- Womb sounds

Of course, rather than simply using these as a 'formula' for comfort and trying to do them all at once, experiment and see which ones work for your baby. Does she respond by calming or should you try something different? For instance, some babies will prefer to be wrapped and held while others may respond better to being worn against your body in a sling without being wrapped.

Warmth Inside your body, your baby didn't experience cool air blowing on his tiny body or entering his lungs and these new sensations can be quite disturbing. So, at first, warm the space where you are going to be with your baby (16–20°C will be a comfortable room temperature for him), and take care not to have fans or air-conditioners blowing directly onto him in warmer weather. If you are popping him into a cradle to sleep, he will be more comfortable (and likely to sleep better) lying on sheets that have been warmed slightly. You do need to take care not to overheat your baby, but you can warm his sheets slightly with a heat-pack before you place him into bed – test the sheets with your forearm to make sure they aren't hot.

Wrapping Just as your newborn was tucked snugly inside your body, supported by the uterine wall, you can provide a sense of security by swaddling him – wrapping him firmly (but not too tightly) in a gauze or muslin sheet in summer, or a soft shawl or bunny rug in winter. With his limbs tucked securely against his body, just as they were in the womb, this will help your baby feel safe as well as inhibiting the 'startle' reflex (a primitive survival response that produces spontaneous, jerky movements and can be disturbing for your baby, especially if his own flailing little arm unexpectedly hits him in the face!).

There are several ways to wrap your baby, and different babies prefer to be wrapped more or less firmly. Some babies settle better when they are wrapped rather tightly (but always leave space to slide a few fingers between the wrap and your baby, to allow movement and chest expansion), while others prefer to be more loosely wrapped. Some babies, especially as they grow and can get their hands to their mouths (usually from about 2–3 months), like to have their fingers free so that they can suck them for comfort. Some babies may have been sucking their fingers while in the womb so these babies may want their hands free from the beginning. Also, do unwrap your baby's hands when you feed him so that he can touch your skin, or you can hold his tiny hands or kiss his delicate fingers. This will enhance bonding and will also provide extra-sensory stimulation as the many nerve endings in his hands and fingers send powerful 'touch' messages to his brain.

Some of the wraps available are very small – these are too easy for babies to wriggle out of and may become tangled around your baby as he wiggles free. Instead, use a larger wrap. From around three months, your baby might start wriggling free, even from a larger wrap. At this stage, discard the wrap in steps: first leave one arm out each time you wrap your baby, then, a few days later, leave both arms out. Once a wrap is too small or your baby is too wriggly, you might like to use a sleeping bag (get one that is just the right size; many of them have arm holes) to keep your baby warm at night.

How to wrap your baby

1. Lay the wrap with a corner facing up, to form a diamond shape. Fold the top corner down towards the centre of the sheet, to form a longer straight edge across the top. Place your baby on the wrap with his shoulders near the top, straight edge.

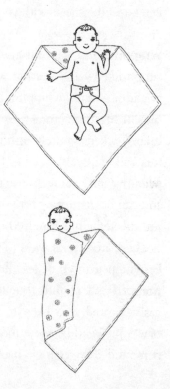

2. Draw one side of the wrap across your baby's body, rolling him a little so you can tuck that edge under him. For a smaller baby (as in this picture), tuck his arms in by his sides, slightly bent across his body, or fold them over his chest, one at a time; for an older baby, leave his hands out so he can discover his fingers.

3. Flip the bottom point of the wrap up towards your baby's head and, if it is long enough, tuck it over the edge that is near his neck.

4. Bring the remaining point across his chest and tuck it underneath him for security.

If your baby has fallen asleep in your arms before wrapping, gently hold him against your shoulder with one arm and wrap him while you are holding him (lying him flat while he is unwrapped may startle and waken him). If this seems too complicated or tends to wake him, lie the wrap in your baby's cot and gently place him on top of it on his side, keeping one hand on him to prevent sudden startles. Gently roll him on his back to quickly wrap, then gently rock (with your hand) or pat him into a deeper sleep, gradually rocking or patting more and more slowly before stopping and taking your hand away.

Wearing your baby and moving Inside your womb, your baby was lulled to sleep by your body movements as you went about your daily work. Now, the motion of being carried in a sling (or front-pack) against your moving body and your comforting heartbeat, as he breathes the familiar scent of your body, will help your baby feel safe. This feeling of familiarity will reduce stress hormones and help your baby relax – and a more relaxed baby will sleep more easily. Wearing your baby may have a balancing effect on his irregular rhythms of waking and sleeping, and is also thought to help him regulate his developing nervous and hormonal system, promoting day waking and night sleeping.

If your baby falls asleep in the sling, you will have two hands free to do a few chores, or you can go out and enjoy a walk. Wearing your baby is especially good if you are in a busy, noisy place such as a shopping centre – your motion, as you hold your baby close, will act as a filter for the extra stimulation and help him to sleep through the bedlam. (However, during the early weeks, venues such as shopping centres will probably be stressful to you as well as your baby, so do consider your own wellbeing, too.) If you are at home and prefer to put your baby into bed when he has fallen asleep, you can gently slip him out of most slings while he is sleeping: simply bend over, lower him towards the cot and unwrap or unclasp the sling at the shoulder (depending on the style of sling). Smooth the sling out under your baby so that it isn't a smothering hazard or, depending on the style, wrap it safely around him, rather than trying to unravel him completely and risk waking him up. By using a sling in the early days, you will get your body used to your baby's weight before he gets heavier. It is best to start with short spells at first and gradually carry your baby for longer periods as your muscles adapt.

> 'Both my children slept on me and in slings during the day for the first three months, and then made the transition to the pram and cot gradually, without any stress. They just both screamed if they were separated from me [during the first three months]. I can imagine that going from inside my womb straight into a pram in a prone position was too scary for them. I enjoyed this bonding time, and I could do more things knowing they were safe and comfortable up against me.'
>
> *Wendy*

In your womb, the gentle movement of the amniotic fluid rocked your baby's little body, even while you were resting. Being still is a new sensation for a newborn baby that will take some getting used to; some babies will crave movement and rocking – and will let you know quite loudly!

From birth, babies learn about their bodies through movement. For instance, gentle stimulation of the vestibular system (the channels of the inner ear) is vital for babies to integrate sensory messages. Such stimulation is provided by constant movement, which is why babies enjoy being rocked or riding in a pram or sling, and older children love to roll and tumble. At first, your baby's movements will be involuntary and the result of what are known as 'primitive reflexes'. Gradually, these early reflexive movements are replaced by deliberate movements such as rolling, crawling, cruising and, later, walking, running and jumping. Instead of seeing your baby's craving for movement in negative terms, accept that this is exactly what he needs to aid his development, and see it as a wonderful justification for spending some quality time together, relaxing in a rocking chair or going for a walk with your baby in a sling. See the checklist below for some ideas on different ways and places to rock/move.

Water Help your baby recall his watery womb world by taking a bath together. Remember that in your womb, your baby was confined, not floating all stretched out, and his womb world was gently bathed in filtered light. By dimming the lights or bathing by candlelight with your newborn, you will help her recall the safety of her womb world and you will be able to hold her close and support her as she gradually relaxes and 'uncurls' her limbs. Bathing together is especially helpful if bonding has been interrupted by early separation or a difficult birth or feeding experience. It can also be a lovely bonding time for father and baby.

Newborns can lose body heat very quickly after a bath, and a cold baby will be more difficult to settle. So, rather than exposing your baby to cool air by laying her flat on a towel and patting her dry, wrap her in two towels and cuddle her. The heat trapped in the towels will dry most of your baby's body as the warmth relaxes her. Then you can remove the damp towel next to her body and with the outer, dryer towel, gently dry her crevices (neck, underarms, groin, between fingers and toes) and dress her. To bathe safely with your baby, it is best to have somebody else to help you get in and out of the bath; if you are on your own, place your baby on a towel that is spread over a baby seat or bouncer next to the bath. When you are comfortably in the bath, reach over and lift her in with you. When you need to get out, place her back in her bouncer, wrap her in the towel to keep her warm while you get dry and pop on your dressing gown, then dress your baby and snuggle together – bliss!

Womb sounds The calming, repetitive sounds of traditional lullabies recall the 'womb music' your baby heard before birth (your heartbeat, and fluids whooshing through the placenta). Baby music that incorporates elements such as the rhythm of a heartbeat or 'white noise' has remarkable soothing effects, especially if played continuously through the night. Of course, your own singing voice or even a gentle, continuous 'shushing' sound is transportable 'music' that doesn't rely on the availability of a CD player, and it will help induce calm and sleepiness just as well as any commercial music – even if you don't have a fabulous voice!

✳ CHECKLIST : ROCKING AND MOVEMENT

- Rock together in a rocking chair.
- Carry your baby in a sling.
- Gently bounce on a fit ball with your baby in your arms.
- Lie your baby in her pram and push her back and forth over a bump between carpet and floorboards or any other small bump on the floor – babies seem to like the rhythm that this creates.
- Sit in a swivelling office chair, holding your baby, and slowly spin one way then the other.
- Hold your baby in your arms and bend at your knees as you lift her up and down (this up and down movement is similar to the movement she would have experienced in the womb as you walked).
- Wrap your baby firmly and lay her on your knees, facing you, with her head well supported in your hands and her feet towards you. Now, keeping your toes on the floor, jiggle your knees up and down one at a time, in a peddling motion.

Food intolerance or allergy

If you or your partner suffers from allergies such as eczema, asthma or hay-fever, or if there is a family history of such conditions, it is more likely that your baby will do so, too. If this is the case, it is worth considering whether excessive crying may be linked to a food sensitivity. Allergies and food intolerance in infants may cause a wide range of symptoms including tummy cramps, nausea, vomiting, gastric reflux (see page 234), silent reflux (reflux without vomiting), breast refusal, frequent night waking, wheezing, dermatitis and rashes. However, before you conclude that any symptoms are allergy-related, other medical causes for your baby's discomfort should be ruled out.

The best way to protect your baby from allergies is to follow the World Health Organization guidelines and breastfeed exclusively for the first six months. Food allergies in exclusively breastfed babies are caused by foods that pass into your milk, not by the milk itself. Some sensitive babies react even to small amounts of some foods in breast milk: the most common culprit is cows' milk protein (in milk, cheese, yoghurt), but chocolate, peanuts, eggs, fish, wheat and citrus can also cause reactions.

Before eliminating foods from your diet, it is worth examining your baby's feeding pattern (see **Lactose intolerance and foremilk imbalance**, page 233). If, however, you think that the crying seems to be related to feeds, jot down his crying times and what you have eaten: if there appears to be a link, one simple solution is to eliminate the suspect food for at least a week (preferably two). If your baby's symptoms disappear, avoid the suspect food in future. (Or, reintroduce a small amount of the food into your diet; if symptoms reappear, you can be pretty certain you have nailed the culprit.) It can take several weeks of trial and error, as you eliminate individual foods, to find the offender/s. But when you do, and you have a more settled baby (and therefore a more settled you), modifying your diet is a small sacrifice to make.

Caffeine Although you may be relying on caffeine hits to help you cope with a crying baby, if you are breastfeeding, this could be the very reason he is irritable. Although one or two cups of coffee a day probably won't affect a baby over three months old, a newborn can take almost 100 hours to metabolise the caffeine in a single cup of coffee, so the caffeine he gets through your milk can accumulate. And don't forget that caffeine is also found in cola drinks, chocolate and, in smaller amounts, tea (including green tea). It is easy to create a vicious circle: baby cries, you drink more coffee, he cries more, and down you both spiral. Caffeine has no nutritional value so why not consider cutting it out altogether and trying decaf, herbal teas or a coffee substitute, especially if you managed without it during pregnancy.

Salicylates Salicylates are chemicals that occur naturally in foods such as fruits, fruit juices, vegetables, herbs, spices, nuts, wines, tea and coffee. They are also present in food colourings and additives, and can trigger food-intolerance symptoms in sensitive people. Babies who are sensitive to these chemicals may be restless and cry a lot. If you suspect food intolerance in your breastfeeding baby, you might like to first try avoiding foods with additives, such as soft drinks (see 'Food intolerance' in the Resources section). Some people find that cutting down is enough, but if you still have problems – and especially if there are family members with food-intolerance symptoms like migraine – you might need to try an elimination diet. Because this is a complex and stressful process, it is essential to be supervised by a dietician.

'There is nothing more isolating than a baby who screams and vomits every time he feeds – there are no offers to hold the baby! I would walk into the doctor's with this chubby, apparently thriving baby and, of course, it would look as though I was simply a neurotic mother. Eventually, through trial and error, I discovered that he seemed sensitive to salicylates: when I stopped eating apples, he calmed down significantly. A dietician supervised my elimination diet while I continued to breastfeed. My son is now thirteen and has no allergies, but is on a strict elimination diet under the supervision of a dietician because food additives have such a detrimental effect on his behaviour.'

Glenda, mother of two

Lactose intolerance and foremilk imbalance All babies are biologically designed to digest milk. But from around four years of age, people from some ethnic backgrounds (non-Caucasian and non-Anglo-Saxon) can no longer do this because they stop producing the enzyme lactase, which helps the body break down lactose (a sugar present in milk). In addition, whatever their genetic heritage, some babies develop temporary lactose intolerance after a gastrointestinal infection, while others exhibit symptoms of lactose or foremilk intolerance: spitting-up; gassiness or colic; or frothy or watery, loose, green bowel motions. This is a result of breastfeeding practices that result in too much lactose-rich foremilk and not enough fat-rich, hunger-satisfying hind milk.

These problems are typically caused by a limited time at the breast (for example, changing sides too often and/or a forceful milk ejection that causes spluttering or makes the baby pull off the breast). If a baby doesn't get the hind milk, he will need to drink more (or more often) to satisfy his hunger, and so consume more lactose. And if he doesn't have enough lactase, he will develop symptoms similar to those of lactose intolerance: diarrhoea, which is further complicated because the milk's low fat content causes the stomach to empty rapidly; or spitting up, because the baby's stomach 'empties in the wrong direction' when he consumes more milk than he can comfortably hold.

The solution here is to allow your baby to nurse on one breast long enough to get the hind milk by letting him decide when he has finished the first breast before you change sides. Another tip, if your baby is diagnosed with lactose intolerance, is to express some foremilk until you feel your milk letting down, before you put him to the breast (and, of course, also let him finish the first breast first). He will then begin feeding on fattier milk and need a lower volume, which will place less stress on his digestive system until symptoms ease.

There are drops available for babies who have difficulty digesting lactose: ask your health carer whether these are relevant to your child's condition. If you are advised to wean (which is occasionally recommended as a temporary measure) but you would prefer to continue breastfeeding, seek another opinion.

Gastric reflux

Gastric (or gastroesophageal) reflux is the regurgitation of stomach contents into the oesophagus. At first, all babies will have 'reflux' to some degree, because their digestive systems are immature. At the bottom of the oesophagus (the swallowing tube), there is a ring of muscle that helps keep contents in the stomach. In babies, this sphincter cannot squeeze shut as effectively as it can in a child or adult, and it undergoes frequent episodes of relaxation. As well as allowing for swallowed wind to be expelled, these relaxations allow food to flow back into the oesophagus. For some babies, this will simply mean a bit of possetting that doesn't bother the baby or have any adverse effects on his wellbeing. At the other end of the spectrum, the process can cause heartburn-like pain, abdominal pain, and/or frequent or recurrent vomiting, which may be responsible for baby distress and symptoms that include wriggling, squirming and 'throwing' themselves off the breast during feeding. Reflux babies may suck voraciously because they are hungry, then pull away out of discomfort; others may want to feed almost constantly, as the natural antacid effects of breast milk may soothe their discomfort. Screaming after and between feeds (especially waking suddenly and screaming – a result of a regurgitation of acid), arching and wakefulness are also symptoms that suggest your baby may have reflux. Babies who are unwell with reflux may also be diagnosed with low weight gain and breathing problems.

According to paediatric gastroenterologist Dr Bryan Vartabedian, author of *Colic Solved* (see **Further reading**) and father of two babies with acid reflux, babies at extreme ends of this spectrum are easily diagnosed, but the babies who are between the extremes can be more challenging to treat, and even doctors can vary in their opinions as to when to treat baby heartburn.

✳ CHECKLIST : IS IT REFLUX?

In his book *Colic Solved*, paediatric gastroenterologist Dr Bryan Vartabedian advises that the presence of one or more of the following signs may suggest that your baby is suffering from GERD (gastroesophageal reflux disease):

- spitting up and vomiting
- constant hiccups
- feeding disturbance
- chronic irritability
- discomfort when lying on the back
- sleep disturbance
- chronic cough and/or congestion.

What can I do about reflux? Firstly, have your baby checked by a doctor – a general practitioner or a paediatrician, or ask for a referral to a paediatric gastroenterologist. (If you are 'blown off', remember, you know your baby best; persist until you get answers to your baby's distress.)

Getting a proper diagnosis of reflux can involve a treadmill of tests, which often simply compounds the distress (yours as well as your baby's). If other medical causes for your baby's pain have been ruled out, before you embark on more invasive testing, consider whether his symptoms may in fact be due to conditions such as foremilk imbalance (see page 233), allergy (milk protein allergy can present with very similar symptoms to gastroesophageal reflux disease) or food intolerance (including reactions to foods that may pass through your breast milk). These conditions can be simply addressed by altering breastfeeding practices such as eliminating offending foods from your own diet, rather than weaning: a child-health nurse, breastfeeding counsellor or lactation consultant can advise you.

Until your baby's system matures, understanding some basic physiology and improving the angle at which he lies and feeds may help you to relieve his distress. After meals, a baby with reflux is – theoretically, at least – best put on his stomach with his head propped up at an angle of about 30 degrees, which causes the stomach to fall forward and close the opening between the stomach and the oesophagus. Remember, though, that this is only theoretical; some infants will cry if put on their stomachs, and if they cry constantly, their stomach will fill with air and then they will start to grunt and strain for relief, which tends to make the reflux worse. (For tips on helping your baby learn to enjoy tummy time, see page 203.)

Perhaps more important than finding·the best position is avoiding uncomfortable positions. It can help to keep your baby upright after feeds, to aid digestion. However, young infants without much control of their abdominal or chest muscles tend to slump when they are placed in a seat (babies with reflux are often extremely uncomfortable in infant car seats). This increases the pressure in their stomachs, which tends to worsen the reflux. Try using a baby carrier that supports baby in an upright position, comforting him as well as leaving your hands free; or try a seat that reclines a bit.

For sleeping, try utilising gravity to aid digestion by raising the head end of the cot: place phone books under the cot legs or place a towel under the mattress (never use a pillow for a baby under twelve months) or use a Baby Wedge, an Australian product designed by the mother of a baby with reflux (see below).

Placing your baby on his left side closes off the sphincter between the stomach and oesophagus, and positions the sphincter above the stomach contents so that regurgitation is less likely. As a result, he may sleep more comfortably on his side – as long as you are there to watch that he isn't rolling onto his tummy while he sleeps. If you are co-sleeping, after feeds, place your baby so that he is facing you, on his left side, with his head supported in the crook of your arm.

A couple of handy products for babies with reflux include a Baby Wedge (babywedge.com.au) – a foam wedge with adaptable bolsters that you can position either side of your baby to elevate him but prevent him from rolling over; and a Safe T Sleep Sleepwrap (safetysleep.com) – similar to a fitted sheet that fits around the mattress, with a wide piece that fastens with velcro around your baby's body. Designed to help reflux babies, the Safe T Sleepwrap also has a piece that fastens over the baby's feet to stop a tiny baby from wriggling under blankets or sliding down to the bottom of the cot when the mattress is elevated. A baby hammock with an elevated head position will keep your baby in a safe and comfortable sleeping position and, as he stirs, may help him rock back to sleep again.

'Both our babies suffered from gastric reflux. The first one used to cry for about half an hour and I would walk him until he was comfortable, then he would sleep soundly. The second one would have crying spells all through the day. I would walk and rock. There were days when I was so tired I wouldn't drive beyond the local shops, five minutes away, because I knew it wasn't safe. For my benefit and my children's, I stayed home and kept life simple. I learnt not to stress if I didn't even read the paper for days.

'Our two-year-old was very articulate and I could explain to him, "Michael hasn't fed and he won't sleep, so I have to walk him up and down. You can walk with us, or this is the time you can play with your blocks, while Michael isn't on the floor." I don't use television until after three in the afternoon. We don't watch any television at the weekends, so I would make a big deal of this being his time to play with toys that the baby couldn't share, like books and crayons.

'My husband works from home in a building outside. Although he didn't come up to the house very often, I knew there was another adult so that if I did finally crack it – when I was sitting on the floor crying – there was someone there. If you have a crying baby, you need to have a good neighbour or another adult you can go to if you are really stressed.

'Basically, the first year is a blur, but you do get your life back. And when they put their head in the corner of your shoulder and finally snuggle up, I just love it.'

Nanci, mother of two

Constipation

Constipation is another tummy trouble that can make for a distressed baby. This problem is rare in fully breastfed babies, because breast milk has laxative properties: it is not unusual for a breastfed baby to have frequent, soft bowel motions in the early weeks and then, in succeeding weeks, to go for several days without a poo – this is not a cause for concern if your baby is comfortable. If, however – whether breastfed or bottle-fed – your baby strains and becomes distressed about having a bowel motion, or if he is being bottle-fed or has started on solids and has hard, dry bowel motions, consult your doctor or child-health nurse to rule out any more serious medical conditions.

Your baby's straining and grunting, especially in the early weeks, may simply be due to immaturity: it takes coordination of abdominal muscles and pelvic-floor relaxation for babies to poo, and this can take a bit of practice to work out. While some parents try to 'help' their baby by using suppositories or stimulating the rectum, in the longer term, this can actually delay your baby's development. Instead, be supportive: try bending his legs towards his chest (don't force) and hold him in a comfortable position, such as sitting in a squat over your forearm facing outwards, and let him work things out for himself!

If constipation is the problem, offer your baby extra water to drink (this is not necessary for fully breastfed babies) and try gently massaging around his tummy in clockwise circles to stimulate elimination of waste from the bowel. If constipation persists in your bottle-fed baby, ask your doctor or child-health nurse whether you should change formulas. For babies over six months old, diluted prune or apple juice (again, check with your child-health nurse) can help keep fluid inside his intestines and soften the stools.

If your baby screams as he uses his bowels, and you notice specks of fresh blood in his poo, his pain may be caused by a fissure (a small ulcerated sore) on the edge of his anus. (You can see this if you lift his legs gently.) An anal fissure may be caused by constipation and certainly will not heal easily if your baby is constipated. To aid healing, remember how you healed your own perineum after birth: sit your baby in a shallow container or basin – the bathroom sink will do – of warm salted water for a few minutes after he has used his bowels, then gently pat the area dry (or use a hairdryer on 'warm') and apply a healing ointment such as zinc and castor-oil cream.

Teething

Although lots of babies are barely bothered by teeth erupting, the experience can turn others (even if they are normally the most placid beings) into little aliens who cry, develop sleep problems and want to breastfeed more frequently for comfort. Some babies may refuse to feed, or may bite down hard with their sensitive gums – strangely, biting seems to bring some relief.

If your baby won't feed, you could try nursing when he has fallen asleep – just pick him up gently without waking him and hold him to the breast (see also **Baby on strike!**, page 142). If you are concerned about his fluid intake, offer homemade icy poles made from expressed breast milk, formula (if you are bottle-feeding) or diluted fruit juice.

Ask your doctor or pharmacist about teething remedies. Meanwhile, try some of the tips in the list below.

✳ CHECKLIST : EASING PAINFUL GUMS

- Rub your baby's gums with your finger (wash your hands thoroughly first, of course).
- Chill a teething ring in the freezer (but remember: don't ever hang a teething ring around your baby's neck, as the cord is a strangling hazard).
- Let him chew on a cool, wet washcloth (pop a damp cloth in the freezer), or a frozen piece of apple inside a muslin cloth (to prevent choking on chewed-off pieces of apple – although he doesn't yet have teeth, he's about to!)
- If your baby has started eating solids, he may enjoy chilled soft foods such as a frozen slice of banana, which will mush down as he gnaws on it (with supervision, of course), or try icy-cold apple puree. Never give hard foods such as carrot, which may be a choking hazard as those teeth emerge and bite little pieces off.

Tension release

Sometimes, crying is simply a baby's way of releasing tension, just as you or I might have a good yell to let off steam or a good cry to release pent-up emotions. According to psychologist Aletha Solter, author of *The Aware Baby*, sometimes babies actually need to yell to release stress and heal trauma. There is a difference between 'leaving babies to cry' and allowing babies to cry in your arms as long as any obvious needs are met. So, holding your baby and talking gently to him as he releases stress can actually be beneficial.

So, what might be stressful to your baby? According to Dr Solter, there is evidence that antenatal and perinatal events are major causes of extensive crying in infants. She quotes research findings (Solter, 2001) showing that babies whose mothers were under pressure during pregnancy or had a difficult birth cried more and woke more often at night. She suggests that crying is a way for these babies to release themselves from that trauma.

A baby's pent-up stress might be manifested in a crying spell at the end of a stimulating day – even though all of her immediate needs are met – as though her immature nervous system is experiencing information overload. Stress-release crying can also be a result of the inevitable frustrations that arise as babies strive to accomplish new skills or reach new developmental stages. This frustration is also likely to make itself felt in an evening crying spell but, thankfully, it passes as your baby masters new skills or adjusts to developmental changes (see page 219).

To implement the crying-in-arms approach, Dr Solter advises considering your baby's needs and why she may be crying even though you are holding her and offering comfort. If there don't seem to be any obvious needs, focus on relaxing rather than frantically trying to stop her tears with one remedy after another. Take your baby to a quiet space and hold her calmly; look into her eyes and talk to her gently, offering reassurance and telling her how much you love her. Listen respectfully to what she is 'telling' you and stay calm yourself (take some deep, slow breaths and consciously let go of tension – this release will pass through to your baby). If you find yourself unable to relax while you hold your crying baby, you could get your partner or another supportive person (if there is somebody else) to hold your baby through the crying spell.

This approach is totally different from leaving your baby to cry alone and even though it can feel awful when you can't 'stop' your baby's crying, she will stop and will either fall asleep or become calm and alert.

'Our third baby would have a lengthy crying spell every evening. This baby had been a "threatened miscarriage". I had bled until I was seven months pregnant, so her early life was probably unsettled, as I was very stressed during the pregnancy. She seemed sensitive to some foods I was eating (I had been eating a lot of citrus fruit from my parents' farm, and cutting this out made a difference). She was very alert and had difficulty switching off from stimulation. She wouldn't calm at the breast like our first two children.

'Somehow, I was quite calm about her crying. I knew deep down that this was not necessarily anything I was doing wrong (perhaps I was more at ease because she was our third child), and that she just needed to be held.

'My husband was studying, so was often at classes in the evening. It meant planning dinner early so I was ready to walk the baby. Many evenings, a good friend would arrive after she had put her own children to bed, and she helped by walking with the baby while I read bedtime stories to the other children, or I would hold the baby and she would read the stories. She was a godsend.'

Carmel, mother of five

Is my baby unwell?

You know your well child better than anyone. Any sudden or uncharacteristic change in behaviour could be a sign that he is unwell or 'coming down' with an illness.

Sometimes, a baby's pain is a symptom of illness – some tummy pains, in particular, require urgent medical care – so any time you have real concerns that your baby may be unwell, it is wise to have him checked by an appropriate health professional. Usually, if your baby is ill, he will have other symptoms too, such as a temperature, a rash, diarrhoea or vomiting, or a distended belly. Or he may refuse feeds, or wake screaming at a time when you can rule out hunger as a cause.

If your baby is unwell or has just been immunised, let him rest (cancel outings, playgroup etc.), give plenty of fluids and some extra vitamin C.

(Vitamin C will pass through your breast milk so increase your own intake via a supplement, rather than drinking extra citrus, which could make your baby cranky if he doesn't tolerate it. If you aren't breastfeeding, you can mix a tiny bit of vitamin C powder in water and give it to your baby – check with a pharmacist or naturopath.) Observe him carefully and if you have any feeling that he is 'not right', have him checked by a health professional. Often, parents can sense that their child is sick even before there are obvious symptoms.

Help your doctor make a diagnosis

To help you describe your baby's symptoms accurately to the doctor, jot down some notes before you phone the clinic or emergency department; you can bet your boots your mind will have gone blank if you have to wait for a return phone call while you're walking the floor with a crying baby. You may need to convince a receptionist that your baby really is unwell and you need an appointment today! It will help if you describe what is happening, other than crying. For example:

• What is your baby's temperature?
• How long has he had a fever?
• Is he lethargic? Cranky? Screaming? Whimpering?
• Is he unable to sleep?
• When did he last feed?
• How much is he drinking?
• Has he tried any new foods recently?
• Does he have a rash?
• Is his skin pale, flushed or mottled?
• What colour is his urine?
• Is he pulling at his ear? Is his ear red?
• Has he been vomiting? If so, how many times? Is there any blood in his vomit?
• When was his last bowel movement? What colour was it? Was it hard, runny or frothy, or did it contain mucus or blood?

Ask questions

When you see a doctor, don't be afraid or embarrassed to ask them lots of questions – it's better to do so while you have his or her attention, rather than ringing back once you're home again. For instance, if a medicine is prescribed, what is it and does it have any side effects? How long are your baby's symptoms likely to last? Should you keep him at home?

Remember, you are your child's advocate. If any advice feels overwhelming or confusing, you could ask your doctor, 'If this was your child, what would you do?' If you feel the need, seek a second opinion and don't hesitate to go back (even hours later) if the symptoms become worse or change. Most doctors are happy to check a child one more time if it will ease a parent's concern.

Soothing the sobs

You will find more comprehensive information about soothing your crying baby in my book *100 Ways to Calm the Crying*, but for now, here is a quick checklist of tips on how to calm your baby, and yourself!

✳ **CHECKLIST : SOOTHING**

- **Learn your baby's language.** By learning your baby's pre-cry signals – wriggling, anxious facial expressions, little grimaces, flailing arms, rooting at the breast, changes in breathing, and little noises that say, 'I am working up to a cry' – you will be able to see when he is bored, frightened, hungry, tired or overwhelmed, and by responding accordingly, you may be able to avert full-blown crying.
- **Protect your baby's senses.** In the early weeks, protect your little one's delicate nervous system by avoiding sudden movements, changes in temperature, loud noises, bright lights and too much handling by 'strangers'. Snuggling your newborn against your bare skin and heartbeat is a perfect way to help him feel secure and snug, just as he was in your womb.
- **Feed her.** Tiny tummies don't hold enough food to go long between feeds – day or night. Babies also have appetite increases to match

growth spurts. If you are breastfeeding, remember: the more your baby sucks, the more milk you will produce. He needs to suck long enough to get the more satisfying hind milk, which is higher in calories. The best way to do this is to watch your baby, not the clock, and allow him to decide when he is finished the first breast, before you switch sides (see chapter 7).

- **Respond quickly.** Despite what some health-care practitioners might tell you, you can't spoil a little baby, but if you leave him to cry, he will become more upset as his crying picks up momentum. Soon, he won't even know why he was crying in the first place – he will just be crying because he can't stop, and he will be much harder to settle. If you are breastfeeding, it is particularly important to respond quickly to hunger cues: a baby who is left to work up to a full-blown cry will have a more disorganised suck and may have difficulty latching on correctly (when a baby cries, his tongue points towards the roof of his mouth, which doesn't allow him to latch on), or he may only suck for a short time before he falls asleep out of exhaustion.
- **Try different carrying positions.** Try holding a crying baby up against your shoulder and walking or gently rocking backwards and forwards or up and down, bending your knees slowly (this is a similar motion to what your baby would have experienced in the womb). Alternatively, try the 'colic carry': lie him face-down across your forearm, his cheek at your elbow and his legs straddled across your arm (see page 113); or tummy-down across your knees, perhaps with a warm (not hot) wheat bag or hot-water bottle on your lap. Or carry him upright with his backbone against you, one hand supporting his bent legs and the other around his chest. Don't, though, hold him in a feeding position (this is especially frustrating for him if dad is doing the soothing), unless you intend to offer a feed.
- **Let him suck up.** Sucking is comforting to babies and helps them relax – and, if you are breastfeeding, you have nature's best comforters right under your shirt! However, if it is inconvenient to offer a breast, or your baby isn't hungry (whether he is breast- or

bottle-feeding) but is comforted by sucking, a dummy can be handy. However, please use dummies with care: the different sucking action between breast and dummy may cause 'nipple confusion' in the early weeks, so it is better to offer a clean finger to suck on if your newborn is unsettled but doesn't want milk, as this will hold his tongue down and encourage a more natural sucking action. (For more on dummies, see page 61.) And if your baby tends to fall asleep on the breast, please don't worry about 'bad habits'; all too soon, your little bundle will be mobile and your opportunities for enjoying quiet cuddles will become scarce.

- **Kick butt**. Studies show that the risk of colic is increased when one parent (no matter which one) smokes. As well as increasing the risk of SIDS, smoking also affects levels of prolactin, the hormone that aids relaxation and milk flow. So, if you can't give up, at least cut down and smoke outside, away from your baby.
- **A gentle touch**. When you first massage your baby, choose a time when he is calm (so that he associates your gentle touch with relaxation), and use warm hands and warm oil. Tummy massage can move wind, encourage digestion and help ease constipation: massage in a clockwise direction (this is the direction that our food travels inside our stomachs). If you alternately massage your baby's tummy and bend his knees, you may release trapped wind. For more on massage, see page 82.
- **Beat the blues**. If your baby has a regular crying time or suffers from colic, try to pre-empt the wails: about an hour before his usual crying time, give him a massage followed by a relaxation bath.
- **Take a bumpy ride**: This often works as a soother. Put your baby in the pram and push it backwards and forwards over the bump where the lino joins the carpet, or over tiles. Or go for a bumpy walk around the garden or up the street. Desperate parents have also been known to resort to a car ride – but don't do this if you are very upset or tired, as your mental state is likely to affect your driving.

'Caitlin used to breastfeed to sleep. She would zonk out into a really sound sleep. Nicholas wouldn't breastfeed to sleep very often. He liked me to sit and stroke his forehead. He would be asleep in five or ten minutes and I would be relaxed, too. The alternative was to leave him standing up yelling in his cot. I couldn't relax with that going on. If they go to sleep contented, they sleep better and we can get things done. Now Nicholas is six, he isn't frightened of the dark. Sometimes he will pad off to the toilet in the night by himself and he loves his bed.'

Emily, mother of two

11

Nurturing yourself

♥

Is your life now defined by a full nappy bin or laundry basket instead of an empty out-tray? Can't fit the baby into a 2 p.m. appointment in your organiser, or have the after-school care arrangements fallen through? (And you thought it would be easier after a few months!)

Is it any wonder that you are terrified of losing control, of suffocating under an avalanche of nappies, of losing your identity, of literally being 'swallowed up' by the job of mothering? You may have discarded the stereotype of the self-sacrificing martyr mummy, but are you causing greater problems by trying to live up to a new 'she who has it all' model?

Men, too, have to come to terms with the changes that a new baby entails. In our macho culture, which values performance above relationships, men are discouraged from talking about their feelings (and their failings). So, often the changes are less widely acknowledged for men than they are for women. Some try to avoid the reality of their changed lives by burying themselves in work. Others struggle on, wondering what their place is.

Losing yourself?

My husband and I had snatched a few hours to have a leisurely lunch together – without kids. It ended up in a heated discussion. He had made a less than complimentary comment about a friend of mine who'd just had a baby, along the lines of, 'Well, didn't she expect a baby to change her life?' The word 'selfish' came in somewhere, too.

I love the man, and he often sees the baby's perspective better than I do, but I gave him an earful about this new mother's perspective. It went something along the following lines: 'Just imagine if you had to give up your job (that you do well, so you get lots of positive feedback) and you were thrust into another one that you had absolutely no training for? What if this new job was complex and unpredictable, but had no clearly defined job description? What if no one ever said you were doing a great job? What if you had nothing tangible (e.g. a pay cheque) to show that you were doing a "real" job? And what if you were totally isolated from your co-workers for most of the day?' Of course it would take some time to adjust – and maybe you would never come to terms with the situation.

You are entitled to mourn your pre-baby life. It is not an indication of selfishness or greed, or that you don't love your baby; it's just that the birth of a child really is one hell of a change that often isn't acknowledged, let alone supported. Because of this, many parents feel that they must deny your feelings. And to survive, they promise themselves that things will soon be back to 'normal'. Well, things will become easier, but there is no going back – 'normal' will be different to the way it was before.

'Lately, I have been finding it a bit of a challenge adjusting to my new role as a mum. I have worked pretty much constantly since I was fifteen years old, with full-time and part-time study along the way. I have had a long time being just me, and enjoyed the freedom this brought and the confidence I gained from an established career. I felt ready to have a baby and thought I was prepared for the major life change that lay ahead.

'My baby is now seven months old and I have loved being a mum so far, but I guess there's a hint of sadness about the pausing of my career or old identity as I create a new identity and have to learn all these new skills in such an important job that has no training. When I got married, I didn't want to become a 'housewife' (I hate that word, but it seems appropriate).

But now that I have a bub, I feel like one (not a very good one either, judging by the mess around here). My partner is really supportive. I think he has also had to adjust to being a dad (and is doing great) but he doesn't really understand the change to my entire life and identity.'

Kate, mother of one

Surrender!

The best way to adjust to having a baby is to acknowledge and accept that things have changed. By surrendering to the changes, you will be able to enjoy precious moments. And no, this doesn't mean raising a white flag and giving up on your hopes and dreams; rather, it means accepting the reality of how things are right now and trying to live in the moment – be 'present', instead of constantly looking ahead and waiting for things to be different: when your baby needs you less, when you stop breastfeeding, when you return to work, when they go to school . . .

The trouble is that most of us subconsciously resist the whole concept of surrender, as it sounds too much like losing control. At work, you tend to draw on your rational mind. But caring for a baby requires more intuition and less analysis. It can be confusing and frustrating when your usual ways of coping – solving problems, making plans, setting goals – become ineffective. The best-laid plans can go astray with one foul nappy just as you are heading out the door. Along with the enormous hormonal upheaval you're going through at this time, glitches like these can seem overwhelming.

'Mothering has some strong lessons to teach us. I find intimate relationships difficult. I discovered I have to fight against *doing* things instead of just *being* in a relationship. To just sit with a child and be with them is hard work. It is easier to be busy. To stop the world and come to their pace is really difficult. The first time I was afraid to let go of the control, but you have to.'

Beth, mother of two

'For me, being a father is a personal-growth journey: being able to acknowledge that there is pain and joy, and being able to tolerate extremes of emotion, from amazingly joyous love to stress and anxiety and fear. When she was born, we became much more spontaneous; we planned less because planning became very difficult. Everything was purely about how the baby was, so we became much more in the here and now.'

Adam, father of one

'You are constantly shifting gears and surrendering to the child's needs and schedules. At first, you have to surrender to the baby's time schedule. As they reach different stages you have to change with them. You have to surrender your conceptions about who you should be and who your child should be. Some women see this as disempowerment. They have become so empowered and aware of their rights, and having a child reverses that. The child's needs have to supersede yours. You need to rationalise this and achieve peace of mind so you don't resent the child. This isn't about being submissive. It is about surrendering your fears and preconceptions.'

Emily, mother of one

What's missing?

As you adjust to your new role, it can help to think about what gave you satisfaction in your previous job. When you work out what you miss most and how that nourished your identity, you may be able to take the good from the old and mix it with the new.

If you miss the social contact, for instance, look for ways to socialise and take your baby with you. This doesn't mean you have to hang out at mothers' groups – although they can be amazingly supportive if you find one that suits you. Perhaps try some volunteer work for a few hours a week – there are lots of worthy causes and most charities are so grateful for your help that you are sure to get positive feedback.

If your previous job was very creative, find a new creative outlet: it could even turn into a money-spinner that you can carry out with baby on board. Many women have started their own business as a result of ideas 'born' from motherhood.

'Birth and mothering have been the catalysts for me finding a place of harmony, where my life and art are woven together. Guiding the energy of my life into creativity is wondrously rewarding and certainly challenging.

'I like to notice things that I experience: birthing, breastfeeding, playing dolls, washing dishes . . . and bring it into my artwork and my writing. I like to notice what is there and take a journey with it, draw it, paint it, read about it or have a conversation around it.

'Artistically being a Mama is a creative heaven; the challenge is often finding the right moments to create something. Each day has a different beat; some days in our family we like to learn together and other times we prefer to follow our interests alone. Often, too, these distinctions can't be made, we just find a harmony where we are learning together and inspiring each other with our projects.

'Children are wonderful at reminding us how to learn and how to live. I try to make art and live my life the way children learn, by one thing leading naturally to the next without coercion. My pursuits are neither more nor less important than the pursuits of my children and I am always trying to honour this by understanding that building their tower out of blocks is just as important as my latest painting. When I remember to honour my children's endeavours, they immediately do the same with mine.'

Chrissy Butler, mother, author, artist

If you are missing intellectual stimulation, find a class. Motherhood and study are entirely compatible and you can learn at your own pace – just a subject at a time, if you like. Seminars or one- or two-day courses and workshops can be enriching and may provide an opportunity to update some career skills for later. Community houses (sometimes called neighbourhood houses) are a great place to find short courses on a range of topics; the environment is supportive and childcare is usually available at minimal cost. Another fascinating way to learn is through online courses – you can do these in your own time and space, at a pace that works for you. Many incorporate audio recordings that you can download onto an MP3 player and listen to as you exercise or drive – or mop the floor.

Ask yourself whether there is something you've always wanted to do. Now is a great opportunity – just do it!

Keeping burnout at bay

'There is no burnout without fire', goes the saying, and there is plenty of fuel for the fires of parenthood. Most of us feel pressured to live up to high, and usually unrealistic, expectations. It's all too easy to judge yourself harshly for not being a 'yummy mummy' with an impeccable home, contented baby, compliant children, doting partner and supportive family members – just like in the glossy mags! So, you keep trying to juggle more and more balls in the air as you meet everybody's needs except your own.

Burnout is a state of total exhaustion – physical, emotional and spiritual – brought on by unrelenting stress. When we are burnt out, we feel we have nothing left to give. Dr Kathleen Kendall-Tackett, author of *The Hidden Feelings of Motherhood*, describes burnout as a loss of enthusiasm, energy, idealism, perspective and purpose. She says that burning out is like the feeling you get when trying to run a marathon at full speed.

Burnout is not a sign that you are failing. In fact, it is generally a sign that you are caring too much – for everybody except yourself! It is also a warning sign that things need to change.

'I didn't realise until it was over; I just thought I was being lazy because I couldn't be bothered cleaning the house or cooking dinner and I was too tired to do anything. I couldn't concentrate properly and I was irritable. Only after I cut some things from my life and started allowing myself to have needs did things get better and I realised how bad it had been. Now, I know what the symptoms are and I look out for them. I put myself and my family first; the truly supportive people in my life will understand.

I recognise that, at the end of the day, it's my kids who suffer if I don't take care of myself.'

Clare

Mothers matter too

While you are busy taking care of your baby, your child, your home and family, it can be all too easy to neglect your own needs, especially your need for sleep. Use the checklist below to help you look after yourself.

✳ **CHECKLIST : LOOKING AFTER YOU**

- **Rest when your baby does.** This is not the time to catch up on chores, study, work or even to have some 'me' time. Make a sign saying 'Mother and baby resting' and hang it on the front door with a notepad so visitors can leave a message. This won't mean you'll never get anything done: while your baby is awake, put her in a sling while you do chores, or place her near you and talk to her as you work. And, if your little one has her longest stretch of sleep between, say, 7 p.m. and midnight (remember, in infant sleep studies, 'all night' is only five hours!), try to get to bed early several evenings a week so you can top up your 'sleep bank'.
- **Eat well.** Breakfast is especially important to maintain your energy for the afternoon. Choose a variety of whole foods (fruit, protein such as eggs or oily fish, wholegrain bread and so on) that are as close to natural as possible. Do not fill up on empty calories from junk food or takeaways, or expect a sugar or caffeine hit to revive you – though you're sure to be tempted at times. Remember that caffeine can create a vicious cycle if you are breastfeeding (see page 231).
- **Take extra B-complex vitamins,** but avoid yeast-based tablets if you are breastfeeding. Make sure your diet contains adequate magnesium (nature's relaxant): if you are breastfeeding, this will pass into your breast milk and help calm your baby, too. Magnesium is found in leafy green vegetables, seaweed and algae products.

- **Drink plenty of water**. Fatigue is one of the first and most common signs of dehydration. Drink whenever you breastfeed your baby, and at mealtimes, and carry a water bottle with you when you go out.
- **Get out of the house** at least once a day, even just to walk around the block. Walking with your baby in the pram or a sling revitalises you, tends to settle a crying baby, and helps you build up stamina. Exercise helps release the neurotransmitters serotonin and dopamine (which keep the lines of communication open within your nervous system) as well as endorphins (which create a sense of wellbeing). A recent clinical trial at Duke University Medical School (Blumenthal et al, 2007) reported that exercise was as effective as Zoloft (an antidepressant that increases serotonin in the brain) for patients with major depression. Also, patients who exercised were less likely to have recurrent episodes of depression. Of course, if you do have symptoms of depression, please seek medical help, as this really is a quality-of-life issue that affects yourself, your baby and your relationship (see chapter 12.)
- **Have a health check**. The tiredness you feel as a new mother is an indescribable shock, but if you are feeling more than reasonably tired, see your doctor. Ask to have your thyroid function and iron levels checked: impaired thyroid function and low iron levels are both reasonably common in the postnatal period, and cause extreme tiredness. Thyroid disorders can also cause symptoms of anxiety and depression, and extreme tiredness can also be a symptom of depression (see symptoms of PND on page 278).

'I have an underactive thyroid and have to take medication every day. After my baby was born, I started feeling really tired. I became very tearful and suffered from insomnia. It seemed like a cruel trick – I couldn't sleep even when my baby was sleeping.

'I went to the doctor. She ordered tests for my thyroid function and haemoglobin. My thyroid levels were way off the scale. I had been so tired that I'd forgotten to take my medication. Also, my system had changed after pregnancy and I needed an altered dosage.

'I had been so shitty that my relationship was shitty and I wasn't able to follow my instincts with my baby. I was swayed by what other people were telling me; it had become a mind-game between my instincts and their advice because I was so fragile. After I got more sleep and coped better, I was able to sort things out.'

Sophie, mother of one

When you are out of balance and feel like yelling or running away, it helps to take stock and consider how you can lighten the load. To be able to nurture your child, you need to nurture yourself, too.

Even if you only take short breaks, there are lots of little things you can do. You can make sure you eat well, exercise, relax and laugh (there is almost always a funny side, though you might have to call a very good friend to help you find it). Take catch-up naps: a fifteen-minute power nap may refresh you when you are flagging, or an afternoon nap may cancel out a sleep deficit (I often catch up with a doze on Saturday afternoon). Take turns with your partner or a good friend to have some 'me' time. Or simply enjoy the moments: the smell of your baby, the laughter of your children, the taste of food you love, the touch of your partner, the sound of a caring voice on the end of the phone.

'I think the hardest part about nurturing oneself is getting around the attitude that time and effort spent on me is selfish time. What rejuvenates me is dreamtime in the garden: wandering around and fantasising about what I will do next; how nice it will be when I can go and pick toma-toes; admiring achievements to date, like listening to the frogs clonking around my new little water feature (we have "pobblegonks", and they clonk!). I love to read – not trash, but good stuff that reconnects me to my intellectual and emotional self. Stuff that may stretch me just a little and remind me who I am beyond the walls of the house. And, while my toddler sleeps, a peep into the cot to see the sleeping angelic face, and to sneak out again and think: *Hmm, perhaps a half-hour nap?* Stolen time is delicious time, and I think it helps to have a little list in my mind of what I would do if I had half an hour, an hour, a day ... so that when it happens, I'm ready to make the most of it.'

Liz, mother of two

'Exercise! I love to get out by myself and go for a paddle on the river.'

John, father of two

Gaining perspective

You may have wondered how your mother managed, without 24-hour shopping, a fast-food outlet on every street corner and a household full of whiz-bang appliances. Sure, in those days many women were full-time mothers, but I believe that they tended to be more realistic about how much they could fit into their lives.

Although I am not suggesting for a moment that we should all become Stepford wives, we could certainly learn from our mothers. Do you, for example, remember wearing the same clothes all day when you were little? Or for more than one day? Well, how many times a day do you change your kids' clothes? And how many times a week (or a day) do you bundle your baby into the car and race to the supermarket when you have forgotten some minor item you could manage without if the shops were shut (or if you had to walk there)? Your mother certainly wouldn't have been 'available' to everybody all the time, as you are with a mobile phone and Internet access. Have you tried simply 'switching off' all technology for a day, a weekend or even a week? I don't give out my mobile number except to immediate family and a small number of friends – and even then, I rarely answer it. I figure I can only do one thing at a time and am not prepared to force myself to multi-task by taking calls while I am driving (I don't own a hands-free device), seeing clients or enjoying time with friends and family.

I feel a deep concern about mothers who have the Internet running all day when little children are around. Although social media may be your 'me' time and a way of connecting with the world, please take care that you aren't disconnecting from your children and giving them messages that you are 'unavailable' or resentful of their presence. It can also be much more uplifting for you to connect to others in real life – at a park, perhaps, with the children in tow. Plus, seeing other grubby kids, messy homes and not-so-yummy mummies in real life can be incredibly reassuring: you're not the only person finding life with small children a challenge.

Forget the windows

If you have a baby who seems to require constant feeding, toddlers who scatter mess and sticky fingerprints all around, or a child who often needs to have his emotional tank topped up, leaving you with nothing to show for your efforts at the end of the day even though you have been working flat out, remind yourself (and your partner, if necessary) that you have been building relationships with your children – arguably the most important job in the world.

One exercise to affirm that you haven't actually been doing nothing all day but watching your littlies make a mess is to pretend you are watching a video-recording of your day: visualise everything you have done from wiping noses and bottoms to cooking meals, paying bills, making appointments, reading stories and whatever else. You will be astounded at how much you have actually achieved and how multi-skilled you are!

Instead of fussing – the dust will wait, I can assure you – take your kids and go for a walk in the park or for a swim. Get some physical exercise and boost your endorphins; cut yourself some slack and try to laugh. This may mean you have to reach a compromise with your partner about domestic priorities, as happened in our household when the kids were small.

'My personal style tends towards organised chaos. My husband, on the other hand, likes order (and cleanliness). One day, when the kids were all little (four of them at that time), he arrived home from work to find me sitting on the floor feeding the baby (again). The boys had made a cubby out of all the chairs and blankets (yes, they had unmade the beds) and the three-year-old was listening to a story as I fed the baby. She had the

blocks and toy cars out around her. He made some unrepeatable comments about the mess, then glanced up and said, "And when was the last
time you cleaned the effing windows?"

'To me, this question was almost hysterically funny. Washing windows
was (and still is) a long way down my list of priorities. (As my children
grew, I paid them to do it!) The next day, I read the kids a fairytale for
inspiration and then gave them pots of paint and told them to paint lovely
pictures on the windows for Daddy. Our windows go from floor to ceiling, and all the bottom panels looked beautiful by the time Daddy came
home. As well, the kids were all bathed and clean, and dinner was ready
(we had played a 'hide the mess' game and popped everything that didn't
fit into toy boxes onto the table, bundled them up in a tablecloth and
stuffed the whole caboodle under a bed). As he came to the door, they
rushed to their Daddy and dragged him to the loungeroom, exclaiming
proudly, "Look at your pretty windows!"'

Pinky

It is helpful to recognise and acknowledge our personal load limit –
exactly how many balls we can keep aloft at once. One way to stay below
your limit is to drop one ball before you throw another one into the air – in
other words, if you take on an extra task, find a way to omit (or outsource)
something else. If, for instance, you volunteer to go on a school excur-
sion or you have an extra meeting, drop off some shirts at the drycleaners
to be ironed and/or buy a lasagne from the deli for dinner. It's better to
know your limits and keep fewer balls in the air than to drop your bundle
entirely.

Making it through the day

It's all too easy to glibly tell mothers to chill out and relax, forget the chores,
love your kids and all will be sweet. The truth is, most of us feel even worse
when our surroundings are in chaos. At the other end of the 'she'll be right'
approach is the 'rigid routine' brigade. Unfortunately, although the idea of

a meticulously planned daily routine can sound like a way to avoid chaos, it can also create added stress: if, for instance your baby won't wake up on time or feed according to scheduled times, you can feel completely over-whelmed. I often get called to visit mothers who tell me something like, 'I feel like a failure – my baby won't wake up for his 7 a.m. feed.' When I ask what time the baby was last fed, they will invariably tell me 5 or 5.30 a.m. Then I check the coffee table, where I usually find a book that advocates a rigid routine that the poor woman has been trying to implement right to the minute. My response, as I offer reassurance and explain that routines can be flexible, is that if you want to get up and start your day at 7 a.m., that's fine – you can have a peaceful shower, wash your hair or eat break-fast undisturbed. Or, if you prefer, you can snuggle down and have some extra sleep while your baby sleeps. Then, if you really want to follow a routine, you can start when your baby wakes for the day.

The early weeks can be the hardest as you struggle with seemingly con-stant interruptions to meet your baby's needs, but at first it is best to watch your baby and follow his lead as he sleeps and eats when his tiny body requires food or rest. It is also important to allow your milk supply to become established so that, later, your baby is more likely to settle into a predictable pattern all by himself because he is contented and well fed.

While predictability is more for your benefit than your baby's when he is very young, as your baby reaches toddlerhood and learns to anticipate what is happening, having a predictable rhythm to his day will encour-age cooperation and confidence. I find it works well for most families to have a gentle but flexible rhythm to their day. Make simple plans that suit your family needs, your baby's needs and, if you have older children, their activities as well. Apart from the fact that rigidly watching the clock and imposing a strict feeding and sleeping regime may not work for your indi-vidual baby, it is also likely to create added frustration as you find yourself trying to race the clock all day, especially if you have older children too. And if you do have appointments, work outside the home or have an older child's schedule to follow (they do need to be at school on time), tweaking your baby's feeds and giving him an occasional top-up before you leave for the school or kinder run is fine, as long as you aren't creating stress for your baby by trying to force her to feed when she isn't interested or making her wait to feed when she is hungry. See the checklist below for some ideas about planning your day.

✳ CHECKLIST : PLANNING YOUR DAY

- Take a good look at what you really need to get done and what you would like to fit in – while being realistic about the size of your to-do list – and work these around your littlies' needs.
- Instead of watching the clock and trying to keep to a strict schedule, break the day up into more flexible segments: early morning, late morning, early afternoon, late afternoon, evening. For instance, if your baby is more alert and happier to be out and about in the mornings, or your toddler needs an afternoon nap, you might plan outings or shopping trips in the morning and have a quiet afternoon at home. Or, if your baby has a longer nap in the morning and is more sociable in the afternoon, you could plan outings later in the day.
- Prepare dinner earlier in the day to avoid early-evening stress (let a slow cooker become your new best friend).
- If you have a toddler as well as a baby, set up an activity before you go to bed at night so that your toddler can start the day engaged in his 'surprise' and you can feed the baby/prepare breakfast/tidy the kitchen in peace. Then, after breakfast, you can head out the door with the baby in a pram or sling, where he can sleep while you walk. Take your littlies to the park, on an outing or a play-date and let your toddler get some physical exercise, too. Or perhaps you could do an outdoor activity at home, such as gardening, while the baby sleeps in her pram nearby. Later, when you get home, you can feed your littlies and have quiet time together or pop your toddler down for his afternoon nap. Your toddler will be much more agreeable about quiet time (and you won't be feeling guilty that you haven't spent any time with him) if you've been able to get out and engage in some activity together.

- Remember that your littlies' continuing development can mean that as soon as you feel you have 'nailed' a routine that works for you, it is likely to change again in just a few weeks, or sooner, as your baby changes his pattern – perhaps by dropping a sleep or having a feeding frenzy for a few days. Littlies can sense when you are feeling stressed and pushing yourself too hard – and you can bet that this will be reflected in their behaviour; they might be more wakeful at night or clingy during the day – so pacing yourself sensibly and being flexible is the key to creating a gentle rhythm to your days.

'I have let Paxton (ten months) be a go-with-the-flow baby. I take him to playgroup on Tuesday, swimming on Wednesday, morning tea with friends on Friday. I have found that he has naturally adjusted his sleeps to before and after these events so that, without trying, we have created a routine that suits. At night time, the three of us have cooked dinner and cleaned up by 6 p.m., ready for Paxton's bath, story, breastfeed and bed. My husband and I decided when we got married that we would not have a TV, which is great now because after Pax's in bed, we clean the kitchen and have some catch-up time with each other, followed by me going to bed early or having some "me" time. TV simply doesn't fit but everything else does, which is wonderful!'

Serena

Keeping up appearances

'Our mums' group started having morning tea at each other's houses, and when it was my turn, I couldn't even make the other women cups of coffee because my baby is so fussy. Now we have started doing lunches. How on earth can I keep up?'

Ali

Ali's distress brings back memories – and some trade secrets that I don't feel pressured to keep to myself any more. I would never have 'made it' in a mums' group full of Martha Stewart clones, either, but if a bit of honesty on my part couldn't have coaxed these girls out of their neatly folded closets, I wouldn't have let them beat me – I would have cheated! I'd have found a fabulous deli that does 'home cooking' and popped out some fresh quiches, breads and dips with a carafe of juice or iced water, and if I'd felt any guilt about not playing waitress, I've have muttered piously about how dangerous hot drinks are around small children!

Most of us feel pressured to put on a good front and show the world we are 'coping'. That's fine if it helps you feel positive, but with your friends it is better to be completely honest (isn't this the measure of a true friend – that they accept us warts and all?).You don't need to add to your stress levels by racing round polishing and cleaning when they come to visit. You might even be making them feel inadequate because they can't maintain the same high standards.

One of my favourite experiences regarding mummy peer pressure occurred at a mothers' group I attended when my kids were little. The coordinator asked all the mothers to introduce themselves in turn, and to tell us something they had enjoyed with their child that week. As we went around the circle, the mums became increasingly competitive: 'I took my child to the park every day,' 'I read three books every night,' 'I have a brilliant new routine and have been able to have special "couple time" every evening with my partner.' (You get the gist?) As I was wondering what to say when my turn came, the woman next to me blurted out, 'I have had an absolutely crap week. The baby has been sick and I haven't done any washing so I am wearing my husband's underpants!' Right there and then I decided I wanted this woman to be my new best friend. I knew there would be no pressure, no performance anxiety, just honesty and a feeling of safety as we shared the mothering load.

Delegate or delete

In your pre-baby career, you would not have hesitated to delegate or delete tasks that weren't productive. Now you not only find it really difficult to delegate (read, ask for help) because you are afraid of being judged, but also because you're not even sure what is 'productive' when you don't have immediately tangible evidence or measured outcomes.

Instead of sweating the small things and feeling that you aren't measuring up to everyone else's perfect mummy achievements (or unrealistic media images that are permeating your fragile mind), write out a list of everything you do – this may take a few days to jot down as you actually do tasks. Now, look at your list and consider whether all of these things have to be done. What could you leave off your list – for now, at least? What can you do less often? And what can you delegate? This may mean hiring some help or perhaps getting your partner or children to take on more responsibility by sharing the load.

It can also help to look at the beliefs and attitudes that might explain why you may not be delegating. Do you, for instance, feel that because you are an 'at home' mother, you 'should' do everything around the home? Are you working outside the home, so feel guilty about asking your children to help? Overcompensating by doing all of the household chores won't do your kids any favours. Eventually, they will have to leave the nest and what could be more devastating than knowing you haven't prepared them for independent living? Also, consider what messages you want your kids to take with them from your modelling: that housework is 'women's work'? That a woman's role is that of domestic servant?

Instead of becoming burnt-out or resentful about how your family members do or don't support you, remember that your partner and children aren't mind-readers. Discuss your needs calmly and ask for help when you need it – and do remember to say thanks, even if you feel it was the other person's duty anyway. We used to have a family clean-up on Saturday mornings: every child would choose a room and take responsibility for cleaning it. In an hour, we were all finished. Everyone would cooperate without complaint, and then we would have a nice leisurely lunch together.

To make things a little easier, below are some tips to help you create order from chaos.

✳ CHECKLIST : CREATING ORDER FROM CHAOS

- **Simplify mealtimes.** Work out a few simple meals and stock your cupboards with the ingredients so that you'll be able to whip up a meal quickly on busy days. (And on the days when you have time, cook extra and freeze leftovers as standby meals.) Serve fresh fruit instead of desserts. Eat some meals on paper plates or have picnics outdoors where the mess won't matter. Prepare dinner early in the day (or grab one of your freezer meals) so you aren't stressed when 'arsenic hour' arrives and you have a grizzly baby or grumpy kids to contend with. Useful appliances are a slow cooker and a rice cooker (you can prepare vegies early, then throw everything into your rice cooker and leave it alone to transform into a delicious risotto. Just add cheese and voila – a healthy meal!) Look for recipes that call for all the ingredients to be simply mixed together, such as Miraculous Quiche (recipe on page 266).
- **Divide your workload.** Don't knock yourself out trying to clean the whole house from top to bottom while the baby is asleep, only to find that you are exhausted by the time he wakes up. Plan one large job each day, such as vacuuming, cleaning the bathroom, or tidying one cupboard or bookshelf, and don't try to do more.
- **Make fewer shopping trips.** Keep a notepad or blackboard in the kitchen and jot down what you need as it occurs to you, then make one weekly or fortnightly shopping trip rather than racing out every day. Or, do your shopping online – most major supermarkets have this facility and they deliver. This will save you money as well as time because, even if you are charged a delivery fee, if you'd gone to the supermarket, you would have been tempted to spend money on extra groceries that you didn't really need.
- **Cut some corners.** Save time by not cleaning the bottoms of cooking pots (after all, black absorbs heat more efficiently!). Throw dishes into a sink of soapy water then come back later to rinse and leave them to air-dry or pack them into the dishwasher. Don't iron anything that crushes easily and, within five minutes of wear, would look like it

had never been ironed anyway. And don't bother to iron or even fold hankies, socks and other small stuff before you put them away. Buy socks all in the same colour and keep them together in a basket or drawer so you aren't searching for pairs. Hang shirts and 'ironable' clothes onto hangers immediately out of the washing machine – this will reduce creases and ironing.

- **Tidy up once, late in the day.** If you have a toddler as well as a baby, it can be frustrating if you try to keep things orderly all day. One late-afternoon tidy will help make you feel relaxed and less flustered as you face the dinner/bath/bedtime rush. It may also prevent friction with partners who have an aversion to coming home to apparent chaos. And aim for efficiency: walk around with a supermarket bag or a basket and collect everything that is scattered. Deliver the contents in one trip (later, if you like), rather than running the length of the house to put each object away separately. (Older kids can collect their own junk from the basket.) Get all kids (of any age, who can walk and talk) to help with tidy-ups. Make it a game at first: as long as you smile, they will never know the difference! Kids under six learn best by imitation, so work with them rather than expecting them to follow orders. And if you want kids to help, consider ways to make things easier for them – hangers that they can reach, for instance, and drawers/toy boxes/baskets with labels/pictures so they can put things in the right places. Also, eliminate things that are outgrown, unused or simply in the way – rotating a small number at a time (by putting the rest away out of sight) will help children enjoy their toys, play more creatively and make tidy-ups easier. It can help to create designated play spaces so mess is contained to one area, rather than scattered all through the house.
- **Wear your baby in a sling or backpack as you do chores.** He'll enjoy the ride and the view, and you'll get extra jobs done. And then you'll feel freer to take a catnap or have some 'me' time while he sleeps.
- **Provide a haven from the chaos.** Keeping small corners attractive, or one room tidy, can provide sanctuary when most of the place is

in a muddle. Little things like fresh flowers look cheerful. Burning essential oils (keep the burner away from small children, or course) makes for a calm and welcoming atmosphere.

- **Lower the lights**. Camouflage mediocre housekeeping by using candlelight (great for disguising dust) or low-voltage light bulbs (better for the environment, too).

- **Be kind to yourself**. Don't feel you have to be an all-dancing, all-singing entertaining mama as well as keeping an impeccable home – some days, you will manage children getting out all the puzzles or wallowing around in messy activities but, on difficult days, cut yourself some slack and give them stickers that are easy to clean up, take them outside and let them 'paint' the fence or a house wall with a small bucket of water and a large paintbrush (while you enjoy a quiet cuppa!), or pop on a DVD while you get a few things done.

Miraculous Quiche

This recipe, which involves no fussy pastry base, can be prepared in 5–10 minutes, even by an exhausted new mum. The added bonus is that there are no pots to watch over and it can be prepared ahead of time.

Whisk together:
3 eggs with ½ cup of self-raising flour (or ½ cup plain flour and ½ teaspoon baking powder), a cup of milk (or half milk/half cream).

Throw in a mix of chopped vegetables:
Try any combination of whatever vegetables you have at hand: tomato, mushroom, broccoli, asparagus, spinach, onions, grated potato or carrot. You can add bacon or chunks of salmon or even sundried tomato – whatever you like in a quiche.

Mix well, pour into a greased pie dish and top with grated cheese.

Bake at 180°C until your quiche is set. (Flour sinks to the bottom during cooking and forms a 'crust'.)

Asking for help

Believing we must be independent and never ask for help has to be one of the most difficult attitudes to unlearn. Yet, believe it or not, people are usually only too glad to help: amongst other things, they can then feel relaxed about asking you to return the favour sometime! But don't let that inhibit you. It is great to reciprocate, but if you aren't in a position to return the favour right now, or the person doesn't need help, you don't have to feel beholden. Maybe you can repay them in some way later, or pass the favour on to somebody else.

If you're uncomfortable about asking for help outright, try an indirect approach, such as leaving vegies on a chopping board on the kitchen bench. If you have a helpful visitor, you might find the whole meal prepared!

'We sent out two cards with our baby-shower invitations. These were for people to fill in instead of buying presents for the baby. On one card we asked people to write a piece of good advice about parenting, and on the other card, they wrote a pledge of support – some way they could help us during the first six weeks, like walking the dog, mowing the lawn or bringing a meal.

'At the baby shower, we all sat in a circle and people read out their cards. There was serious advice and very funny advice, and then they read their pledges of support. As new parents to be, it felt as though we were surrounded by a lot of love and commitment.'

Sue, mother of one

Saying 'no'

The flip side of asking for help is learning how to say 'no'. It seems that this is a difficult undertaking for most women: a 1999 survey in the US magazine *Working Mother* found that only one-third of mothers set limits and boundaries with others, and 54 per cent wanted to learn to say no when asked to take on an extra activity.

It can be difficult to say no, even to the same old 'users' who are miraculously unavailable when you need them, especially if they catch you unawares. You might have to learn their cues: 'Are you going to be home today?' may mean, 'I need somebody to leave my kids with while I go shopping/out to lunch/to the hairdresser.' If you have a 'friend' like this, have a few ready answers. If they are the kind who drop by without calling first and ask whether it's okay to leave the twins with you for a couple of hours, try saying, 'Sorry, I'm just rushing to the doctor. Little Johnny has been vomiting.' (Keep your handbag/nappy bag near the door.)

It can be much more difficult to say no to activities that are related to your child in some way – like committees, meetings and school activities – but it is important to prioritise. If the time required is going to compromise the family balance (or your own personal balance), then you need to be strong and decline. Sometimes, you can offer an alternative: instead of going to meetings, I've often said, 'I'm sorry, I can't get there. Can you delegate me a task I can do in my time?' or 'Would you like me to write a press release/put up some posters/phone somebody?'

When you have babies or little children, you may also have to guard your energy levels and learn to decline invitations to potentially tiring events. This may take some negotiating and support from your partner – or perhaps you can juggle your time and/or have an afternoon nap to fill your 'sleep bank', or organise extra help so you can sleep in the next day.

Sharing the load

Even the most recent studies seem to show that women in a relationship still do most of the housework. Nobody has ever included me in one of those surveys: if they did, it might tip the balance in favour of the guys!

It can take a radical shift of consciousness for both partners and lots of ongoing negotiation to find a balance around sharing the workload of caring for a home and family. I was conditioned to be a 'good wife': my mother used to clean my father's shoes before he went out – without her – every Saturday night. On the other hand, my husband was the baby of the family and, until we married, lived with his widowed mother who looked after his every need. That was a hard act to follow.

For my partner and I, the breeze of change blew in when I was pregnant for the first time. One day, as we were getting ready for work, he asked me where his clean shirts were. 'Oh,' I said, 'there weren't any in the wash.' As he glanced towards the pile of clothes on the floor, I patted my burgeoning belly, sighed and told him, 'I just can't bend down and pick those up any more.' We have come a long way since then. One evening, a little friend had come to play with our youngest child. Our eldest son was ironing (I taught my kids early how to use a washing machine, and by high-school age, I put a laundry hamper in their rooms so that their clothes were their responsibility – if they ran out of clean clothes, they didn't complain to me!). The little visitor exclaimed, 'Everyone in your house does ironing!', at which our littlie looked puzzled and asked, 'Who does the ironing at your place?' 'Only my mum,' said the visitor. Ours quickly advised him, 'You better learn to iron, or you'll never get a girlfriend.'

How you negotiate the workload (including the paid work) in your relationship is, of course, your business. And how you divvy things up will depend to a great extent on the dynamics of your relationship. Sometimes the division will not be exactly equal: one of you could be facing extra pressures, or work arrangements will present difficulties. If things are out of balance for too long, though, talk about your feelings. Don't become a martyr to your spouse or to your kids. This is likely to make you resentful, and resentment will eat away at your relationships and your soul.

'This is my second family. I have a son and daughter in their early thirties, and a three-year-old. The first time round I was young and ambitious. I saw my job as a provider. I always had two jobs and my wife looked after the children. I was working so hard, the dog would bark when I came home and the kids would call me "Mister". I have learned that, at the end of the day, the money doesn't matter. That song "The Cat's in the Cradle" is so apt.

'I have quite a good relationship with my older kids now, but when you don't spend the time with them when they are little, they become very independent of you. When it would be nice to see more of them, they don't need you – they have their own lives. I am enjoying spending time with Anna as a little person and helping shape her values.'

Angus, father of three

Dealing with guilt

Parent-blaming has become an industry. There are shelves of best-selling books devoted entirely to the sins of mothers and fathers – the sins that are screwing up our kids and defining our family lives as 'dysfunctional'. If you are parents of a newborn, your greatest fear might be that you will screw up your child for life if you don't get every single detail of nurturing absolutely perfect; you might feel that any slip-up could either create bad habits or cause irreparable damage.

There are therapists who caution us against becoming 'toxic parents' or 'parents who love too much'. We could be guilty of 'emotional incest' or we could become 'enmeshed'. We could be over-responsible or we could be neglecting our duty. (But hey, it mightn't *all* be our fault – we can lay part of the blame on our parents for the dodgy job they did bringing us up!)

Much of this blame – particularly for children's mental health – is laid on mothers. (Many fathers I speak to claim that they don't have any feelings of guilt about their efforts at child-rearing, and don't even understand what I'm talking about – a good thing for them!)

None of us sets out to be a bad parent. In fact, it's probably our desire to be 'good' parents that causes us to be so ridden with guilt (or guilt's companions: shame and embarrassment) when we or our children muck up or when we simply can't live up to our own or other's high expectations. Often, the standards bar is set far too high and the support level far too low for the multi-tasking mother.

'I operate a manufacturing business from home. I also have a part-time job as a television newsreader. Juggling is my middle name, although often it's guilt that I juggle as well as tasks. If I'm at the post office, I wince that I'm not making balloon animals for my three-year-old. If I'm trading gurgles with my newborn, I feel the unsent invoices burning a hole in my desk. Playgroup? I'm jumping and grooving and thinking of marketing strategy.'

Christie, mother of a six-month-old and a three-year-old

Good guilt!

It's helpful to remember that guilt and other associated feelings may be triggered by external forces (like unrealistic media images) and that they may arise out of situations over which you have no control. However, they are your emotions and you can't afford to ignore them, just in case they are an early warning sign that all is not well with your choices. You don't have to be driven by guilt, but you do need to learn to differentiate between the guilt you feel for short-changing your child and the guilt you feel about not meeting unrealistic and limiting expectations. Perhaps we should sort our guilty feelings into 'good guilt' (which motivates us to explore options and try to make improvements) and 'bad guilt' (which stirs us into beating ourselves up unnecessarily). Having said that, I barely have time to sort the laundry, let alone guilt!

It doesn't matter whether your children have homemade cookies in their lunch boxes or whether you feed them baked beans on toast for dinner. But if your kids have parents who feel utterly lousy about themselves most of the time, this will negatively impact their self-esteem. And if you feel guilty about being a lousy parent, you are likely to try to compensate by letting your kids do whatever they please or by buying them lots of things. Another negative about guilt is that dwelling on it can take you away from the present and stop you enjoying your baby right now.

Guilt is really only legitimate if you have let another person down. If you feel guilty, it can help to ask yourself where the feeling is coming from. Are you really letting your child down? What are your true responsibilities? What can you change? Where can you find support?

A cheer squad

We all need a cheer squad – people who reinforce our sense of worth, as parents and as people. Being a parent is an enormous job, especially if you have kids with special needs or you are on your own. A support group can be an invaluable source of help and information, in all sorts of situations. You may be dealing with an ongoing crisis, such as an illness in the family. You may be getting negative feedback about your style of parenting. Or you may just want to share a positive environment with like-minded people.

Becoming a parent gives a whole new meaning to the term 'network'. To form your own network, list five people (besides your partner, if you have one) you feel you could call on for help. Next, write down the kinds of support you would find most helpful – then set out to find it. Your list should include a neighbour you can call in an emergency; an experienced mother who will offer support without judging you; and several 'back-up' people. To this list, add emergency contacts such as your family doctor, a local hospital, and the poisons information hotline. You might also want access to breastfeeding help, emotional support, a supermarket and/or fruit shop that delivers and, for desperate situations, the local pizza takeaway. Keep your list of helpers (with contact details) next to the phone.

Many parents find support on the Internet. This isn't the same as a face-to-face chat or a real shoulder to cry on, but there is somebody out there around the clock and it can be amazing to discover that parents all over the world have similar concerns and feelings. If this appeals to you, do some surfing and find some sites that support your parenting style and provide good health information. Consider subscribing to relevant online newsletters.

'Mothers' groups and playgroups have been my lifeline. As a new mum, I made the most of every other mum I met. I would pick their brains. The best people to ask for advice are the people who are in there doing it. They know how you are feeling. Over the last month, I've been asking other mums, 'What do your kids eat?' I was concerned my kids weren't eating enough of the right sorts of food. One mother suggested adding it up over a week rather than worrying every day. That made sense and now I am relaxed about it.'

Elli, mother of two toddlers

'I have been going to a men's group for the past five years. It is leaderless. For about two-and-a-half hours, we just talk about our lives. There are rules about confidentiality and one person talking at a time. It is about what people bring to the group. Out of nine guys, only two are not health professionals, but we all have an interest in self-growth. At first; only one of the guys was a father; now, almost half of us are fathers and we look to him [the first father] as the "experienced" one. Mostly, when men get together, the focus is on an activity rather than talking. For us, there is no 'action'; here, the activity is sitting and talking. It is really nurturing to simply share experiences without advice or problem solving.'

David, father of a toddler and a baby

Supporting each other

Parents can offer each other support by being honest and non-judgemental. I feel saddened when I see mothers bickering about parenting choices (men don't seem to play such silly games). Issues such as how you feed your child (breast or bottle?); how you sleep (co-sleeping or cot or separate bedrooms?); how you educate (public or private?); and so on can be incredibly divisive. It would be nice if mummies remembered to play nicely, took a step back and realised that whatever our chosen parenting style, it is hard work and most people cross over stereotypes anyway. It can take time to work out a parenting style that suits you and your child, and it can also take time to get used to this brave new role. So, instead of categorising other parents and perhaps dismissing the possibility that you may actually have a few things in common – despite feeding or transporting your babies differently – try to see things from their perspective.

Also, try reaching out: next time you are at a shopping centre and see another mother struggling or 'losing it', offer her a hand. If you can't manage that, at least give her a smile. Too often, mothers are judged harshly by anyone who is present at the time. One local mother who smacked her toddler in a shopping centre was followed to the car by a man who took her registration number and reported her. This 'good Samaritan' could simply have offered to push the mother's trolley so she could carry the child. Instead, the mother had to endure the distress of facing a child-abuse charge (which was dismissed) in court.

Another mother whose toddler threw a tantrum in a supermarket car-park found herself the subject of a newspaper's parenting column. The writer was highly critical of the mother's solution to the tantrum problem – she reached into her trolley and gave the kid a piece of chocolate (shock horror!).

We are all responsible for the quality of parenting that children receive – all children, not just our own. And the quality of care many kids get could be improved with a little support for their parents. You do have a responsibility to report genuine abuse, but we all have bad days and who knows how any one of us will deal with a particular situation until we are in it ourselves?

An Ad Man's Woman

'I knew I'd be a perfect mother. And my perfect baby would be a credit to my perfect mothering. I knew, too, that I would never 'let myself go' – that I would always be immaculately groomed and, eventually, surrounded by a whole family of perfectly clean, perfectly behaved children and a perfectly adoring husband in a gleaming, perfectly sparkling home.

'Of course, back in those perfect days BC (Before Children), I also pictured babies either peacefully sleeping or smiling Heinzfully day and night. I imagined toddlers cutely toddling (never climbing or spilling) between afternoon naps and bedtime stories. I visualised crisply Fabulon-ed children, happily playing in sandpits (never mud). I would take my perfect brood for frolics in the park, with my long red hair (semi-permanent, naturally) blowing in the breeze. Then I would feed my hungry little human beans and tuck them into bed before a gourmet dinner for two, prepared with my own perfectly manicured hands. I'd be simply irresistible and he'd love how my hair shone.

'Alas, I wasn't like the TV mothers. I learned that happiness was not a dry nappy. I had nightmares about drowning under piles of nappies. I felt as though I was drowning in breast milk. In the supermarket, another shopper whispered, "Excuse me, your milk is leaking." Can you imagine a better start to the day? I automatically made an embarrassed check. It was the carton in the trolley she had been referring to!

'I gave up being a Wella Woman sometime during the first year of motherhood. The baby woke up every time I was about to wash my hair (and whenever my beloved told me he loved how my hair shone), and there would be another centimetre of regrowth.

'In between mopping up the spilt milk, I only ate half as much. And when the children didn't empty their plates, it would be half as much again. I used to look great in a mini, too! There were night howls and musical beds. I started asking, "Have you got any protection?"'

'Oh ad man, ad man, show me the way,

To be that perfect woman every day.

Yes, I'll shave and deodorise every inch of me.

I'll be an ad man's woman – naturally.'

Manic Mothers

12

Postnatal depression

♥

The harsh realities of new parenthood – when the long-awaited child doesn't sleep, eat and smile like the dream child in the soft-focus TV ads – can come as a complete shock. This is compounded by our feeling that we must put on a happy face in order to show the world that we are in charge. This not only adds to our own sense of inadequacy, but prevents us from reaching out for the kind of support that could make things much more bearable for us, our partners and our children.

'People would say, "You must be so happy!" Part of me was thinking: *I should be happy, I am a father.* But our lives had changed so dramatically that we were tired and stressed for weeks and months. I had to get used to the changes in the relationship with my partner. One day I was the centre of attention and the next day I wasn't. There were times when I wondered what was going on. I would wonder: *Does this mean there is anything wrong with me, or with me as a father?'*

Richard, father of a one-year-old

'It takes a lot of energy to be faced with the completely new every day. It's like being in a new country and not being able to speak the language or read the signposts. I found it quietly terrifying that I was no longer able to do things confidently. Things other women were doing so easily such as changing nappies, feeding the baby and having a shower every day. I was utterly lost in this new country.

'I walked around in a capsule of exhaustion. I had never not coped before, except when I was sick. I couldn't understand how I couldn't manage to find the time to take a two-minute shower during the day. I wondered what was wrong with me. I felt embarrassed and guilty because I thought I was the only one feeling like that. It seemed to me that other women coped. Other women brushed their hair, other women fitted back into their clothes after giving birth. Other women didn't alienate their partners by being a bitch. Other women had partners who understood. Other women's babies slept.'

Erina Reddan, author of Baby Daze

Crying more than your baby?

Evidence suggests that as many as 40 per cent of women experience some distress in adjusting to the demands of motherhood. Some of these women will cross over the line from distress into postnatal depression (PND). It is also becoming more widely recognised that fathers, too, can experience adjustment difficulties and depression after the birth of a baby.

The passing 'baby blues', where you are weepy for no apparent reason in the days following the birth (typically between the third and fifth day after delivery), affect up to 80 per cent of women. About 10 to 15 per cent of women develop moderate to severe postnatal depression, requiring medical treatment. One mother of four who experienced PND with her first child but has been well after subsequent births compares the two states: 'There is a vast difference between tiredness and the black despair of postnatal depression.' At the other end of the spectrum from the baby blues is postpartum psychosis, a severe psychiatric disorder that affects only two or three in 1000 women; symptoms include delusions and manic behaviour, and help should be sought urgently. Although this is not common, women who do experience postpartum psychosis usually become ill within days of their baby's birth so are likely to be either in hospital or at home with somebody present who can get appropriate care very quickly (call your GP or the hospital where your baby was born for referrals). And, although it is frightening for family members to see a new mum 'unravelling', sufferers will recover with prompt and effective treatment.

> 'I had heard about the baby blues, but I sailed past the third and fourth days and thought: I must be fine – I'm not going to get the blues. Then, on the fifth day, I got up to do the vacuuming. I plugged in the cleaner and it wouldn't go, so I plugged it into another outlet and it still didn't work. I picked up the machine and hurled it out the back door, then started crying uncontrollably.
>
> 'Normally, a little thing like a broken vacuum cleaner wouldn't worry me at all – I would just have said, "Damn, it doesn't work." But all that day, the smallest thing would trigger another bout of tears – something on television or a comment from my mother, or nothing at all. I took everything personally. I cried uncontrollably for about twenty-four hours, and then, just as suddenly, I stopped. I have been fine ever since.'
>
> *Hayley, mother of a six-month-old*

Postnatal depression (PND) can develop during pregnancy, immediately after birth or slowly in the weeks or months that follow. It can occur after a live birth, a still birth, an easy birth or a complicated delivery, a miscarriage or a termination. Symptoms of PND include:

- mood swings and extreme irritability (your partner can't get anything right, no matter how hard he tries)
- sleep disturbances unrelated to the baby's needs (this seems like a cruel joke – your baby is sleeping soundly and you are wide awake)
- appetite disturbance
- chronic exhaustion
- hyperactivity (ironing at 3 a.m.?)
- uncontrollable crying

- loss of memory or concentration
- anxiety or panic
- unrealistic feelings of inadequacy or guilt
- loss of libido

Postnatal depression – just like any form of depression – is a serious condition that can be damaging to the whole family, not just the sufferer. Yet the condition is not widely acknowledged or understood in the community; women in its clutches have been told to 'Snap out of it' or 'Pull yourself together', and partners have been given well-meant but inappropriate advice such as, 'Take her out to dinner.'

PND has been attributed to various non-clinical factors, including the changing role of women, the low status of mothering, the medicalisation of childbirth and unrealistic expectations of motherhood. In fact, it is more likely that a range of interrelated biochemical, psychological and social factors – hormonal and other physiological changes during pregnancy and after the birth, stress or trauma in early life, or a family history of mental or emotional illness – predisposes people to depression.

Kathleen Kendall-Tackett, author of *The Hidden Feelings of Motherhood*, describes depression as 'an illness that affects your mind and body and that both your body and mind contribute to depression. For instance, a chemical imbalance in our brains can influence our emotions and on the other hand, our thoughts, experiences and behaviour can affect the biochemistry of our brains. The "up side" of this is that we can make conscious choices to create and support a healthy brain biochemistry, such as making dietary changes and exercising daily – carbohydrates and exercise can increase levels of serotonin, a calming chemical. And, because looking at events negatively can elicit the release of cortisol (a stress hormone), that can increase your susceptibility to depression, it can help to implement some stress management and relaxation techniques such as meditation, as well as trying to maintain a positive outlook.'

Another factor in the incidence of depression, especially in postnatal women, could be diet: a US study (Hibbeln, 2002) identified a link between low levels of DHA (an essential fatty acid found abundantly in dark-fleshed fish such as salmon and tuna) and PND. It showed that maternal levels of DHA become depleted as the body automatically provides for the developing infant's needs during pregnancy. Low levels of DHA can lead to reduced concentrations of serotonin, which has been linked to depression.

Another US study, at the University of Arizona Medical School (Freeman, 2006), showed that increasing the intake of DHA reduced symptoms of postnatal depression in women who had already been diagnosed with the condition.

Whatever the cause, it is essential to seek medical attention if you develop depression at any time, as it can have devastating effects on your relationships with your partner and children as well as your own health – the chronically elevated cortisol levels that characterise anxiety and depression can suppress your immune system and have been linked to atrophy of the hippocampus, a brain structure responsible for memory and learning.

> 'When my husband went to work I would sit in the rocking chair crying. It was like paralysis. I wouldn't answer the door or the phone. I wouldn't go out. If I did manage to go out I was too scared to come home to an empty house. It was an enormous effort just to go to the supermarket. I would watch other mothers enjoying their babies. I wondered why I didn't feel like that. I loved him but it was as though there was a wall between us.'
>
> *Evelyn, mother of one*

Family impact

PND can impact on those nearest and dearest to you. It is not uncommon for women to turn on their partners, and for partners in turn to be distressed because they can't 'fix' the problem.

> 'I couldn't understand why I was being rejected in so many ways. I came home from work and tried to help by bathing the kids and doing the housework. But because of her mindset, if I helped, I was trying to show her up. If I didn't, I was a lazy sod. I was angry at other people who,

because my partner's illness was invisible, thought she was weak. Sometimes I was angry at her, but then I felt extremely guilty. My feelings of helplessness were heightened because of my work as a personnel manager with a large city company. I have counselled people who wanted to slash their wrists, but I couldn't get through to my wife.'

Chris, father of two

Depression, if left untreated, can not only affect the way you interact with your baby and children, but can lead to serious longer-term outcomes: the stress of an angry or withdrawn mother will in turn increase cortisol levels in little ones, and this has been shown to have adverse effects on infants' developing brains, possibly increasing their predisposition to depression and anxiety.

This isn't meant to make you feel guilty for having an illness that is no more your fault than, say, a broken leg. And I would like to stress that children are unlikely to be deprived if the illness is treated promptly. In fact, so long as you get early treatment and appropriate support, it is more likely that you will feel as though you have missed out on precious time with your baby, rather than that your baby will suffer adverse effects because of your illness.

So, if you are experiencing some of the symptoms listed above or seem to be suffering more than the 'baby blues', it is important to acknowledge the possibility that you may have depression and to seek help so that you can receive appropriate treatment, recover and enjoy your children.

'I couldn't bear to be home alone so I used to walk my baby in the pram, up and down the local shopping strip. One day, I walked into the doctor's surgery to ask about a little sunspot on my face. He must have seen I was depressed.

'He said, "Is there anything else you would like to ask me about?"

'I replied, "No, I'm fine."

'He said, "Are you sure? I'm more than willing to listen."

'I bolted because I felt so ashamed. I had a beautiful baby. I thought: *I should be happy.* I lost the perfect (and only) opportunity I had to ask for help – I let the pressure to be the perfect mother stop me. Then I spiralled into a deep depression.

'I would wake up in the morning feeling that I couldn't look after myself, yet knowing that I had to get up and feed and dress a baby. When I was feeding my baby and laughing with her, it was the biggest act. What I really wanted was for my mother to come and look after me. I felt I had to be extra happy in front of my child because I had read about all the harmful effects of depressed mothers, so I would be laughing with her and crying at the same time, my emotions were so mixed up. When I played with my baby and blew raspberries on her little neck, I would tell her, "I'm sorry you got such a failure of a mother." At playgroup, I would listen to women judging other mothers. I couldn't tell them how I was feeling, or they would be talking about me next.

'When I had my second baby, I would take my baby and toddler out in the pram together and people would look into the pram and say, "Oh, you've got a boy and a girl. Aren't you lucky!" I would grit my teeth and squeeze my mouth into a smile and say, "Yes."

'I was beyond asking for help and other people didn't see it. Finally, when my youngest child was three (I had been unwell since my first child was born) and my eldest was five, I was sitting in the lounge one night with a handful of pills. I said to my husband, "You have to help me or I will take these and you can have [the kids] and look after them all by yourself." I thought they would be better off without me. He took me straight to the doctor. I was in hospital for three months.'

Ruth, mother of two

Help available

The good news about PND is that it is treatable. And, the sooner you get help, the more quickly you will recover. There is a range of treatments, from psychological therapies to medication – and yes, there are safe medications for women who are breastfeeding. So, if you suspect that you or your partner may be suffering from PND, you can discuss this with your maternal and child-health nurse or your GP, or you can call one of the services listed in the Resources section of this book.

Lisa Fettling experienced PND after her first baby. She stresses the importance of waiting until you are well before becoming pregnant again, and of setting up support networks for any subsequent pregnancies. When I interviewed Lisa, she said:

'When I had my second baby, I chose my obstetrician on the basis of which hospital my psychiatrist would go to. I wanted them to "meet in the corridor" if I became unwell again. I found a fantastic obstetrician. He didn't dismiss my fears and say, "Don't worry about it [happening again]." He simply reassured me that if it happened, we could deal with it early. I felt more confident knowing that he was watching me closely and that if PND, recurred it was treatable.'

Lisa points out that the pressure on women to be 'good' mothers discourages them from seeking help. She says, 'It is up to everybody – neighbours, friends and family – to recognise the symptoms of depression and know where to go for help. Because postnatal depression has such a devastating effect on the whole family – partners, children and worried grandparents – early intervention could prevent an enormous amount of distress.' (See **Resources** for more about Lisa.)

'Two months before my third baby was born, I began experiencing feelings of extreme anxiety. I'd had two children with no difficulties so I tried to talk myself out of the feelings, but still I had this overwhelming sense that something was dreadfully wrong.

'Within hours of the birth of my baby, I had lost touch with reality. I was hearing voices which were telling me to harm myself and my baby. There was just a tiny thread of reality holding me back.

'With shock waves rippling through the family, I was admitted to a general psychiatric unit, rather than a mother/baby unit specialising in the treatment of postnatal mood disorders.

'At psychotherapy sessions, I heard about other people's genuine hardships. I thought: *I have three beautiful children, a husband who loves me, no mortgage – I have no right to be like this.* Nobody bothered to explain that I had an illness that was treatable and that I would get better. I thought: *This is my lot in life, now.* I felt that my family would be better off without me. I was advised by a psychiatrist that I needed more adult stimulation and that I should return to my former employment as a maths/science teacher. It was absurd – I couldn't add two and two together! How could returning to work suddenly give me back my faculties?

'After I was well again, I harboured fears that my illness would affect my two older children in the longer term. I was concerned they'd be scarred for life. Then, a year or so later, as we were driving past the hospital, one of the children commented, "That's the hospital where Mummy went." I could see he seemed to be remembering. I asked, "What do you remember?" He said, "They had pretty fish in the tank."'

Leanne, mother of three

Someone to hear me

We usually associate grief with death and dying. But there are many losses in life that we need to let ourselves mourn; they don't all involve a death and are not all marked by any rituals or cards, yet they are profound nonetheless. These may include the experience of miscarriage, or the loss a mother feels when she has missed precious moments of her child's infancy because she was ill with PND. It may be the shattered dreams of parents whose child is abused or becomes seriously ill, or who has a disability or other difficulties.

In the case of pregnancy loss, for instance, there tends to be little acknowledgement outside the family, and fathers in particular may be overlooked altogether.

'While I was wrapped in the knowledge that others were there for me, I didn't realise that [my husband] Peter wasn't enjoying a similar sense of empathy from them. I was shocked, therefore, when he pointed out that all the cards that came with the flowers and all the letters that people had taken the time to write were addressed to me alone. All he said was, "They were my babies, too."

'You can't deny that the majority of adult men have been brought up to behave in ways which show they are strong, tough, unbreakable, incapable of deep sorrow, and free from emotional baggage. These are now outdated expectations of manhood, which make the open expression of grief unacceptable. It is hard enough for most men to externalise their emotions through tears or words, but doing so is even more difficult if they see the attention, the flowers and the care being directed towards the mother. When this happens, the traditional expectations he has been brought up with are reaffirmed, and instead of reaching out for love and support in his own right, he gives what he has left to his partner. The tragedy is that he is often left wanting.'

From A Silent Love *by Adrienne Ryan*

Virginia Lafond, a Canadian social worker and author of *Grieving Mental Illness*, advocates deliberate, conscious grieving as a means of facing the reality of an illness or loss. She offers practical strategies for getting in touch with and managing your feelings to help you regain a sense of control over your life. One way to do this is to work out what feeling you are experiencing and to accept that it is okay to be feeling this way. Then try asking yourself: How can I work with this feeling? What can I do in a constructive way to help me cope?

When you are grieving and feel sad or angry (anger is a legitimate emotion, often an expression of pain or fear), it helps to talk to somebody who cares. This doesn't have to be a professional, just a supportive person. If they don't 'hear' you, find someone else and don't let that experience invalidate your pain. If you hurt, you hurt – you don't need to wear a plaster cast to prove it.

If you find you can't come to terms with a loss, can't accept it or find a sense of peace, it is wise to seek help from a professional. Just as you go to a dentist or doctor when you have physical pain, it is important to get help for emotional pain. For the sake of both yourself and your loved ones, ask for help – again and again – until somebody listens.

13
Body image

♥

The messages on the magazine stand are loud and clear: yummy mummies look gorgeous and slim as soon as possible after giving birth. (Think Reese, Britney and Catherine Zeta-Jones, who, incidentally, was lauded for putting herself in the hands – or should that be on the treadmill? – of a personal trainer just hours after her first baby was born so that she could fit into her slinky wedding dress.) Those who don't are likely to have their wobbly bits blown up in full-colour cover shots. But if trim and taut are terrific, where does that leave the rest of us who are soft, round and droopy?

When you are exhausted and overwhelmed by the relentlessness of caring for a baby, and when you can't even recognise the body you see in the mirror, it doesn't help to have your man ogling a babe on the television. It is a sad reflection on our times when women with new babies feel that they need to live up to some ideal of a yummy mummy come perfect mother come domestic goddess.

Body image and self-esteem are so strongly connected in the West that beauty issues become inextricably linked with self-esteem. Instead of being able to say, 'I feel unhappy,' you say, 'I am fat,' and when you allow judgemental comments and unreal expectations to chip away at your self-esteem, it becomes all too easy to believe that how you look is who you are: that fat signifies an inability to take control of your life while a lean, toned body is a triumph of order over nature's raw energy. Struggling to maintain an 'ideal' body shape can be less about health or appearance and more about trying to be in control. Soon, you move away from being aware of your body and its feelings; instead, your body becomes an object to be either punished or rewarded. (If you are a good little body, I will buy you new clothes . . .). Remember, there is a person in there and she deserves to be treated with love and kindness, not to mention a little respect.

'When I was overwhelmed in the early months and feeling less than "hot", it wasn't so much about my body image – I never looked like the babes on television before I had a baby, so why would I expect to look like one now? If I could get a bit of space for myself – even to read a book in bed for half an hour without either a baby or partner making demands on me – I felt much better. I didn't have the energy to care about trying to be hot. I figured that my partner was a bit like a starving man: he would be grateful for any crumbs he got. And the more supported I felt, the more likely he was to get "dessert".'

Lara

Your pregnant body

From the moment your pregnancy becomes visible, you can be certain that some people will take the liberty of making comments such as, 'My, you are getting big!' or 'I bet you'll be glad to get your figure back,' when really, your greatest concern is more likely to be, 'How will I get this baby out of my body?'

Your feelings about your body during pregnancy reflect your views on sexuality, your partner's views, and the views that have been handed down to you about what it means to be a woman. They will also vary depending on whether it's your first pregnancy or a later one, whether the pregnancy was a surprise or planned, and so on. It can take a while to adjust to your new body, especially if body image has been important to you. Some women despair ('Now my body's ruined, anyway') and start binge-eating. Others are so terrified of putting on weight that they exercise or diet excessively during pregnancy, which can result in a low birth weight for the baby and a predisposition to prematurity or to mental or physical problems. (And, contrary to popular opinion, a small baby does not necessarily mean an easier birth.) Evidence suggests that women who feel unattractive before or during pregnancy are much more likely to gain too little weight prior to giving birth.

A pregnant body is, however, governed by factors beyond the control of diet and exercise. Your body shape and size are to a large extent genetically determined, and when you are pregnant, your partner's genes also come into the equation. (If he tops 1.8 metres and you are only up to his armpit, you could well be carrying a big baby.)

Vicki is a photographer who specialises in beautiful black-and-white images of pregnancy. She is tiny but has a tall partner and gave birth to a bonny 4.5-kilogram boy.

'I had a dreamy image of pregnancy. All the pregnant women I saw had beautiful bodies. I had only ever seen one woman with stretch marks. Now, I realise that the ones who didn't feel comfortable with their bodies didn't come to have them photographed.

'I was fascinated by my body as it grew, but at around five months I felt as though my skin couldn't possibly stretch any more. All of a sudden, I was covered in stretch marks. Only now (a year later), people are being honest and saying, "You were so big – we felt sorry for you."

'I made a plaster cast of my belly and decorated it while I was pregnant. I'm so glad I did that.'

Vicki

Your post-birth body

Though you may be feeling extra vulnerable after the birth of your baby, making it difficult to come to terms with your new, larger body, don't be in a hurry to shed those extra kilos straight away. The additional weight you carry after giving birth is part of your baby's life-support system. While you are pregnant, your body stores fat to ensure that you have extra nutrients available for breastfeeding. About six months of breastfeeding tends to whittle weight off without you having to make any special effort, although some women do hold that extra weight until after their baby is weaned.

In any case, dieting doesn't work. Reducing your food intake merely signals your metabolism to slow down (your body goes into famine mode and stores fat), and when you increase your intake again – boom! Back comes the weight. Also, reducing your food intake while you are breast-feeding may disrupt your milk supply. And rapid weight loss may release toxic residues (such as pesticides) into your milk as your body fat breaks down. Listen to your body signals: rest when you feel tired and eat nutritious foods when you feel hungry.

Once your bleeding has stopped (or after six weeks, if you have a caesarean), try some gentle exercise: just as an athlete returns to training slowly after an injury, your body needs time to recover from the birth. Take your baby walking (in a pram or a sling) as soon as you feel up to it, gradually increasing the distance you walk. Exercise, of course, also releases endorphins that enhance your general wellbeing, and an increased milk supply is the likely result.

One form of exercise you can (and should) do soon after the birth is to tone up your pelvic floor muscles. In fact, it's important for all women to do pelvic floor exercises throughout life, not just in the first weeks after having a baby. You may be just fine right now, after one baby, but your pelvic floor may be weakened after subsequent babies or as a result of the hormonal changes that occur at menopause. Then, all of a sudden, you find yourself peeing every time you laugh, cough or sneeze, and you may then need specialist help or even surgery. It's much better to be religious about doing pelvic floor exercises now – and you can start these during pregnancy.

Fortunately, you can do these exercises anywhere, any time – and no one will know. All you need to do is to draw in your vagina and urethra as though you were gripping a tampon, squeeze and hold for about five seconds, and then let go before repeating. Try five squeezes ten times a day (but don't worry too much about counting – just do it!) If you find yourself forgetting to do the exercises, remind yourself by putting brightly coloured stickers in various places around the house, or use other cues such as waiting at traffic lights, during television commercials or as you chop the vegetables.

Don't bounce into a heavy gym regime too soon after the birth, as the hormonal changes you've undergone put you at risk of overstraining joints and ligaments, and weakening your pelvic floor. In addition, heavy exercise could restart lochia (the vaginal blood loss that occurs after birth) and your milk supply could be affected as nutrients are redirected. Drink lots of water before and during exercise so that you don't get dehydrated.

It can also be helpful to your changing body in the early weeks to wear special-purpose, supportive underwear such as a stretchy but firm belly band or a pair of support shorts; this will aid in guiding your muscles – especially your abdominals and your pelvic floor – back into place.

Above all, be kind to yourself and be realistic. It took nine months for your body to change shape, so it's unlikely to be restored in just a few weeks.

'I had a tiny, superficial graze after the birth. The doctor asked if I wanted it stitched. He looked across at my husband and said, "Cosmetically, it would be better to have it stitched." What the hell did he mean by that? That I would need to wear cover stick if I didn't have stitches? By the way, I didn't have any stitches and it healed beautifully.'

Jenni, mother of one

'My brain has shrunk'

Many mothers feel that, while their body has stretched, their brain has shrivelled. Don't worry if you seem to be a little forgetful, or have difficulty following the thread of a conversation other than the 'goo goo, gaa gaa' kind; blame it on your hormones and take heart – things will get better (your brain did not slip out with the placenta). In fact, your hormones influence your mind for several months after you have a baby.

You might feel frustrated or disconcerted by these changes in mindset, but look on the bright side: you are learning all sorts of new skills that will be useful later – even in the corporate world. I bet you can prioritise in a split second (answer the doorbell or watch baby in the bath? Easy!). You will become a great listener and be able to cut straight to the chase in a disagreement (who had that toy first?). You will develop expert negotiation skills, and you will develop more patience than you ever thought possible.

This is a very special time. You can't ever get it back again. Be kind to yourself and enjoy every precious moment getting to know your baby, without feeling pressured to grasp the finer points of every article in the *Financial Review*.

'You look great!'

These three little words are powerful. They can counter all the negative messages that you may be giving yourself about your body and put a spring in your step for hours. Consider how much effort you put into making sure your little one looks gorgeous. Do you take the same care of yourself?

Superficial though it may sound, making an effort to look great is an expression of who you are, whatever your shape or size. When you go out there and say, 'I am me. I feel great about who I am,' it isn't long before your confidence attracts compliments like, 'You look great!' Let's face it, nobody is likely to say, 'Hey, I love your personality,' or 'Wow! You are such a kind person.' So you might as well accept compliments on behalf of your kick-arse shoes or your radical new hair colour.

Also, the more you look after your appearance and the better you feel about yourself, the better people will treat you (try waiting in a queue at the butcher's wearing tracksuit pants and baby drool, then go back in your business suit and see which end of the chop you get). So, instead of buying another impossibly cute outfit for your little (and not so little) ones, try to resist and think like a role model. Show your partner and kids you believe in yourself: buy yourself something pretty. It doesn't have to be expensive – even a new lipstick can make you feel a million dollars. You're worth it.

Unmasked at the pool

'We'll meet at the pool,' they said. 'Bring your bathers.'

They were twenty-something mums. I was a forty-something mum with a Bonus Baby (the baby you have when your other ones are big enough to tie their own shoelaces, run their own baths or even drive their own cars).

I used to be a twenty-something mum. I used to spend most of the summer at the pool with my other babies. In those days, 'forty-something' meant kilos to me. With a bikini top nicely rounded out by lactating bosoms, I didn't have a body-image problem. Nowadays, if it wasn't all so soft (and so far south), I'd be nicely rounded all over. The babies I had when I was a twenty-something mum do nothing to enhance my fragile body image. 'Blue goes with everything,' they tell me; it's the varicose veins they're referring to. Today, I'm a mistress of camouflage. I know just what to wear to conceal my biggest assets. But – at the pool? T-shirts over bathers are fine – until they're wet!

Before the Bonus Baby became a socialite, I used to put him into the pool with the big kids. Later, he loved being taken to the pool by a big brother (the bonus for the big brother was that the Bonus Baby was a babe-magnet). But this time, I was trapped. His big sweet eyes with curly lashes looked trustingly up at me. It was bathers on for both of us – no excuses – and into the pool with all the trim, taut, terrific twenty-something mums and their kids. And the nanas (or were they also mothers of Bonus Babies?). And the granddads (or were they just older fathers?). Splashing and playing, laughing and yelling and playing 'ring-a-rosie'. Well, at least I could keep my face out of the water, couldn't I?

Uh-oh. Big sweet-eyes with curly lashes looked trustingly up at me, begging me to go under. Down I bobbed. Up we came again. And there I was, hair dripping, mascara running – completely unmasked. Big sweet-eyes looked up at me, smiling. I was smiling too. It felt just as good as it used to when I was a trim, taut, terrific, twenty-something mum.

Oh, what a friend we have in Tim Tams

Are your darkest hours marked by chocolate binges? (I knew the lights were dim the day I realised I was dunking the baby's rusk in my cup of tea, and he was sucking on my Tim Tam). Do you reach for a sweet treat to give you a lift when you feel low on energy? Yet, when you are feeling strong and motivated and relaxed, you probably don't even have junk food supplies in the house.

Instead of seeking comfort by feeding our faces, we need to nourish our hearts, souls and minds with kindness and love. As parents (and particularly as mothers) we are conditioned to nurture everybody around us, from our kids to stray animals. But we need to be kind to ourselves, too, otherwise our nourishment tanks become empty and we become fragile, with nothing to give to anybody.

✳ CHECKLIST : **NOURISHING YOUR WHOLE SELF**

- Listen to beautiful music.
- Take a walk in the bush or a park (with the baby in a sling or backpack); watch the waves; walk barefoot in the sand; relax under a tree (in your backyard or in a park) while the children play.
- Surround yourself with aromas, colours and textures that make you feel happy, or peaceful, or lively (whatever your need is at the time). Put some essential oils in a burner, fill a vase with colourful flowers, snuggle under a fluffy rug.
- Read stories and poetry to inspire you and transport you to another place; have a nap to refresh your body and mind; take a bubble bath by candlelight to soak away your cares.

- Express yourself. Write (including all the things you might never actually tell anybody – it's a great release); paint or draw (with the kids if necessary, but use good-quality paints, pastels or pencils – you are worth it); sing (even if only a baby could love your voice); dance (with your child if you can't find another willing partner!).
- Pamper yourself with a facial or massage. No, you don't have to do it yourself; if money is an issue, go to a student clinic at a hair and beauty college. Natural-health colleges offer lots of other inexpensive treatments, too.
- Reach out to others. Call a friend or give someone a hug – they will feel nourished, too.
- Choose a delicious and special treat. Savour the moment, really taste what you put into your mouth, and enjoy.

'This sounds a little crazy but I love driving to work. I switch between radio stations and occasionally an old eighties song I love will come on – I pump up the volume and sing out really loud like a crazy woman.'

Amanda, mother of two

14

Relationships

♥

You promised a baby wouldn't come between you. But these days, fore-play has diminished to, 'Are you awake?' and the response is most likely to be, 'No, I'm asleep, but feel free to help yourself.'

The reality is that all the frozen casseroles in the world can't prepare you for the effects a new baby will have on your relationship. Having a baby changes things dramatically – forever! There can be so many overwhelming emotions flowing between you and your partner and your baby that, some days, the rosy glow of romance can seem more like a feeble flicker. Either of you may feel you have nothing left to give as you confer your body, your mind and your soul on your child. This is normal, and not a sign that either of you is faulty or that your relationship is on the proverbial rocks. The newborn period is a 'season' and, just as the winds of autumn or the frosts of winter pass, things will become easier.

Planning for change

Most couples plan for and arrange physical support when they are expecting a baby, but are less prepared for the inevitable and profound changes in the dynamics between them. The demands of caring for a baby can create difficulties for couples who are used to exclusive time together or who may have unresolved feelings about their own early experiences. It is a good idea to talk these matters through during your pregnancy, to bring to light what feelings may arise and to discuss who you may be able to share these with.

Jealousy is not just for left-out dads or usurped toddlers, but at least their feelings are usually acknowledged. You may find you have similar twinges as your partner gives all his adoration to the baby and hardly seems to notice you, especially if he takes to calling you 'Mum'.

Resentment, a close cousin of jealousy, can also be a big dampener on a relationship. You feel trapped as you see him driving off to work, joining the 'real world'. He feels trapped as he drives off to work, knowing you have a 'free' day to meet friends for coffee or lunch. In spite of all the rational role planning, emotions play havoc if you can't empathise with each other's adjustment to new responsibilities. If this happens, it's important to share your feelings with your partner. It is also helpful to learn to recognise when your partner is feeling stressed and to know what kind of support you expect from each other.

It's sensible to develop good communication skills well before your baby is born; under stress, you fall back on what you know best – which, unless you've practised more effective says to communicate, tends to involve yelling and screaming. It is vital, during the sometimes-stressful newborn period, to listen to and respect your partner's feelings, and for them to do the same for you.

This is also a time when financial intimacy is important. Money is up there with sex and communication as a major war zone between genders. Before your baby is born, it is helpful to discuss this with your partner – to recognise your different money personalities and to accept your strengths and weaknesses regarding spending or saving. Life shouldn't be a power struggle with the power balance held by the biggest earner – although this is often the case.

'I was most surprised by how little time there is for the two of you and what this means for your relationship. Different opinions on childcare can impact on your relationship, too. Perhaps you just assumed your partner would think the same way, so you didn't talk about it.'

Amelie, mother of two

Talking, not shouting

When the going gets tough, the tough keep talking. Your partner is not a mind-reader. If things are bothering you, discuss your feelings – and try to do it without sounding as if you are accusing or blaming. The easiest way to do this is to use 'I' statements ('I feel upset when . . .') rather than 'you' statements ('You make me feel . . .').

If you feel you are being verbally attacked, instead of shouting, try to be patient (take some deep, slow breaths) and listen to what your partner is trying to express. If you feel unsupported, or that your partner is wrong or being unfair, try to see things from their perspective – this works well with kids, too, so practise, practise, practise! You don't have to agree with what you hear (remember: if two people agree on everything, one of them isn't thinking), but if they feel listened to, the conflict will often dissolve. If you both feel affirmed, you can draw back from self-righteous, defensive positions and work together on a solution. The alternative is likely to be a major argument that results in nothing but bitter feelings.

If you have difficulty expressing how you feel, or believe you aren't being heard, try putting it in a letter. Because the written word is so powerful, keep the note for a few hours and read it over before you pass it on; when things are less heated, you may want to tone it down a bit if you have been very expressive. The same tactics apply to letters as to verbal expression: try to express how you are feeling without blaming or accusing.

Consider also that we all feel more motivated when our efforts are acknowledged. Show appreciation for helpful gestures, compliment each other, and, above all, keep talking. Simple expressions like 'Thank you', 'I'm sorry' and 'I love you' mean a lot. Use them every day. (If you end up calling each other 'Mummy' and 'Daddy', it might be time for an 'I' statement – 'I am me!')

'At first, I got so child-absorbed and so sleep-deprived (or is that depraved?) that I think I blew things out of proportion. Yet I knew it was vitally important to tell my partner exactly how I felt, in a non-blaming way. It sounds a bit "Dr Phil", but I had to tell him how his actions (or inaction) made me feel. Even if it seemed like I was being petty, I still made myself say it. I used to get shocked when he would open up and say that some of my actions made him feel bad and unloved! No matter how silly the leading circumstance, the emotions are very real and need to be in the open. We often end up laughing at ourselves and that is always a good thing.'

Amanda, mother of two

'Planning' spontaneity

Whatever the age of your child, there will be no 'spontaneity' in your daily life without careful planning! You will have to make plans for everything, from a walk in the park or a dash to the bank to a deep and meaningful conversation with your partner or dinner for two – let alone lovemaking. Paradoxically, you will learn the true meaning of 'impromptu' as you find yourselves making spur-of-the-moment plans to take advantage of your baby's routines (or lack of them).

Even if there is a shortage of uninterrupted time alone, don't neglect spontaneous cuddles, backrubs, talking and listening to each other. Take advantage of the moments to give each other 'I care' messages.

'We occasionally give each other cards – not just for birthdays or anniversaries. It is a nice, tangible affirmation. Sometimes we have a bath together by candlelight when the kids are in bed, and going out for a coffee or a meal gives us uninterrupted time to talk and keep in touch.'

Parents of five

When sex is a pain

It may seem incredible that when a four-kilogram baby has just passed safely through your vagina, the slightest nudge from a penis can have you crossing your legs in fear. But all that fiddling about in your fanny during the birth – not to mention forceps, scalpels, needles and thread – has affected your most important sex organ: your brain.

After giving birth, some women feel a new sense of power and pride in their bodies and are eager to affirm their sexual feelings. Other women feel completely violated by the birth. If the birth was a traumatic experience for you, or even if you had a reasonably 'normal' delivery but there was lots of poking and prodding, vaginal penetration and even foreplay may trigger flashbacks to labour and birth.

If you are experiencing prolonged physical pain, though, it is unlikely to be all in your mind – deep bruising and scars can take weeks to heal. A persistently painful perineum can be treated by a gynaecologist, obstetrician or women's-health physiotherapist (call the physiotherapy association in your state) and may involve ultrasound therapy. Many women say that it is the possibility of pain on entry that worries them, and that gentle penetration (perhaps with extra lubrication) can make all the difference. If you have continuing difficulties, seek help from a professional such as your obstetrician or a women's health physiotherapist. This is a quality-of-life issue, so if your concerns are dismissed, be persistent or seek help elsewhere.

If you are physically healed but simply don't have any libido, it could be that your testosterone levels have dropped. This can be caused by tiredness and, in some women, by breastfeeding (though some studies show that breastfeeding women in fact have an increased libido). Body image, too, can affect how desirable you feel. Talk about your feelings and make an effort – perhaps arrange a 'date' with your partner. Even if you don't go out, get in some treats and a DVD, have a nice meal or a bath together (by candlelight – not so threatening if body image is causing performance anxiety), use some aromatherapy (try a mix of ylang ylang and patchouli oils), and put on some music that is meaningful to you both. Your relationship needs as much nurturing as your baby does.

The birth experience can affect either partner's feelings about love-making, and it can take time to heal both physically and emotionally. But you can work together to re-educate your body to experience pleasure.

✳ CHECKLIST : POST-BIRTH LOVEMAKING

- Use a condom for your first post-birth encounter, regardless of contraception. After a few weeks of abstinence, your partner may ejaculate in a flash and the condom might slow him down.
- Lowered hormone levels may make your vagina uncomfortably dry. Keep a lubricant under the pillow to allow for spontaneity. If dryness continues, ask your doctor about oestrogen creams or pessaries: be sure to mention if you're breastfeeding, as some creams are absorbed into the bloodstream and may have adverse effects on your baby.
- Practise your pelvic-floor exercises during foreplay (as well as when you are scrubbing the spuds or doing the dishes). When your muscles contract there is a surge of blood flow to the area, which improves lubrication and arousal as well as nourishing healing tissues. For the same reason, aim for an orgasm a day! No, this isn't goal-oriented sex: but orgasm stimulates the pelvic-floor muscles to contract.
- If you are fearful of experiencing pain (or causing it) during intercourse, enjoy a glass of wine together before you make love (though see also **Breastfeeding and alcohol,** page 151).

A note for dads

You want sex. You think that making love will reassure your partner that your feelings for her haven't changed. But she feels all 'touched out' after giving to your baby. She may want cuddles, but withdraws because she suspects that cuddles will lead to sex. You withdraw because you don't want to pressure her – or perhaps you feel rejected.

According to childbirth educator and relationship counsellor Rhea Dempsey, gender differences can also affect intimacy between partners. In her work, Rhea uses the acronym CISS, which stands for Communica-tion, Intimacy, Sensuality and Sex. When I interviewed her, Rhea said, 'The pathway to bonding and connection is biologically in opposite directions for men and women. For women, communication leads to intimacy, which leads to sensuality and then to sex. Women want and need to feel connected through sharing the effort and joy of caring for their child, and then they are more open to sensuality and sex. For men, feelings that they are on the outside of the close mother–baby unit (which, of course, is necessary for the baby to thrive) can see them also wanting to restore the connection with their partner. Men are programmed to do this through sex which, instead of being seen as a pathway to intimacy and communication by the mother, is often seen as a demand that can be overwhelming on top of the unrelenting needs of the baby.'

So, although lovemaking was probably the main expression of your connection with each other before you had a baby, now you may need to find other ways to stay close. Keep up your physical connection in non-sexual ways such as massage or cuddles, without pressure to have sex. If you are sensitive and supportive during the early weeks and months, your patience will be rewarded as your partner's love and respect grows and, consequently, her interest in you returns at a higher level.

'I honestly don't think that men think the same way as we do. I want him to buy me flowers "just because he thought of me". He thinks that his deep love for me is conveyed when we make love.'

Mandy, mother of two

Passion postponed

Coitus interruptus is not just a family-planning method for teenagers and optimists. When you do get around to making love, even if your baby is sleeping soundly, you can bet your boots he will yell just as you get to the moment of bliss. This seems to have little to do with hunger or being disturbed by noise and more to do with a primitive survival response. It is probably related to the same deep connection between mother and baby that has a mother waking just before her baby stirs, or triggers a milk let-down as her baby cries – even if she's up the street and her baby is at home.

Candles and bouncinettes become sex aids when you have a baby. You are less likely to be interrupted if your baby is awake when you make love, and little ones are mesmerised by flickering candlelight. (Much later, you can try sending junior to check the letterbox!)

Are you awake?

If your baby hasn't yet arrived and you want an idea of what's in store, think of how tired you were in the first three months of your pregnancy and multiply it by any number from ten upwards. This exhaustion can have a ripple effect on your relationship, especially if you are taking most of the responsibility for baby care and your partner's life has barely changed. Whatever the age of your kids, exhaustion combined with childcare and other demands can see you collapsing, comatose, any time there's a break in your schedule.

The reality is that tiredness will be a feature of your life for the next eighteen years (at least). It eventually palls, though, as an excuse for postponing lovemaking. If you find yourself becoming resentful of your partner's demands or you are 'holding out' because he isn't pulling his weight around the house, discuss how you feel. Sometimes, the most stimulating foreplay can be help with the dishes or any of the other million tasks that need doing before you finally get time to relax. Share your chores and take turns to nurture yourselves and to sleep so that you each have some energy left over to share with each other. For some tips about conserving (or regaining) your energy, see **Keeping burnout at bay**, page 252.

Mixing friendships and parenting

Nobody ever tells you how madly and deeply you will fall in love with your baby – or how this will affect your relationship not only with your partner but also with your friends. Friends who drift away because they can't cope with your new love may drift back when they have babies of their own. Or they may not. Other friends may drift away because you disagree about parenting styles. If you value your friendships, you may have to accept that there is more than one way to bring up the perfect baby.

Sharing friends as a couple can be nourishing to your relationship. You can learn different ways of connecting and discover that you aren't alone in the struggles that are an inevitable part of being parents (dealing with kids' behaviour, holidays, and even learning how other couples share the workload).

Some ways you could socialise as a couple include:

- Take turns with another couple in spending a Saturday night at each other's houses. Take the babies and a plate of food to share. Or form a men's cooking club: the guys cook the meal while the ladies relax, chat and look after the kids. Use paper plates so that the clean-up is easy.
- A couples' book club might give you something to talk about besides wees and poos – although you may have to be past that stage before you find time to read. Of course, you could always kill a couple of birds with the one stone and discuss a parenting book.
- If you are new to the area, or are the first among your friends to have a baby, why not invite several couples from your mothers' group to get together? Or former members of your antenatal class? Or put up a notice at your infant-welfare clinic? If you choose to have a structured group, set some ground rules about how often you meet and what you are prepared to spend if you are planning social activities. (This suggestion may work for forming your own mothers' network, too.)

Grandparents

Until you had your baby, you probably lived a busy and independent life that didn't really include your own parents on a day-to-day basis – at least, not since you left home, met your partner and developed your own network. While some families remain committed to regular family gatherings as their children grow, often these become limited to special celebrations such as birthdays and holiday events.

However, the birth of your child is incredibly exciting and special for your own parents. It is also important for your littlies to enjoy this very special family connection, so you do need to consider how you will nurture the relationships between your own parents and your child. Feelings between you and your parents are likely to be tense, at times, as you adapt to this new kind of relationship with each other and work out how you can share each other's lives in a way that works for everyone. But it is worth making an effort to tread gently because, despite any criticisms you may have of your own upbringing, your parents did the best they could with the resources they had at the time, and they really do deserve respect. It's also worth acknowledging that they have experience that you don't yet have, even though it will be different from your own and things may have changed a lot since you were a baby. Although advice changes, babies don't, and grandparents can be a valuable source of support and advice if they are welcomed by you to share this very special time. It can help to imagine how you would like to be treated by your child when they grow up. Most likely, you would want to be acknowledged with dignity and consideration. How disappointed would you feel if your own child treated you rudely and perhaps just as a convenience, called on for babysitting, with little other interaction or acknowledgement? Or, as one set of grandparents I recently heard of were told, 'You need to go to grandparents classes; you are totally out of date.'

'I feel a yearning to see my grandchildren. It's a deep primal urge that I find hard to explain – they are my child's children and it's like an invisible umbilical cord is reaching beyond my own children into another layer of little ones, even though they are not "mine" in the same sense.

'I feel really hurt that I am excluded from their lives on so many levels. I have questioned many times whether I have caused offence in some way, but I am pretty sure I have not been intrusive or interfering – certainly not intentionally. My son and daughter-in-law are wonderful parents so I have no need to give advice or criticise, but they live a busy life and I am in a queue behind their friends, their work lives, their social lives . . . I have been told not to "drop in", yet when I phone to make an "appointment", it is never convenient. Even when I try to make longer term arrangements, they will be 'booked up' all week, or arrangements will change at the last minute and I will receive a text message telling me not to come – often because a friend is visiting. I try very hard to change my own arrangements to fit in with them, but I would never tell them they can't visit me because I am "having friends over". It seems that it is always up to me to make the effort to see the little ones – they rarely initiate a visit to my place, even though we only live a half-hour drive apart.

'Although the exclusion hurts me personally, this rejection is a much deeper pain – I feel as if I have been slapped every time I am told it doesn't suit for me to see my grandchildren. At one level, I really don't believe there is any intended malice, but I have cried many tears because it can be weeks between visits, despite repeated efforts on my part. I have no idea how to express my feelings to make this different without sounding like an emotional bitch or offending them, creating even more distance. I feel I am grieving for the loss of a very important relationship – with my own child's children. I love these littlies and I would love to share their lives – to hold them and laugh with them and watch them grow. As a grandmother, I know all too well how fleeting these childhood moments are and when they are gone, they are gone forever.'

Anna

Surviving the in-laws

You may have heard a million jokes about mothers-in-law, but when it comes to dealing with your own, up close and personal – and especially when you become a parent – it isn't always easy to see the funny side. Unfortunately, we can't choose our in-laws – they come as part of the package along with the person we fall in love with. And here lies the root cause of most problems: the difference in upbringing between ourselves and our partners. Each family has its own values and traditions as well as ways of behaving as a family – one family will talk to each other every day while another will go weeks between phone calls; one family might tell each other everything while another may have clear boundaries about what issues are private, even between family members; some families will be outspoken and not at all backwards about offering advice while others may express disapproval in more subtle, but none-the-less intrusive ways.

To deal more calmly with interference, try to see the other person's perspective. If your mother-in-law seems all too ready to undermine you, it may be a sign that she needs to increase her own self-worth, albeit at your expense. After all, she brought up the partner you love and have a child with, so she probably feels some credit is due. At some level, your mother-in-law may be feeling that she has to compete with you for the love and respect of her own child (that is, your partner); your different parenting style may be a threat to the way she brought up your partner (or you, if it is your own mother who is being critical). On the other hand, grandma may be genuinely trying to make things easier by sharing her hard-earned knowledge, or she may simply want to be more involved with her grandchild.

Ultimately, the issue here is not who 'wins', but how to encourage a positive relationship between your child and their grandparents. So, when you disagree with in-laws (or with your own parents), it is worth remembering the old adage, 'You catch more flies with honey than vinegar.'

✳ CHECKLIST : GRANDPARENT RELATIONSHIPS

- Find common ground. Because your relationship with your child's grandparents will be an ongoing one, it is important to try to find some common ground. Try asking for grandma or grandad's opinion on a fairly neutral topic or invite them to be more involved, then give them positive feedback. For instance, 'Would you like to give him his bath?' Or, 'He loves it when you take him to feed the ducks.'
- Stay calm. If you are confronted by unwanted advice from your mother or mother-in-law, no matter how well-meaning, you can either tell her honestly – but politely – that you feel undermined by her advice, or you can simply stay calm, take a deep breath and respond like this: 'This works well for us,' or '[Baby's name] feels happy when we . . .' Another option is to thank grandma for her tips

and say, enthusiastically, 'I'll remember that,' then choose which
information suits you and your little one, and discard the rest.

- **Share new information**. You might like to share some up-to-date
  information with grandparents by commenting enthusiastically
  about a new book you have discovered or some written information
  or research that reinforces what you are doing. It will work better
  to do this proactively, before you are bombarded with out-of-date
  information, so that she isn't put in a situation where she feels
  defensive.

- **Refer to authorities**. If all else fails, you can deflect unwanted advice
  by bringing in the big guns: 'Our lactation consultant/paediatrician/
  child-health nurse says . . .'

- **Maintain a united front**. If your partner starts to side with his or her
  mother against you, it is only natural that you will want to cut the
  apron strings between them – with a very sharp pair of scissors! But
  again, the best advice is to remain calm and, when you are alone with
  your partner, enlist their support by telling them how you feel without
  becoming angry or putting them in a situation that makes them feel
  they must 'choose' between you and their mother. It is also important
  to tell your partner how much you value their parenting efforts ('You
  are a great dad/mum! I love the way you . . .'); then help them to see
  how vulnerable this criticism makes you feel and how much you need
  their support so you can be a confident, competent parent.

- **Agree on what really matters**. It can be difficult to stand up to
  your parents, but if you and your partner can agree on what really
  matters, and if you can support each other, then you are more likely
  to succeed in setting boundaries. Sit down together and make a list
  of what bothers you about each other's families, and decide which
  issues are worth standing firm on. What you feed your baby or how
  you choose to discipline your child may be priorities that you won't
  compromise on, for instance. But if your mother-in-law wants to iron
  your husband's shirts 'properly' or complains about how you mow
  the lawns (or don't), perhaps you could let this one go or share it as a

mother-in-law joke. After all, you, your partner and child are a family now, and it is time to establish your own values and traditions.

• **Give listening a chance.** Although they may not always be overly diplomatic about giving you advice, by being patient and listening to your parents, you may well pick up some very valuable pieces of wisdom and some practical tips as well.

Naughty (indulgent) grandparents

As parents, it can be difficult to be 'vegetables and boundaries' to our children while grandparents can be 'ice-cream and fun', especially if they were harsher on us when we were growing up. But if you are struggling with grandparents who indulge your kids, it might help to see things from your parents' perspective: when you were a child, your own parents may not have had the resources – time, money and sleep – to 'spoil' you as they do your children. They see it as a rite of passage to enjoy their grandchildren in a very different way. And, if they don't get to see their grandchildren often, buying new clothes or toys can be a way for grandparents to feel connected.

As parents of a baby (or toddler), you need to take responsibility for your little one's wellbeing on a day-to-day basis. It is your job to guide and teach your child and, right now – just as for your parents when you were a child – the buck stops with you when it comes to your child's health and wellbeing. This can make it difficult to step back and decide whether grandma's spoiling is really undermining your parenting and damaging your child's wellbeing, or just part of a very special connection between your child and her grandparents. Disagreements in this case can often be about food – grandma may think it's fine to give your baby ice-cream, for instance, but these days there is evidence that this can cause allergic reactions.

If you really do feel that grandma is overstepping the mark and 'spoiling' your child, it is a good idea to let her know how you feel – gently, of course. Remember, the relationship between her and your child is important in the long term. And so is your own relationship with your mum or your partner's mum. For now, you will need to be firm around what your baby eats, for instance, but you don't need to restrict cuddles or rocking or holding from grandparents. As your baby becomes a toddler, if food choices are an issue, you could try explaining that your child gets very excited and behaves badly when he eats too many lollies, but he loves crackers and dip or peeling his own mandarins. Grandmas do like to carry 'treats' in their bags, so try to guide her so that she has something suitable that won't create conflict between you. Or, if you would rather grandma spent time with your child instead of simply buying things for him, rein-force what a lovely time your little one had at the park or helping grandma cook, or suggest some activities that you know your child enjoys. A more subtle way to inspire special activities, rather than material things, is to give grandma an appropriate but beautiful activity book, such as *The Little Big Book for Grandmothers* (see Further Reading).

Despite subtle protestations, or even unsubtle ones, you may not be able to tame an indulgent grandma. If all your efforts to rein in your 'naughty nana' fall on deaf ears, you might simply need to take a chill pill and accept that a bit of spoiling, even if it seems over the top right now, probably isn't doing any long-term harm, and it may be creating some very special memories for your children

'I mind my two-year-old granddaughter one day a week. I know how consistent her parents are about her daytime sleep, but she is so excited when she is at my place that I can't get her to sleep – even though we have quiet time and stories and cuddles at her sleep time. I felt really guilty that she would sleep in the car on her way home, then she would be up late for her parents. Then I realised that it is only one day a week, so now I am more relaxed and just enjoy having fun with her, whether she sleeps or not.'

June

'Our kids' grandparents lived a long way away from us and we didn't get to see them much, so when we did, it was good for them to give the kids lots of attention. My father-in-law used to give them chocolate before tea and wait for me to rouse, but I figured it was one or two weekends a year, and why not? It was only ever a little bit – not enough to mean they wouldn't eat their tea. He would put sugar on their Weet-Bix, too, which I never did. (I was a mean mummy.) My dad used to give the kids jelly snakes, which is how they still remember him. And my parents would give the kids dessert even if they didn't eat their vegetables ("Ice-cream fills a different hole to peas," my dad would say, and, "You can't spoil a child with love.") Now, my dad and in-laws are gone and my kids have only one grandma, who still lives a long way away. And at eighty-seven, who knows how long we will have her?'

Phillipa, mother of four now-teenage children

Kissing strangers

Early parenthood is touted as a danger time for affairs. He's supposed to feel neglected and she is supposed to want to reaffirm her desirability. (I want to know where they get the time, let alone the energy!)

An affair does not have to be a sexual relationship, and in fact it is emotional intimacy that often poses the greatest threat to a relationship. Nowadays, of course, Internet relationships are flourishing: they encourage even more intimacy because people tend to share their private thoughts in more detail online than they would over the phone or in person. Also, they provide both fantasy and a refuge.

It's a good rule of thumb not to do anything with a person of the opposite sex (or the gender that you prefer) that you would not do if your partner were standing next to you. This absolutely excludes talking to that person about problems with your partner, which creates a triangle that almost invariably leads to relationship breakdown. It is a breach of faith. Whine to your mates, not to a potential sexual partner. And, if you have a mate who is a potential sexual partner, then don't confide in them, either. If you are having problems with your partner that make you feel like you need to cosy up to someone else, sort out the problems with your partner.

Otherwise, you will not only damage your relationship, but probably screw up the poor sucker you are confiding in.

If a partner has an affair, the pain will be lasting. A breakdown in trust can take years to repair. And, because this pain affects both of you, it will inevitably hurt your child too, whether or not you choose to stay together. If you feel dissatisfied, distrustful or can't talk any more, please seek outside help. Seeking help is not a slur on your ability to cope – it is the most mature way to deal with your situation. And it may take just a couple of sessions with a counsellor to set you on the right track – and save your relationship.

A Parents' Valentine

A loaf of bread

a glass of wine

backrubs in labour

milky breasts

stretchmarks

little night howls

passion postponed

watching sunrises together

(as the baby falls asleep)

fingermarks on the wall

mess on the floor

monsters under beds

lust left until later

fish and chips in front of the telly

meetings

sports

teachers' reports

headlice

worms

teens who need to talk at midnight

desire delayed

chocolates

cuddles

my family

your family

mortgage repayments

working back

the dog on heat

receding hair

going grey

sharing jokes

come what may

carnations from the supermarket

bubble baths for two

passion

lust

desire

and you!

Pinky

Resources

♥

Allergies and food intolerance
Allergy Free

1300 662 250

allergyfree.com.au

Information and support for allergy-free households; personal and baby products available online.

Food Intolerance Network of Australia (FINA)

fedupwithfoodadditives.info

Hosted by Sue Dengate, the author of books on allergies and food intolerance, including *Fed Up* and *The Failsafe Cookbook*. Offers a wealth of information and resources including a list of food additives, articles, parenting stories, links and a free newsletter.

Breastfeeding
Australian Breastfeeding Association

(03) 9885 0855

breastfeeding.asn.au

Lactation Consultants of Australia and New Zealand (LCANZ)

lcanz.org

The professional organisation for International Board Certified Lactation Consultants (IBCLCs) in Australia and New Zealand. Via the site, you can find a professional to help with breastfeeding difficulties.

Parenting information and support

Infant Heath Centres

See under 'Child Health Centres' in your local *Yellow Pages*.

Child and Youth Health South Australia

cyh.sa.gov.au

Offers a wealth of information about parenting and child development; useful whatever state you live in.

Parenting helplines

ACT: 13 20 55

New South Wales: 13 20 55

Queensland & Northern Territory: 1300 30 1300

South Australia: 1300 364 100

Tasmania: 1800 808 178

Victoria: 13 22 89

Western Australia: 1800 654 432

Names vary from state to state, but offer a similar service, including information, advice and referrals.

Raising Children Network

raisingchildren.net.au

Supported by the Australian Government, includes a wide range of information about child health, development and behaviour.

World Health Organization

who.int

Up-to-date information about child health, including infant growth charts, which use breastfed babies as the standard and are a great resource if you are concerned about your baby's weight gains.

Bonnie Babes Foundation

(03) 9800 0322

bbf.org.au

Telephone, individual and group counselling for miscarriage, prematurity, stillbirth and neonatal loss.

National SIDS Council of Australia Ltd

(03) 9819 4595

sidsaustralia.org.au

Support and information about Sudden Infant Death Syndrome (SIDS).

Playgroup associations

National: playgroupaustralia.com.au; 1800 171 882

New South Wales: playgroupnsw.com.au

Northern Territory: playgroupaustralia.com.au/nt

Queensland: playgroupqld.com.au

South Australia: playgroupaustralia.com.au/sa

Tasmania: playgroupaustralia.com.au/tas

Victoria: playgroup.org.au

Western Australia: playgroupwa.com.au

Postnatal depression

beyondblue

beyondblue.org.au/postnataldepression

This government-funded mental health initiative includes a postnatal depression support service.

Dona Maria Postnatal Support Network

1300 555 578

A telephone support service staffed by health professionals.

Lisa Fettling (postnatal depression counsellor)

0407 943 938

lisafettling.com.au

Lisa is the author of *Postnatal Depression: A guide for Australian families*, and *Women's Experience of Postnatal Depression: Kitchen table conversations*. She offers individual, group, couple and family counselling in Melbourne. Her web site includes information about postnatal depression as well as her services.

Northern Queensland Postnatal Distress Support Group

(07) 4728 1911

nqpostnataldistress.com

PANDA (Post and Antenatal Depression Association Inc.)

1300 726 306

panda.org.au

Offers a phone helpline (national) and a services directory (Victoria only).

Post & Antenatal Depression Support & Information Inc. (Canberra)

(02) 6232 6664

pandsi.org

Postnatal Depression Support Association (WA)

(08) 9340 1622

Postnatal Disorders Clinic, Mercy Hospital for Women (Victoria)

(03) 9270 2501/2884

Relationship services
Relationships Australia
1300 364 277

relationships.com.au

New Zealand Resources
La Leche League New Zealand
(04) 471 0690

lalecheleague.org/LLLNZ

Parentline (based in Christchurch)
(03) 381 1040

Parents Centres New Zealand
(04) 476 6950

parentscentre.org.nz

Childbirth and parent education and support, including playgroups and the magazine *Kiwi Parent*.

Royal New Zealand Plunket Society
(04) 471 0177 or 24-hour helpline: 0800 933 922

plunket.org.nz

Web sites to watch
pinkymckay.com
My site has informative articles, comprehensive links to local and international health and nurturing sites, books, DVDs and downloadable digital recordings of interviews with leading health and early child development professionals. You can also subscribe to my ezine for regular updates and events.

askdrsears.com

The site of Dr William Sears and his sons, who are paediatricians. Very informative, offering evidence-based information about all aspects of parenting.

attachmentparenting.org

The site of Attachment Parenting International offers educational materials, research information and consultative, referral and speaker services to promote parenting practices that create strong, healthy emotional bonds between children and their parents.

aaimhi.org/documents/position%20papers/controlled_crying.pdf

This is the link to the Australian Association of Infant Mental Health's policy statement on controlled crying – interesting reading!

centreforattachment.com

The Centre for Attachment is a New Zealand-based agency dedicated to providing support, education and training for families, organisations and communities on optimal child development and attachment. Grounded in research, CFA translates the findings from neuroscience, mental health and psychology to everyday life situations such as mother–infant bonding, feeding and sleeping, family development and relationship health.

sarahjbuckley.com

Australian author of *Gentle Birth, Gentle Mothering*, Sarah Buckley is a family physician, an internationally acclaimed expert on pregnancy, birth, and parenting, and the mother of four. Her web site includes superbly researched articles that will help you to make gentle, loving choices for your family.

References

♥

Bartick, M., & A. Reinhold, 'The Burden of Suboptimal Breastfeeding in the United States: A pediatric cost analysis', *Pediatrics*, 2009.

Blumenthal, J.A., M. A. Babyak, M. Doraiswamy, L. Watkins, B. M. Hoffman, K. A. Barbour, S. Herman, W. E. Craighead, A. L. Brosse, R. Waugh, A. Hinderliter & A. Sherwood, 'Exercise and pharmacotherapy in the treatment of major depressive disorder', *Psychosomatic Medicine* 69 (7): 587–596, 2007.

Dewey, K. G., 'Growth Characteristics of Breast-Fed Compared to Formula-Fed Infants', *Biology of the Neonate*, 74: 94–105, 1998.

Doan, T., A. Gardiner, C. L. Gay & K. A. Lee, 'Breastfeeding increases sleep duration of new parents', *Journal of Perinatal and Neonatal Nursing*, 21(3): 200–206, 2007.

Fergusen, D. M. et al, 'Breastfeeding and subsequent social adjustment in six to eight year old children', *Journal of Child Psychology and Psychiatry and Allied Disciplines*, 28: 378–86, 1987.

Field, T. 'Massage Therapy for Infants and Children', review in *Journal of Developmental and Behavioural Pediatrics*, 16: 105–11, 1995.

Field T., S. M. Schanberg, F. Scafidi, C. R. Bauer, N. Vega Lahr, R. Garcia, J. Nystrom, & C. M. Kuhn, 'Tactile/kinesthetic stimulation effects on preterm neonates', *Pediatrics* 77:654–8, 1986.

Freeman, M. P. et al, 'Randomized dose-ranging pilot trial of omega-3 fatty acids for postpartum depression', *Acta Psychiatrica Scandinavica* 113: 31–35, January 2006.

Fleming, P. & P. Blair, 'Safe environments for infant sleep: community and laboratory investigations or folk wisdom?', *Symposium on Breast Feeding, Parental Proximity and Contact in Promoting Infant Health*, paper delivered University of Notre Dame, South Bend, September 1998.

Freudenheim, J., et al., 'Exposure to breast milk in infancy and the risk of breast cancer', *Epidemiology* 5: 324–331, 1994.

Fukuda, K. & K. Ishihara, 'Development of human sleep and wakefulness rhythm during the first six months of life: Discontinuous changes at the 7th and 12th week after birth', *Biological Rhythm Research*, Vol. 28, Issue S1: 94–103, Japan, November 1997.

Horwood, L. J. & D. M. Fergusen, 'Breastfeeding and later cognitive and academic outcomes', *Pediatrics*, vol. 101, no. 1, January 1998.

Hibbeln, J., 'Seafood consumption, the DHA content of mothers' milk and prevalence rates of postpartum depression: A cross-national, ecological analysis', *Journal of Affective Disorders* 69: 15–29, 2002.

Hunt, J., *The Natural Child*, New Society Publishers, Canada, 2001.

Ip, S., M. Chung, G. Raman, P. Chew, N. Magula, D. DeVine, T. Trikalinos, J. Lau, 'Breastfeeding and Maternal and Infant Health Outcomes in Developed Countries', *Evidence Report/Technology Assessment No. 153* (Prepared by Tufts–New England Medical Center Evidence-based Practice Center, under Contract No. 290-02-0022), AHRQ Publication No. 07-E007, Rockville, MD: Agency for Healthcare Research and Quality, April 2007.

Kendall-Tackett, K., *The Hidden Feelings of Motherhood: Coping with stress, depression, and burnout*, New Harbinger Publications, USA, 2001.

Kinsley et al, 'Motherhood improves learning and memory', *Nature* 401: 137–8, 1999.

Lafond, V., *Grieving Mental Illness: A guide for patients and their caregivers*, University of Toronto Press, Toronto, 1994.

Mitchell E. A. & J. M. D. Thompson, 'Co-sleeping increases the risks of the sudden infant death syndrome, but sleeping in the parents' bedroom lowers it', *Sudden Infant Death Syndrome: New Trends in the Nineties*, Scandinavian University Press, Oslo: 266–269, 1995.

Morton, J, J. Y. Hall, R. J. Wong, L. Thairu, W. E. Benitz & W. D. Rhone, 'Combining hand techniques with electric pumping increases milk production in mothers of preterm infants', *Journal of Perinatology*, July 2, 2009.

Pearce, J. C., *Evolution's End: Claiming the potential of our intelligence*, Harper Collins, US, 1992.

Reddan, E., *Baby Daze: Becoming a mother and staying you*, Hodder Headline, Australia, 2000.

Ryan, A., *A Silent Love*, Penguin Books, Melbourne, 2000.

Sark, *Succulent Wild Woman: Dancing with your wonderful self*, Fireside/Simon & Schuster, New York, 1997.

Scholz, K. & C. A. Samuels, 'Neonatal bathing and massage intervention with fathers, Behavioural effects 12 weeks after birth of first baby: The Sunraysia Australia Intervention Project', *International Journal of Behavioural Development*, Vol. 15, no.3: 67–81, 1992.

Sherburn, R. E. and R. O. Jenkins, 'Cot mattresses as reservoirs of potentially harmful bacteria and the sudden infant death syndrome', *FEMS Immunology and Medical Microbiology*, 42: 76–84, 2004.

Solter, A., *The Aware Baby*, Shining Star Press, Goleta, California, 2001.

Sunderland, M., *The Science of Parenting*, Dorling Kindersley, London, 2006.

Underdown, A., J. Barlow, V. Chung, S. Stewart-Brown, 'Massage intervention for promoting mental and physical health in infants aged under six months', *Cochrane Database of Systematic Reviews*, Issue 4, 2006.

University of Bristol, *Avon Longitudinal Study of Parents and Children*, available at http://www.bristol.ac.uk/alspac, Bristol, ongoing.

Weaver, Clair, 'Why tears at bedtime are good for babies and mothers, finds study', *Sunday Telegraph*, 14/3/10.

West, D. and L. Marasco, *The Breastfeeding Mother's Guide to Making More Milk*, McGraw-Hill Companies, USA, 2009 (see makingmoremilk.com).

Zeedyk, S., '"What's life in a baby buggy like?": The impact of buggy orientation on parent–infant interaction and infant stress', *Talk To Your Baby* (National Literacy Trust early-language campaign), UK, November 2008.

Further reading

♥

Brown, K., *Mother Me: A mum's guide to balance, well-being and harmony*, Macmillan, Sydney, 2008.

Buckley, S. J., *Gentle Birth, Gentle Mothering: The wisdom and science of gentle choices in pregnancy, birth, and parenting*, One Moon Press, Brisbane, 2005.

Bumgarner, N., *Mothering Your Nursing Toddler* (rev. ed.), La Leche League, Illinois, USA, 2000.

Cox, S., *Baby Magic*, Australian Breastfeeding Association, Melbourne, 2009.

Cox, S., *Breastfeeding with Confidence*, Finch Publishing, Sydney, 2004.

Day, Jill, *Breastfeeding ... naturally* (2nd ed.), Australian Breastfeeding Association, Melbourne, 2004.

De Crespigny, L., M. Espie, & S. Holmes, *Prenatal Testing: Making choices in pregnancy*, Penguin, Australia, 1998.

Dengate, S., *Fed Up: Understanding how food affects your child and what you can do about it*, Random House, Sydney, 1998.

Doe, M. & M. Fayfield Walsh, *10 Principals for Spiritual Parenting: Nurturing your child's soul*, Harper Collins, New York, 1998.

Gerhardt, S., *Why Love Matters*, Routledge, East Sussex, 2004 (see why-lovematters.com).

Gethin, A. & B. Macgregor, *Helping Your Baby to Sleep*, Finch, Sydney, 2007.

Grille, R., *Heart to Heart Parenting*, ABC Books, Australia, 2008.

Heller, S., *The Vital Touch*, Henry Holt & Company, USA, 1997.

Jacobsen, H., *Mother Food for Breastfeeding Mothers*, Pagefree Publishing, USA, 2004 (see mother-food.com).

Kendall-Tackett, K., *The Hidden Feelings of Motherhood: Coping with stress, depression, and burnout*, New Harbinger Publications, USA, 2001.

McKay, P., *Breastfeeding Simply*, ebook available at pinkymckay.com.au/breastfeedingsimply, 2009.

McKay, P., *Sleeping Like a Baby*, Penguin Books, Melbourne, 2006.

McKay, P., *100 Ways to Calm the Crying*, Penguin Books, Melbourne, 2008.

McKay, P., *Toddler Tactics: How to make magic from mayhem*, Penguin Books, Melbourne, 2008.

McKenna, J., *Sleeping with Your Baby: A parent's guide to co-sleeping*, Platypus Media, Washington DC, 2007.

Naish, F. & J. Roberts, *The Natural Way to Better Babies*, Random House, Australia, 1996.

Naish, F. & Roberts, J., *The Natural Way to Better Birth and Bonding*, Doubleday, Australia, 2000.

Sunderland, M., *The Science of Parenting*, Dorling Kindersley, London, 2006.

Tabori, L., *The Little Big Book for Grandmothers*, Welcome Books, 2002.

Torqus, J. and G. Gotch, *The Womanly Art of Breastfeeding* (7th ed.), Plume Books, USA, 2007.

Van de Rijt, H. & F. Plooij, *The Wonder Weeks: How to stimulate your baby's mental development and help him turn his 8 predictable, great, fussy phases into magical leaps forward*, Kiddy World Promotions B.V., US, 2010.

Vartabedian, B., *Colic Solved: The essential guide to infant reflux and the care of your crying, difficult-to-soothe baby*, Ballantine Books, USA, 2007.

West, D. and L. Marasco, *The Breastfeeding Mother's Guide to Making More Milk*, McGraw-Hill Companies, USA, 2009 (see makingmoremilk.com).

Acknowledgements

♥

Firstly, I would like to thank all the mothers who have been a part of my life and an influence on my work: my own mother; the mothers of La Leche League New Zealand who guided and supported me when I was a new mother; and the wonderful mothers I work with every day as they do the awesome job of nurturing their little ones gently and consciously. I would also to acknowledge the mothering organisations who have 'spread the word' about my work through invitations to speak or write and who do such a wonderful job of supporting mothers without fanfare or financial reward, such as the volunteers of the Australian Breastfeeding Association, the Playgroup Association, the Bonnie Babes Foundation and the numerous support groups for parents who face the challenges of multiple births, premature babies and babies with special needs

To all of the mothers who have shared your stories: even if your personal story doesn't appear in this book, I sincerely appreciate the time you took to share your experience. You have given me a deeper insight and your experience will surely validate another mother.

To all of my colleagues who work with parents, I am deeply grateful to you for your support and the wisdom you have shared through our discussions as we have 'fixed the world of mothers and babies' – Dr Jillian Opie, Lauren Porter, Tracey Gibney, Margaret Callaghan, Dr Sarah

Buckley, Dr Kathleen Kendall-Tackett, Susan Shaw, Barb Glare, Lynne Hall, Anne Kohn, Robin Grille, Professor James McKenna, Dr Helen Ball, Elizabeth Pantley, Yvette O'Dowd, Maureen Minchin, Dr Jenni James, Shaughn Leach, Rebecca Glover, Anne Thistleton, Merrin Bradbury Butler, Marion Stott, Dr Jane Williams, Deborah Loupelis, Donna Sheppard-Wright and Carey Brauer.

My deepest gratitude and admiration goes to my amazing cheerleader and agent, Jacinta Di Mase; Kirsten Abbott, my publisher at Penguin, who told me 'this needs to be a BIG book!', then supported me to get it done as my world whirled with mothers, babies, overseas trips and speaking engagements. And to my wonderfully conscientious copy editor Nicci Dodanwela, whose attention to detail is essential to an 'overall effect' person like me!

I also want to thank my family – my husband, children and beautiful grandbabies who have kept my home and life full of the joy of babies up close and personal for many years. You are the inspiration that motivates me to my goal – that every mother with a baby in her arms also has a smile on her face!

Index

Also by Pinky McKay

100 Ways to Calm the Crying

100 Ways to Calm the Crying addresses the reasons babies cry, from the normal developmental changes that may make them more sensitive, to painful conditions such as colic and reflux. Along the way, Pink McKay offers gentle strategies to help you calm and connect with your baby, practical tips to help you cope with crying and sleepless nights, and ways to identify symptoms that may require professional help.

Toddler Tactics

Do you automatically cut toast into fingers?
Appreciate finger painting as much as fine art?
Hear 'no' a million times a day?

If the answer is yes, then *Toddler Tactics* is for you. Being the parent of a toddler can be exciting, inspiring and exhausting – all at once! Your adorable little baby has now become a moving, grooving tot with attitude, and it will take all your patience and skill to deal with these changes. Parenting expert Pinky McKay explains what to do at each stage of development and offers fuss-free advice on:

- communicating with your toddler
- discipline and good manners
- good eating habits
- routines for play and sleep
- toilet training
- family dynamics

Toddler Tactics is bursting with practical strategies for making the toddler years the exhilarating experience they should be.

Sleeping Like a Baby

Are you obsessed about your baby's sleep? Do you feel 'weak' because you can't leave him to cry himself to sleep? Do you need to relax more and enjoy being a parent?

Parenting expert Pinky McKay offers a natural, intuitive approach to solving your little ones' sleep problems and gives practical tips on how to:

- understand your baby's tired cues
- create a safe sleeping environment
- gently settle babies and toddlers
- feed infants to encourage sleep

Sleeping Like a Baby is a must-read for stress-free, guilt-free parenting and offers down-to-earth and heartening advice on helping babies (and their parents!) to sleep better.